Tolkien in the
New Century

To
Thomas Alan Shippey, PhD,
Walter J. Ong, S. J., Professor *Emeritus*,
St. Louis University,
who shows us each old stone in the tower,
without forgetting the view of the sea:
þú eart mægenes strang ond on móde fród / wís wordwine.
You are strong of body and sage of mind, / wise word-friend.

Tolkien in the New Century

Essays in Honor of Tom Shippey

Edited by
John Wm. Houghton,
Janet Brennan Croft,
Nancy Martsch,
John D. Rateliff
and Robin Anne Reid

McFarland & Company, Inc., Publishers
Jefferson, North Carolina

LIBRARY OF CONGRESS CATALOGUING-IN-PUBLICATION DATA

Tolkien in the new century : essays in honor of Tom Shippey /
   edited by John Wm. Houghton, Janet Brennan Croft,
   Nancy Martsch, John D. Rateliff and Robin Anne Reid.
       p.   cm.
   Includes bibliographical references and index.

   ISBN 978-0-7864-7438-7 (softcover : acid free paper) ∞
   ISBN 978-1-4766-1486-1 (ebook)

   1. Tolkien, J.R.R. (John Ronald Reuel), 1892–1973—
Criticism and interpretation.   I. Shippey, T.A., honouree.
II. Houghton, John William, editor of compilation.
III. Croft, Janet Brennan, editor of compilation.
IV. Martsch, Nancy, 1945– editor of compilation.
V. Rateliff, John D., editor of compilation.   VI. Reid,
Robin Anne, 1955– editor of compilation.
PR6039.O32Z8446 2014
823'.912—dc23   2014009351

BRITISH LIBRARY CATALOGUING DATA ARE AVAILABLE

On the cover *left to right*: Tom Shippey by Catherine Shippey (used
with permission); J.R.R. Tolkien (b&w line drawing by Patrick Wynne
after a photograph by Roger Hill, published in *Mythlore* 52 [14:2],
Winter 1987); *background image*: clearing in cypress tree forest
(© Siri Stafford/Lifesize/Thinkstock)

Printed in the United States of America

McFarland & Company, Inc., Publishers
  Box 611, Jefferson, North Carolina 28640
    www.mcfarlandpub.com

Table of Contents

Preface

The stimulus for this collection was the 2008 retirement of Thomas Alan Shippey, PhD (Cantab.), from the Walter J. Ong, S.J., Endowed Chair in Humanities at St. Louis University in Missouri. Shippey has published more than a dozen articles since 2008, so the term "retirement" is used loosely. In the call for papers, the editors cited Shippey from the Foreword to his 2001 *J.R.R. Tolkien: Author of the Century:* "The dominant literary mode of the twentieth century has been the fantastic.... [W]hen the time comes to look back at the century, it seems very likely that future literary historians, detached from the squabbles of our present, will see as its most representative and distinctive works books like J.R.R. Tolkien's *The Lord of the Rings....*" (vii). If, as seems likely, that prediction comes true, those historians will also be compelled to acknowledge the work of Prof. Shippey.

This collection has benefited from several sessions in the Tolkien at Kalamazoo track of the Medieval Institute at Western Michigan University's annual International Medieval Congress, including a 2009 roundtable session in honor of Tom Shippey. Thus, our thanks are due to the "Tolkien at Kalamazoo" interest group, and especially to its first organizer and presiding spirit, Jane Chance, and to her successor, our colleague, Robin Anne Reid. Her fellow editors would also acknowledge the long-standing contribution to Tolkien studies and fandom of Nancy Martsch, whose regular, and on-going, publication of *Beyond Bree*, newsletter of the J.R.R. Tolkien Special Interest Group of American Mensa, not only led to two of the pieces included in this volume but also produced the series of "Bree Moot" conventions, for the second of which the guest of honor was T.A. Shippey.

Finally, the editors wish to thank Dr. Salvatore Attardo, Dean, College of Humanities, Social Sciences & Arts, and Dr. Arlene Horne, Vice Provost for Research and Dean of Graduate Studies, Office of Research and Sponsored Programs, both of Texas A&M University-Commerce, for generous grants to defray the expenses of licenses to reprint copyrighted material.

Introduction

by John Wm. Houghton

In Part I: Memoirs, this collection begins with six brief essays which will give an introduction to Tom Shippey as seen by his colleagues and friends in academia and fandom. In "Counseling the *Scippigræd:* How T.A. Shippey Taught Us to Read," John R. Holmes, having coined a new Old English word for "those counseled by Shippey," offers a 10-step formula on how to be like him, along with an overture to his own essay elsewhere in the volume. David Bratman's "Shippey: The Philologist and the Critics" recalls the impact of Shippey's first edition of *The Road to Middle-earth*, of his conference appearances, and of his classroom teaching. In "Tom Shippey, and a Few New Leaves on Some Old Roots and Branches," E.L. Risden discusses Shippey's scholarship particularly in the light of that author's most recent book, *Roots and Branches* (again with some foretastes of his own essay in this collection). Todd Jensen's "A Talk by Tom Shippey" depicts him speaking to fan gatherings during his time in St. Louis; Jessica Yates sketches Shippey's role in U.K. fandom in "Tom Shippey and the Tolkien Society"; and my own piece "Shippey Amongst the Mercians" juxtaposes Shippey with an earlier literary lion.

In Part II: Answering Questions, the first five essays in the body of the collection respond directly to issues Shippey himself has raised. Nancy Martsch, in "The 'Lady with the Simple Gown and White Arms' *or* Possible Influences of 19th and Early 20th Century Book Illustrations on Tolkien's Work," answers Shippey's 2008 call for studies of the influence on Tolkien of now-unfashionable 19th and 20th century authors by considering the illustrations (yet more obscure, in that they are frequently omitted from modern reprints) which accompanied these stories in the editions in which Tolkien originally encountered them. In "Places Where the Stars Are Strange: Fantasy and Utopia in Tolkien's Middle-earth," Robert T. Tally, Jr., responds to Shippey's observations on the role of the fantastic in 20th century literature in the light of the "utopian critique of fantasy." Fredric Jameson's contrast of utopia and fantasy, Tally argues, "overlooks the utopian function and potential of fantasy," while utopian assessments of Middle-earth as reactionary and escapist take Tolkien's Other-world to be more clear-cut than it actually is. E.L. Risden's "Middle-earth and the Waste Land: Greenwood, Apocalypse, and Post-War Resolution" takes Shippey's characterization of Tolkien as a post-war writer and his observations about the mythical element in Modernism as the starting point for a detailed comparison of eschatological landscapes in Tolkien's novel and T.S. Eliot's archetypal Modernist poem. Verlyn Flieger's "The Jewels, the Stone, the Ring, and the Making of Meaning," by way of answering Shippey's question "What is a Silmaril?" assesses the effectiveness of those jewels, the Arkenstone, and the One Ring as vehicles for the theme of "the danger of uncontrolled desire," arguing that the series shows a development in Tolkien's ability to match symbol and meaning. Shippey has pointed to, on more than one occasion, the "fellow feeling" between Tolkien and the *Beowulf* poet. In "Tolkien and Apposition," Leslie Stratyner argues that the resemblance runs far deeper than such obvious elements as the Anglo-Saxon sources of the Rohirric culture, reaching to the "bone and sinew" of Tolkien's prose in his use of his Old English predecessor's appositive style.

In Part III: "Philological Inquiries," we turn from answering Shippey's questions to applying his methods of literary criticism. John R. Holmes, in "Keeping Counsel: Advice in Tolkien's Fiction," considers advice, such as Frodo's *gnomon* "Go not to the Elves for counsel, for they will say both no and yes," as a form of semantic displacement from the present to the future. The *Scippigræd* will, he suggests, want to begin by considering carefully the grammatical tensions of Gildor's reply, "Elves seldom give unguarded advice, for advice is a dangerous gift, even from the wise to the wise, and all courses may run ill," with its curious overlay of modern and Old English syntactical structures. In "Tolkien's Wraiths, Rings and Dragons: An Exercise in Literary Linguistics," Jason Fisher explores "creation from philology" in tracing the roots and branches of *wraith, writhe, ring, willow* and *worm* to show how Tolkien moved from "purely philological ruminations" to "explanatory narratives." Applying the models of Northrop Frye and Giambattista Vico to close readings of utterances of Finrod, Galadriel, Frodo and Elessar Envinyatar, B.S.W. Barootes' "'He chanted a song of wizardry': Words with Power in Middle-earth" considers the overall pattern of decline in Middle-earth as it appears specifically in the diminishing (and renewed) power of language.

Part IV: "The True Tradition," pursues another typical Shippey concern in considering Tolkien's interactions with his medieval antecedents. In "Inside Literature: Tolkien's Explorations of Medieval Genres," John D. Rateliff surveys a range of works from outside the Middle-earth cycle to show how

Tolkien's imitations of medieval forms and genres developed his ability to give his more purely modern works a medieval appeal. "'Poor Sméagol': Gollum as Exile in *The Lord of the Rings*," by Yvette Kisor, recognizing how widespread the theme of exile is in *The Lord of the Rings* and how widely Old English literature influences the novel, argues that, despite the presence of the exiled Noldor and the exiled Númenóreans, it is actually Sméagol who best exemplifies the Old English exile. John B. Marino's "The Presence of the Past in *The Lord of the Rings*" examines the ways in which the much-discussed "large history in the background" (*Letters* 333) of the novel regularly haunts the present, evoking the nostalgic sentimentality of the *Ubi sunt?* trope from both the characters and the reader. Finally, in "Night-wolves, Half-trolls and the Dead Who Won't Stay Down," Marjorie Burns uses Tolkien's boyhood encounter with Sigurd and Fafnir in Andrew Lang's *Red Fairy Book* as the starting point for a study of the representation of various Norse monsters in Tolkien's *legendarium*, beginning with the remembered wolves of Icelandic sagas.

In both *The Road to Middle-earth* and *Author of the Century*, Shippey is careful to attend to Tolkien's shorter works, both for their ability to illuminate the central cycle and for their own sake; the essays in Part IV: Perspectives from Outside the Cycle follow that example. David L. Dettman, in "Väinämöinen in Middle-earth: The Pervasive Presence of the *Kalevala* in the Bombadil Chapters of *The Lord of the Rings*," takes the recent publication of Tolkien's "'The Story of Kullervo' and Essays on *Kalevala*" as occasion to expand on earlier studies (including his own) of the Finnish elements in "The Adventures of Tom Bombadil" as well as the related sections of *The Lord of the Rings*. Having argued elsewhere that "the story of Túrin in all of its various recensions" shows Tolkien reflecting in fiction on the questions of the heroic ethos which he also considers in "Ofermod," Richard C. West turns, in "'Lack of Counsel Not of Courage': J.R.R. Tolkien's Critique of the Heroic Ethos in *The Children of Húrin*," to the roles secondary characters play in the examination of heroism, largely through their similarities to, and differences from, Túrin himself. In the final essay, "'Alone Between the Dark and Light': 'The Lay of Aotrou and Itroun' and Lessons from the Later *Legendarium*," Kristine Larsen uses a consideration of Tolkien's attitude toward occult practices, particularly astrology, to expand into a wide-ranging consideration of his continuing effort to develop a clear "differentiation between miracle, magic, enchantment, mechanism, science and art in his pre-Christian (yet admittedly Catholic) sub-creation."

A list of Shippey's work on Tolkien since 2004 (the date of his last published bibliography) is featured as an appendix.

Abbreviations and Other Conventions

(Based largely on those of *Tolkien Studies*.)

Works of J.R.R. Tolkien

Anderson — *The Annotated Hobbit*. Ed. Douglas A. Anderson. Rev. ed. Boston: Houghton Mifflin, 2002.

"Aotrou" — "The Lay of Aotrou and Itroun." *Welsh Review* 4, no. 4 (1945): 254–66.

ATB — *Adventures of Tom Bombadil*. Boston: Houghton Mifflin, 1963.

BMC — "Beowulf: The Monsters and the Critics." *MC* 5–48.

Finn — *Finn and Hengest: The Fragment and the Episode*. Ed. Alan Bliss. Boston: Houghton Mifflin, 1983.

FR — *The Fellowship of the Ring*. 2d ed. Boston: Houghton Mifflin, 1987.

H — *The Hobbit*. Fiftieth anniversary edition. Boston: Houghton Mifflin, 1987.

Lays — *The Lays of Beleriand*. Ed. Christopher Tolkien. The History of Middle-earth III. Boston: Houghton Mifflin, 1985.

Legend — *The Legend of Sigurd and Gudrún*. Ed. Christopher Tolkien. Boston and New York: Houghton Mifflin Harcourt, 2009.

Letters — *The Letters of J.R.R. Tolkien*. Ed. Humphrey Carpenter, with assistance of Christopher Tolkien. Boston: Houghton Mifflin, 1981.

Lost Road — *The Lost Road and Other Writings*. Ed. Christopher Tolkien. The History of Middle-earth V. Boston: Houghton Mifflin, 1987.

Lost Tales I — *The Book of Lost Tales, Part One*. Ed. Christopher Tolkien. The History of Middle-earth I. Boston: Houghton Mifflin, 1984.

Lost Tales II — *The Book of Lost Tales, Part Two*. Ed. Christopher Tolkien. The History of Middle-earth II. Boston: Houghton Mifflin, 1984.

MC — *The Monsters and the Critics and Other Essays*. Ed. Christopher Tolkien. Boston: Houghton Mifflin, 1984.

Morgoth — *Morgoth's Ring: The Later Silmarillion, Part One*. Ed. Christopher Tolkien. The History of Middle-earth X. Boston: Houghton Mifflin, 1993.

Narn	*Narn I Chîn Húrin: The Tale of the Children of Húrin.* Ed. Christopher Tolkien. Boston and New York: Houghton Mifflin, 2007.
Nom	"Nomenclature of *The Lord of the Rings*." Wayne G. Hammond and Christina Scull. *The Lord of the Rings: A Reader's Companion.* Boston and New York: Houghton Mifflin, 2005. 750–782.
Peoples	*The Peoples of Middle-earth.* Ed. Christopher Tolkien. The History of Middle-earth XII. Boston: Houghton Mifflin, 1996.
RK	*The Return of the King.* 2d ed. Boston: Houghton Mifflin, 1987.
S	*The Silmarillion.* Ed. Christopher Tolkien. Boston: Houghton Mifflin, 1977.
Sauron	*Sauron Defeated: The History of the Lord of the Rings, Part Four.* Ed. Christopher Tolkien. The History of Middle-earth IX. Boston: Houghton Mifflin, 1992.
Shadow	*The Return of the Shadow: The History of the Lord of the Rings, Part One.* Ed. Christopher Tolkien. The History of Middle-earth VI. Boston: Houghton Mifflin, 1988.
Shaping	*The Shaping of Middle-earth: The Quenta, The Ambarkenta and The Annals.* Ed. Christopher Tolkien. The History of Middle-earth IV. Boston: Houghton Mifflin, 1986.
"Silmarillion"	(In quotation marks and without italics) The body of legend in general, as opposed to the published version of 1977.
TL	*Tree and Leaf, including the Poem* Mythopoeia. Boston: Houghton Mifflin, 1989.
TOF	*Tolkien On Fairy-stories.* Ed. Verlyn Flieger and Douglas A. Anderson. London: HarperCollins, 2008.
Treason	*The Treason of Isengard: The History of the Lord of the Rings, Part Two.* Ed. Christopher Tolkien. The History of Middle-earth VII. Boston: Houghton Mifflin, 1989.
TT	*The Two Towers.* 2d ed. Boston: Houghton Mifflin, 1987.
UT	*Unfinished Tales of Númenor and Middle-earth.* Ed. Christopher Tolkien. Boston: Houghton Mifflin, 1980.
War	*The War of the Ring: The History of the Lord of the Rings, Part Three.* Ed. Christopher Tolkien. The History of Middle-earth VIII. Boston: Houghton Mifflin, 1990.

Works on J.R.R. Tolkien

Author	T.A. Shippey. *J.R.R. Tolkien: Author of the Century.* Boston and New York: Houghton Mifflin, 2001.
Carpenter	Humphrey Carpenter. *Tolkien: A Biography.* Boston: Houghton Mifflin, 1977.
Chronology	Christina Scull and Wayne G. Hammond. *The J.R.R. Tolkien Companion and Guide: Chronology.* Boston: Houghton Mifflin, 2006.
Companion	Wayne G. Hammond and Christina Scull. *The Lord of the Rings: A Reader's Companion.* Boston: Houghton Mifflin, 2005.

Encyclopedia	*J.R.R. Tolkien Encyclopedia: Scholarship and Critical Assessment.* Ed. Michael D.C. Drout. New York and London: Routledge, 2006.
Guide	Christina Scull and Wayne G. Hammond. *The J.R.R. Tolkien Companion and Guide: Reader's Guide.* Boston: Houghton Mifflin, 2006.
Invention	*Tolkien and the Invention of Myth: A Reader.* Ed. Jane Chance. Lexington: University Press of Kentucky, 2004.
Medievalist	*Tolkien the Medievalist.* Ed. Jane Chance. Routledge Studies in Medieval Religion and Culture 3. New York and London: Routledge, 2003.
Road	Tom Shippey. *The Road to Middle-earth.* Revised and expanded. Boston and New York: Houghton Mifflin, 2003.
Roots	Tom Shippey. *Roots and Branches: Selected Papers on Tolkien.* Ed. Thomas Honegger. Cormarë Series 11. [Zollikofen]: Walking Tree, 2007.
Scholarship	*The Lord of the Rings 1954–2004: Scholarship in Honor of Richard E. Blackwelder.* Ed. Wayne G. Hammond and Christina Scull. Milwaukee: Marquette University Press, 2006.

Counseling the *Scippigræd*: How T.A. Shippey Taught Us to Read

JOHN R. HOLMES

The Christening of Alfred Ætheling of Wessex in 849 may have played a role in his greatness. Alfred's father, Æthelwulf, had wanted to establish his own name-prefix, *Æthel*, which means (more or less) "noble," as the sign of the royal line: he gave it to his first four sons and a daughter. By the time his sixth child came along, however—his fifth son—there didn't seem to be any point in giving him the *Æthel-* prefix, since there seemed to be no reasonable chance this infant could ever be king. But wishing the lad wisdom and happiness, Æthelwulf named him *Ælfred*, "advised by elves." While we have no historical proof that Alfred actually received counsel from elves, there is no evidence to the contrary, and the boy certainly prospered as if he had. Alfred, Elf-counsel, not only outlasted four older brothers to become king, but also would be the only English monarch known to history as "The Great."

When it's naming day for Tolkienists, may they be similarly graced. May the best writers who write about J.R.R. Tolkien be named, not *Ælfred*, but *Scippigræd*, the Shippey-counseled, and may they write as if they listened to that counsel. Oh, but what a terrible burden for Mr. Shippey. "When did I agree"—we can imagine his complaint—"to stand godfather to any idiot who's read *The Road to Middle-earth* or *Author of the Century*? I never signed up for this!" Well, Prof. Shippey, that's too bad. It's your own fault for writing so well. And reading so well. And teaching the rest of us to read Tolkien.

There is, however, another burden that comes with the name *Scippigræd*. It is the burden of counsel itself. It is a paradox that the wisest, who are most qualified to give advice, are often also the most reluctant. Many of the very good reasons for that reluctance will be explored in another essay on the motif of advice in Tolkien's fiction elsewhere in this volume (87–96). But one reason that we the *Scippigræd* may not relish the image of Prof. Shippey as guru is that the routinization of "advice" in modern popular culture has embarrassingly sentimental associations. While advice in the form of writing could have valid mythic associations on the highbrow end—such as runic spells, Gudrún's warning runes to her brothers in the Eddaic *Atlamál* or the leaves of the Sibyl in the *Aeneid*—we can't escape the lowbrow end: the newspaper Advice Column. And not even the most fanatical *Scippigræd* would want to see a "Dear Tom" column in *Mallorn* or *Mythlore* or *Tolkien Studies*.

Granted, the newspaper advice column has a loftier pedigree than one might think, a history nearly as old as the newspaper itself. A London biweekly, *The Athenian Mercury*, launched what was probably the first advice column, to which Jonathan Swift would later correspond, in 1690. Daniel Defoe imitated it in *The Review* in 1704. But not even the literary pedigree of Swift and Defoe could rescue the thought of our premier Tolkien scholar answering tortured missives from readers who sign themselves *Lēofgeornost* or *Slæplēas*[1] *in Sēættliburh*. Could you imagine the letters?

Dear Dr. Shippey,

I have just finished my PhD dissertation on *Roverandom*, which I think is even better than my MA thesis on Tolkien's emendations of *Ancrene Wisse* (perhaps you've read it), which in turn was even better than my undergraduate thesis on the influence of the *Bhagavad Gita* on "Fastitocalon," which was an expansion of my high school senior project on Sanskrit rhythms in Tolkien's verse.

My question is: how can I become a great Tolkien scholar like you?

Expectantly,
Hopeful in the Heartland

Broad and bald as this sample may be, putting it in writing demonstrates how nearly impossible it is to give good advice. Even if there were a fan or an academic un-self-conscious enough to ask the question that directly—"How can I be like Shippey?"—how would any of us (let alone Professor Shippey) answer such a question? Some of the Tom-advised in academe may already have asked themselves that question, and even worked out their tentative answers in fear and trembling, but can that answer be reduced to advice for others? A ten-step formula?

How to Be Like Tom Shippey

1. Be educated in the great 19th-century tradition of comparative philology—quickly, before the scholars in that field are all dead. Oops. Too late.

2. Read everything that Tolkien would have read in his lifetime. (A good starting point is Shippey's list at the end of *The Road to Middle-earth*.)

3. Corollary to #2: learn all of the languages Tolkien knew. And on the assumption that Tolkien was modest about such knowledge, learn any language he *might* have known.

4. Play rugby in your youth—quickly, before that youth is gone. Oops. Too late.

5. Read every science fiction and fantasy work influenced by Tolkien (that is, virtually everything in the genre written after 1965).

6. Write with clarity, humanity, humor, and *panache* (see *Road* 128 for the etymology of *panache*).

7. Use individual words as lenses through which to see Tolkien's mind at work. Do not, however, rest with etymology: be sensitive to the layerings of meaning in the word as it has survived, and to the *way* it has survived.

8. Enrich the field of Old English studies as greatly as you have influenced Tolkien studies. Quickly, before the field is absorbed by literary theory. Oops. Too late.

9. Do not restrict your reading either to fantasy or to Germanic philology. If the *Scippigræd* are to make the case for Tolkien's canonicity, we need to know more of the canon than just *Beowulf*. Nor can we accept uncritically Tolkien's jests about not having read anything written after 1400.

10. Never listen to advice.

(Logicians will recognize #10 as a conundrum: "never listen to advice" is, of course, a bit of advice.)

If you have been drawn to this volume honoring the contributions of Tom Shippey to Tolkien scholarship, then you don't need my advice, which is: Read as much Shippey as you can. Never mind, then. Go on to the other essays.

NOTE

1. The acutely *Scippigræd* will of course immediately think of Tolkien's comments on the *–léas* suffix in *Slæpléas* from his 1951 philological note on Middle-English *Losenger*. Cf. J.R.R. Tolkien, "Middle English 'Losenger': Sketch of an etymological and semantic enquiry," *Essais de Philologie Moderne* (1951), 63–76.

Shippey: The Philologist and the Critics

DAVID BRATMAN

In the last chapter of *The Lord of the Rings*, Sam notes that he can still identify the very tree that Frodo hid behind in their first encounter with a Nazgûl. The memory is that vivid. In much the same way, though more pleasantly, I can still identify the bus stop in Seattle where I was waiting one day in 1983 when I realized that the book I was reading was the most insightful study of Tolkien I had come across yet—or have in all the years since.

What I can't remember is which of the brilliant insights of Tom Shippey's *The Road to Middle-earth* sparked that realization. Possibly it was the bit in chapter 3 where he notes that though "There is not much in common between the language" of Balin's and Bilbo's mutual farewells in chapter 18 of *The Hobbit*, "nevertheless it is perfectly clear that they are saying the same thing" (67). This comes as the sweet climax of a whole section on Tolkien's ironies in juxtaposing Bilbo's elaborate modern linguistic discourse against the plain ancient heroic saga talk of the other characters. Other scholars had discussed Bilbo as out of place in the heroic Northern world before, but none had done so in purely linguistic terms, and none had shown how, at the end, the two styles meet in amity.

Linguistics, or more properly philology, was Shippey's business as it had been Tolkien's. Viewing Tolkien's work through this lens was uniquely rewarding, but it's not Shippey's only strength as a Tolkien scholar.

In subsequent years, as his book's fame grew, I began to see Shippey at conferences. One of the less-remarked of his biographical resemblances to Tolkien is that they were both rugby players, and Shippey looks and acts like a rugby player: big, bald, blunt, and forceful. Combined with his intelligence, this means he gives conference presentations that really keep the audience awake. One of my favorites was his presentation at the 1992 Tolkien Centenary Conference in Oxford, showing that Tolkien's thoughts about war paralleled those of more "canonical" authors like Orwell, William Golding, and T.H. White. This was one of the seeds that gave rise to his rousingly polemical subsequent book, *J.R.R. Tolkien: Author of the Century*, which could have been subtitled, "Why So Many Critics Hate Tolkien, and Why They're Completely Wrong." And it proved its case.

A few years ago I had the privilege of watching Shippey give a guest lecture to Diana Pavlac Glyer's class on the Inklings at Azusa Pacific University (Azusa, California). So if you place him in front of this class of college lit students in the frying pan east of L.A. and tell him that they're reading *All Hallows' Eve* by Charles Williams, he'll begin like this: "It's one of the rules of the novel, that your characters have to be alive from the start. No; let's have them dead: it's different."

And he just went on like that for an hour, throwing off one insightful quip after another, some of them of only tangential relevance. On Aleister Crowley: "He was called 'the wickedest man in the world,' but he wasn't that wicked. Or if he was, he wasn't that good at it." On the Renaissance: "In school, I learned that everything gets invented in the Renaissance: gunpowder, America, stuff like that. As I got older, I realized this was complete nonsense." And much more that I didn't get the chance to write down.

We are greatly fortunate to have a scholar so articulate, so resourceful, and so forthright in his views in Tolkien and Inklings studies. May his shadow never grow less.

WORK CITED

Shippey, T.A. *The Road to Middle-earth*. First American Edition. Boston: Houghton Mifflin, 1983.

Tom Shippey, and a Few New Leaves on Some Old Roots and Branches

E.L. Risden

Most of us inevitably and aptly associate Tom Shippey's work on Tolkien with philology, an approach to scholarship and literary enjoyment that for this audience requires no defense. But many of us know him also as a generous mentor, a staunch representative of academe's old—and still worthwhile—values: not effete gentility, but tenacious rigor and tireless pursuit of understanding joined with love of the subject matter and good talk with anyone interested in it. While other highly visible members of the *duguða* retreat among those of their own class, often skipping out on the bar tab, Tom is buying another round of drinks at the local pub for all the wide-eyed *geogoðum* and drawing everyone into conversations that would have left Sam Johnson quietly attentive. I once saw Tom after a conference session eagerly searching about for a young student who had given a disastrously awful paper—one that a thoughtless professor had probably insisted the student submit without actually having read it, setting up the student for embarrassment. Tom wanted to make sure that someone said at least something encouraging to the presenter who must have sensed in the audience something between pity and hostility. I suspect Tom would not admit to having done it, particularly since many of his scholarly essays have their genesis in a textual or linguistic problem the answer to which someone else has got wrong, but our current generation, bent on turning every decent argument into postmodern politicized quarrel, would do well to note that even correction works best delivered through knowledge tempered with kindness. Even the old Germanic heroes—as Tom has shown in his discussions of "How the Heroes Talk"—for all their love of grim irony, allowed their opponents the opportunity to save face. How much more should we do so with our fellow scholars, elder and younger alike!

Many of Tom Shippey's essays on Tolkien and philology that treat both old errors and new understandings appear in what probably remains Tom's least-known work: *Roots and Branches: Selected Papers on Tolkien by Tom Shippey*. Most of us keep as regular companions *The Road to Middle-earth* and *J.R.R. Tolkien: Author of the Century*, but the aptly named *Roots and Branches* returns us to scholarly greenwood to recall the roots that have come before us, to nourish the leaves and new branches that will come after—even the most fragile of them—and to fight any encroaching scholarly waste land. Shippey's new book plots no new course—other than to urge continuing interest in Tolkien and philology in both text and film—but it collects many of the essential steps that developed into or from those earlier, better known books, comprising papers published or delivered over approximately the last twenty-five years. Those papers address Tolkien's life, his scholarship, his well-known and lesser-known works, ongoing debates on Tolkien's work, and even *The Lord of the Rings* cinematic trilogy, all through the lens of philology and by means of an enormous fund of general learning: approaches we can hardly overvalue in these times when most of us face diminishing funds on all sides. In this brief essay I'll call attention only to a few of the leaves that feed those old roots and branches to hint at the breadth and depth of the scholarship involved.

Tolkien, of course, worked in the crease between his own fervent Catholicism and his admiration for the "pagan" Germanic "theory of courage"; the "'flavour' of Snorri and of Norse tradition as a whole" derives in part from its "endemic good humor," Shippey observes, and Tolkien adapted that tone in different ways but continually through his fiction (*Roots* 27–28). That familiar and somewhat familial sense of humor sets Tolkien apart from T.S. Eliot and much of the Modernist generation and has probably contributed to some critics' sense that Tolkien's work lacks what Matthew Arnold might have called the "high seriousness" necessary for canonicity (see my essay in this volume [57–64] for more on Tolkien and Eliot). But Tolkien also borrowed from that world a tension between heroic courage and the rising Christianity, its tendency toward proverbiality, and its fear of the corrupting influence of the "dragon-sickness" (greed, or the "disease of ownership," 349), even as he echoed from the later Finnish *Kalevala* the sorrow of "dispossession and replacement" (34). His persistent attention to words and names, details that eluded most scholarship, led him on a mission of search and rescue; he felt himself "a kindred spirit of the poets, not only cleaning and restoring what they had written, but going on to use it in the way they had intended" (178)—that is, creatively, not merely scribally. On page 193 Shippey hints at a nominal connection: from Old Norse *tulkr* to English *tolke*, "spokesman"—not far at all in sound from *Tolkien* (though Tolkien decisively rejects this etymology and any connection with his surname [*Letters* 428–9]). But Shippey stresses that philology produces more than hints, if one pursues it correctly and energetically. A textual problem triggers imagination, because it is not, finally, merely a textual problem: it invokes a mythological explanation and implies an essential "real-world meaning," which, to be true to one's calling, one must pursue and refine over a lifetime (349). Names, if we pursue them, as Tolkien knew and as Shippey so appropriately recapitulates, lead to stories, "myths," and to some extent Modernism, as Eliot suggested, had "made it possible to replace narrative method by 'mythical method'" (*Author* 313). War, the waste land, and the declining greenwood had highlighted the necessity of myth-making and the further, more intense interpretation of myth as a means—as Joseph Campbell would say—to throw ourselves into the midst of life with all its grit and gore. Our survival in the wake of our own destructiveness has perhaps come to depend on it.

The very first essay in *Roots and Branches*, "Tolkien and the *Beowulf*-Poet," focusing on Tolkien's constant fascination with names and place names in the Anglo-Saxon heroic poem, notes that "the conclusion he [Tolkien] drew from such continuities between ancient poetry and modern life" is that "the heroes of antiquity *had not gone away*. They were still there, in the landscape, in names, and probably in the gene-pool" (18, emphasis in original). We can only hope that the same holds true for the next generation of our most heroic scholars. In the final essay of the volume, on Peter Jackson's adaptation of *The Lord of the Rings* for film, Shippey asserts that while Jackson "may not have been able to cope with all the ramifications of Tolkien on Providence" [as, he adds, few have], he "certainly succeeded in conveying much of the ... narrative core ... the difference between Prime and Subsidiary Action, the differing styles of heroism, the need for pity as well as courage, the vulnerability of the good, the true cost of evil" while showing the courage to retain the "sad, muted, ambiguous ending of the original" (386)—more than one dare ask of any filmmaker or any novelist, however great and however scholarly. In an essay on "Heroes and Heroism," Shippey asks his readers "once again to reflect on work," what we do regularly for a living: "it is the Great Unsaid of fiction, and of criticism" (268)—our daily work effects the embodiment of our creative impulse. Who could better understand that impulse in Tolkien than the person whose career follows, parallels, and in its critical range and magnitude exceeds that of his predecessor? Who has better infused our resolve to sustain the greenwood that Tolkien left us—and also the critical incisiveness that Eliot helped resuscitate? Tom Shippey concludes *Roots and Branches*, punning on his own earlier title, with the hope that Jackson's films will help "new readers facing a new experience, and finding once again Tolkien's road to Middle-earth" (386)—in a sense, to unveil to a new generation a world that can profitably absorb their attentions. He need not have felt concern at that, as his own writing, teaching, lecturing, and friendship have posted a new generation of readers, teachers, and scholars eager, if not endowed with quite so much wizardly power, to point and guide the way from the waste land to that *Road*.

A Talk by Tom Shippey

TODD JENSEN

I first learned of Tom Shippey's work on Tolkien when I checked a copy of the then newly published *The Road to Middle-earth* from the library, in the mid 1980s. I found it immensely enjoyable. I had noticed from first reading *The Hobbit* the strong echoes of Norse mythology without the explicit use of any characters or events from the Norse myths, and Shippey's description of *The Hobbit* as set in what he called an "asterisk-world" that explored the stories behind blurred references (such as the possible odyssey of the dwarves behind the Catalogue of Dwarfs in the *Elder Edda*) delighted me. I also liked his discussion of the contrast between the everyday speech-patterns of the hobbits, as representatives of modern man, with the more archaic manner of the Elves and the Men of Gondor and Rohan, and his exploration of how the Ring illustrates Tolkien's thoughts on evil (especially its careful blend of two theories—of evil as a malevolent outside force and as a temptation from within). I checked it out many times thereafter.

In 1995, I was fortunate enough to meet Tom Shippey himself at Bree Moot 2, when it was held in St. Louis, Missouri, and to hear him speak at the banquet on Tolkien's use of old half-forgotten legends (such as the wood-woses—who became the Woses of Drúadan Forest—and the ettens, whose name appears in the Ettenmoors). I also briefly listened to him chatting on the origins of the Arthurian legend with a few other attendees (Shippey was of the opinion—whether he still is, I do not know—that Arthur was mythical, since we simply have no solid evidence for his being real, and used the phrase "smoke without fire" to express his argument).

Six years later, I met Shippey again when he gave a talk on Tolkien at Left Bank Books, in St. Louis's Central West End, in the summer of 2001. His second book on Tolkien, *J.R.R. Tolkien: Author of the Century*, had just been published, and I bought a copy at the bookstore that evening, which he autographed for me. The talk was also a delight; but one memory that most stands out to me is Shippey's singing the old school song of King Edward's School, which Tolkien attended, and commenting how it may have inspired Bilbo's reflection that defeat may be splendid at the Battle of Five Armies. Since then, I also bought a paperback edition of *The Road to Middle-earth*—a revised edition, with, thus, more material than the original edition that I read in the mid-eighties (additions which do not deprive it of its virtues at all)—though, alas, this one not autographed.

Shippey's writings on Tolkien remain to this day among my favorites, and I recommend both *The Road to Middle-earth* and *J.R.R. Tolkien: Author of the Century* to all who have not yet discovered them. Professor Shippey, I thank you.

Tom Shippey and the Tolkien Society[1]

JESSICA YATES

I joined the Tolkien Society in Autumn 1972, and as a Londoner became a member of the Northfarthing Smial at the same time as the Smial was organising regularly monthly Innmoots, and meetings in members' flats and houses.[2] Belladonna Took (Vera Chapman), the Society's founder and Secretary, soon recruited me to help her, and it was my ambition to bring journalists and scholars into the Society to join the fans.

Rayner Unwin (of Allen & Unwin, Tolkien's publishers) told us that Humphrey Carpenter had been commissioned to write the official biography of J.R.R. Tolkien, and so the Committee booked him for the 1976 AGM-Dinner. That day I had just been elected Secretary, and had noted several reviews in the *Times Literary Supplement* of Old and Middle English books, signed T.A. Shippey: his reviews often mentioned Tolkien. Moreover, the library where I worked had acquired the *Mastermind Quiz Book* and the questions on Tolkien and science-fiction had been set by Tom Shippey, of St. John's College, Oxford. I therefore asked Carpenter if he knew of Shippey, and he was positive about him; so was Rayner, who said that "he was writing a book for us." Thus I wrote to Tom at his college in 1977, the Year of *The Silmarillion*, to ask if he would call on us at our Saturday evening party at Oxonmoot, at the Welsh (Prancing) Pony that September. He turned up, and soon made himself at home in the bar!

My next move was to invite him to be our Guest of Honor at the 1978 AGM-Dinner. This was in Birmingham (Brummoot), and Rayner Unwin and Tom comprised a double act to celebrate *The Silmarillion*. Tom gave us some titbits from his research for *The Road to Middle-earth*, and we were all absolutely gobsmacked by our first experience of his unique insight into Tolkien's sources. Much of the material he gave us would go into *The Road* by way of his essay, "Creation from Philology in *The Lord of the Rings*" in Salu and Farrell's *J.R.R. Tolkien: Scholar and Storyteller.*

Shippey went on to be our GoH again at the 1980 AGM-Dinner in York. I remember reading the typescript of the first chapters of *Road* in the car going up from London to York. The transcript of his talk ("Tom Shippey Speaks...") in a characteristic Q and A style, was published in the Tolkien Society's series *Digging Potatoes, Growing Trees* (Vol. 1, 1997), as were his talks at our Dinners in 1983 and 1991 (Vol. 1, 1997 & Vol. 2, 1998). He also reviewed *An Introduction to Elvish* for us in *Mallorn* 13.

Returning to the York AGM, on the Sunday he showed us round Tolkien's Leeds, and sent us a short article ("A Wose by any Other Name") for *Amon Hen* about the fact that Tolkien lived near Woodhouse Lane, and that probably made him think of the woodwoses in *Sir Gawain and the Green Knight.* (The cover of that *Amon Hen* depicted Éomer confronting Aragorn, Legolas and Gimli, Éomer's helm bearing a white plume or *panache*, as Shippey had discussed in his talk.)

Tom's scholarship and admiration for Tolkien had been noted some ten years earlier, though I did not know it until Belladonna showed me the rare booklet (a gift from Rayner Unwin?) entitled *An Afternoon in Middle-earth*, published by the Cannon Hill Trust, Birmingham, 1969. The afternoon began with readings, then Donald Swann performed some of his Tolkien songs (from his song cycle *The Road Goes Ever On*), Tolkien's Allen & Unwin secretary Joy Hill spoke on the Tolkien cult, and the concluding discussion panel comprised Mary Coghlan, a psychologist, Naomi Lewis, the children's book critic, and Tom Shippey, at that time a lecturer at Birmingham University. The date: November 30, 1969. The booklet included a handwritten welcome from Tolkien, articles about him, on the cult, and on the newly restored Sarehole Mill, near Tolkien's childhood home in Birmingham.

Shippey's book on Tolkien came out in Autumn 1982, celebrated at Church House Bookshop, near Westminster Abbey, our usual venue in those days for Tolkien/Lewis events, at which he gave a talk on the righteous pagan (from chapter six of *Road*). We hosted him at our first Tolkien Society Workshop in 1986, and again at Beverley in 1989, where he gave a talk on "Tolkien and 'The Homecoming of Beorhtnoth'" (*Roots* 323–339). I think it was then that we awarded him Honorary Membership of the Society. He wrote us a nice piece for *Amon Hen* 100 in 1989 on "Tolkien's Academic Reputation Now" (*Roots* 203–212). He gave the keynote speech at the 1992 J.R.R. Tolkien Centenary Conference in Keble College, Oxford: "Tolkien as a Post-War Writer," and another one on "Tolkien and the *Gawain*-poet" (*Roots* 61–77). He then gave a talk on "Grimm, Grundtvig, Tolkien" (*Roots* 79–96) at our 1997 Seminar.

We saw less of him once he had moved to the United States, and were delighted when he retired back to the UK. He gave a lecture on "'A Fund of Wise Sayings': Proverbiality in Tolkien" (*Roots* 303–319) at our Tolkien 2005 international conference in Aston University, Birmingham, and we look forward to welcoming him to future events and reading more of his writing.

May I end on a personal note: whether on Tolkien, other fantasy and SF writers, or Old and Middle English literature, his work is always well worth reading. As an independent scholar I admit that most of my longer published articles, and those I am working on, owe something to a hint from Tom's work (sometimes I even disagree with him!); and it's for his ever-cheery welcome and courteous arguments that I greatly value Tom Shippey.

Notes

1. With thanks to Charles Noad of the Tolkien Society for producing a Shippey/Tolkien Society timeline at very short notice!

2. Smials are discussion groups of the Tolkien Society, which hold meetings ("moots") at inns and elsewhere. The Tolkien Society has two or three yearly gatherings, the Annual General Meeting (AGM) for business, Oxonmoot, its annual convention, and workshops and seminars. Tolkien Society publications are the bimonthly newsletter *Amon Hen* and the journal *Mallorn*. [Eds.]

Works Cited

Holloway, Leslie, ed. "An Afternoon in Middle-earth." Birmingham, England: Cannon Hill Trust, 1969.

Shippey, Tom. "Creation from Philology in *The Lord of the Rings*." *J.R.R. Tolkien: Scholar and Storyteller*. Ed. Mary Salu and Robert T. Farrell. Ithaca: Cornell University Press, 1979. 286–316.

_____. "An Introduction to Elvish." Rev. of *An Introduction to Elvish,* ed. Jim Allan (1978). *Mallorn* 13 (1979): 7–10.

_____. "Tolkien as a Post-War Writer." *Scholarship & Fantasy: Proceedings of* The Tolkien Phenomenon, *May 1992, Turku, Finland*. Ed. K.J. Battarbee. *Anglicana Turkuensia* 12. Turku, Finland: University of Turku, 1993. 217–236. Rpt. *Proceedings of the J.R.R. Tolkien Centenary Conference*. Ed. Patricia Reynolds and Glen H. GoodKnight. *Mallorn* 33 / *Mythlore* 21.2 (#80) (Winter 1996): 84–93.

_____. "Tom Shippey Speaks at the Tolkien Society Annual Dinner, Cambridge, April 23, 1983." *Digging Potatoes, Growing Trees*. Ed. Helen Armstrong. Peter Roe Memorial Booklets 5. Swindon: The Tolkien Society, 1997. Vol. 1, 31–52.

_____. "Tom Shippey Speaks at the Tolkien Society Annual Dinner, Norwich, April 13, 1991." *Digging Potatoes, Growing Trees*. Ed. Helen Armstrong. Peter Roe Memorial Booklets 6. Swindon: The Tolkien Society, 1998. Vol. 2, 13–23.

_____. "Tom Shippey Speaks at the Tolkien Society Annual Dinner, York, April 19, 1980." *Digging Potatoes, Growing Trees*. Ed. Helen Armstrong. Peter Roe Memorial Booklets 5. Swindon: The Tolkien Society, 1997. Vol. 1, 6–30.

_____. "A Wose by any Other Name." *Amon Hen* 45 (1980): 8–9.

Swann, Donald, and J.R.R. Tolkien. *The Road Goes Ever On: A Song Cycle*. Boston: Houghton Mifflin, 1967.

Shippey Amongst the Mercians

John Wm. Houghton

Tom Shippey famously directs our attention to the Mercian element in Tolkien's *legendarium* (e.g., *Road* 122–123; "Tolkien and the West Midlands: The Roots of Romance," *Roots* 39–59). This is eminently appropriate, Shippey himself having been born (like Tolkien) overseas but educated (like Tolkien) in Birmingham: yet there is at least a bit in Shippey of another Midlander. The other literary Mercian, a son not of upstart Birmingham but of its ancient northern neighbor, Lichfield (and, coincidentally, a student in Pembroke College, where Tolkien was a fellow for the two decades during which he held the Rawlinson-Bosworth Professorship), was Samuel Johnson, LL.D. Shippey has yet to attract his Boswell, but like the author of the *Dictionary* his literary output is enviable and his generosity notorious; his conversation can be bracingly magisterial, and he travels surrounded with a bodyguard of anecdote.

Like many people, I made my first acquaintance with Tom Shippey in 1986, not through Tolkien studies—though he had already made a mark in that field, having published the first version of *The Road to Middle-earth* in 1982—but through the PBS series *The Story of English*, in which he memorably imagines a bit of English-Danish horse trading.[1] I actually met him nine years later, for a dinner at the Crazy Fish Grille in Clayton, Missouri (a few blocks from the apartment of which we eventually became sequential inhabitants), during which he kindly agreed to be the volunteer Guest of Honor for a shoestring-budget convention, Bree Moot 2. The fact that he would spend the time with, and give a paper to, such a group illustrates, on a small scale, both his generous nature and the way his career has consistently spanned the gap between academia and fandom. Indeed, he has inspired a certain level of fandom of his own: for some years, otherwise serious scholars at Western Michigan University's annual International Medieval Congress made a game of being the first to sight Shippey, a contest which ended the year a party ran into him over hamburgers at Waldo's, a local Kalamazoo watering hole, before the conference even began.

I once heard Tom introduced with the comment (attributed by the presenter to yet another scholar) that he tended to conduct academic arguments with the same vigor he once brought to the rugby pitch. And there is a certain amount of truth in this; one can, without too much effort, imagine someone applying to him Boswell's response to Johnson's comment "Well, we had good talk": "Yes, Sir; you tossed and gored several persons" (Boswell IV, 168n 582). Having heard him say in the commentaries of the DVD version of Jackson's *Lord of the Rings* that whereas Tolkien's critics had accused him of flogging a dead horse, he knew that he had a Derby winner, one can detect the same note of glee in his demolition of Edmund Wilson and C.N. Manlove in the first chapter of *Road*. At the same time, however, he has been characteristically encouraging and helpful to other scholars. Many an evening over the years at the aforementioned Waldo's found him in the conversation pit in front of the fireplace, deep in lively discussion with graduate students from two continents (a scene I have myself seen duplicated, *mutatis mutandis*, at such other gatherings as the annual meeting of the august Medieval Academy of America). Asked for a blurb for a forthcoming book, he has been known to reply, not only with the requisite quotable quote, but with corrections to Old English citations in the text.

Perhaps my favorite Shippey story is one he tells on himself. Stripped of his own colorful details, it goes like this: Conversation over sherry in an Oxonian Senior Common Room had turned to the question of the national origins of names. Shippey observed that one older Fellow's name was obviously (say) German; the gentleman in question insisted that it was English. After several rounds of this, Shippey finally said, "Well, look here, not to put too fine a point on it, but I'm a philologist and you're a mathematician. Why are you *so* sure that you're right about this?" To which the other man replied, "Because Tolkien told me so."

In 1739, Dr. Johnson published in four monthly numbers of *The Gentleman's Magazine* a biography of the Dutch physician Herman Boerhaave (1668–1738). Summing up the (other) polymath's career, Johnson wrote:

> Nor was he unacquainted with the art of recommending truth by elegance, and embellishing the philosopher with polite literature: he knew that but a small part of mankind will sacrifice their pleasure to their improvement, and those authors who would find many readers, must endeavour to please while they instruct.
>
> He knew the importance of his own writings to mankind, and lest he might, by a roughness and barbarity of style, too frequent among men of great learning,

disappoint his own intentions, and make his labours less useful, he did not neglect the politer arts of eloquence and poetry. Thus was his learning, at once, various and exact, profound and agreeable [Johnson Vol. 14, 154–184].

"Learning ... various and exact, profound and agreeable": the one great Midlander might have been looking across the centuries to compliment the other.

NOTE

1. "Mother Tongue," at about 20 minutes.

WORKS CITED

Boswell, James. *Life of Johnson.* Third edition. Ed. George Birkbeck Hill. London: Charles Dilly, 1887. The Classic Literature Library. N.p., n.d. August 9, 2012. http://www.classic-literature.co.uk/scottish-authors/james-boswell/life-of-johnson-vol_04/ebook-page-168.asp.
Johnson, Samuel. "Herman Boerhaave." *The Works of Samuel Johnson.* Troy, New York: Pafraets, 1903. The Samuel Johnson Sound Bites Page. Frank Lynch, July 22, 2012. August 9, 2012. http://www.samueljohnson.com/boerhaave.html#17.
"The Mother Tongue." *The Story of English.* Episode 2. Dir. William Cran. PBS/BBC. 1996.

The "Lady with the Simple Gown and White Arms" *or* Possible Influences of 19th and Early 20th Century Book Illustrations on Tolkien's Work

Nancy Martsch

Young John Ronald opened the red-bound book. There, at the back, was his favorite part: "The Story of Sigurd." Turning the pages, he saw pen-and-ink drawings of Fafnir the dragon, of stalwart Sigurd.... He was reading *The Red Fairy Book*, edited by Andrew Lang, with illustrations by H.J. Ford and Lancelot Speed. It had been published in 1890.[1]

Tom Shippey, in a Guest Editorial for the Tolkien Society's journal *Mallorn*, suggested areas of Tolkien studies which he thought needed further consideration. No. 2 on the list was "the influences on [Tolkien] of writers of the nineteenth and twentieth centuries, so often now deeply unfashionable, forgotten and out of print ..." (*Mallorn* 3). Since Shippey issued his call to arms in 2008, additional studies of these writers' works have been published, but usually only of the text (probably because the illustrations are seldom reprinted).[2] But often these nineteenth and early twentieth century works were illustrated. I propose that we need to consider the illustrations in addition to the text when searching for possible influences on Tolkien's writing. We know that Tolkien acknowledged a picture as the "Origin of Gandalf."[3] Might not other pictures, especially those he saw in his youth, have inspired his imagination as well?

For this essay I have selected a particular image, which I will call "the lady with the simple gown and white arms," which was popular in nineteenth century illustrations. I hope to demonstrate that the descriptions of the beautiful ladies in Tolkien's *The Lord of the Rings* fit this image well.

The modern reader, leafing through the pictures in *The Red Fairy Book*, may notice that many of the ladies—regardless of the story being illustrated—look very much alike. This is especially true of the illustrations by Lancelot Speed.[4] Lancelot Speed (1860–1931) was a well-known Victorian illustrator whose work included the *Fairy Books*, *The Blue Poetry Book*, *Eric Brighteyes*, and many others, some of which Tolkien undoubtedly read as a boy.

I have selected two of Speed's illustrations to accompany this essay, "The Princess and the Spiders" and "Men turned and looked," because (a) Tolkien saw these illustrations,[5] and (b) they are excellent exemplars of the type. But this should not be taken to imply that Tolkien was influenced by *these particular illustrations*. Many other illustrators depicted the "lady with the simple gown with white arms" too.

The "lady with the simple gown and white arms" reflects the 1890s ideal of feminine beauty. She has a slender waist (sometimes the shape of the corset is visible), long hair often bound up exposing the slim neck, Greek profile, white skin. She is clad in a simple gown, usually light in color, either loose or fitted, with a girdle around the waist or hips, a low neck, and—the most consistent feature—bare arms. The gown may be sleeveless or with draped sleeves open to the shoulder. Sometimes the gown is augmented with a mantle.

The simple gown may have been influenced by Greek and Roman styles; the light color could reflect Classical influence or imply "primitive" unbleached wool or linen; and it is easy to render in pen-and-ink. Bare arms and shoulders were (and still are) the standard for ladies' evening dress, only today they're fashionably tanned, not white.

The "simple gown with white arms" was used to represent everything from fairy tale ladies to the legendary past to the Dark Ages of Europe. It was seen in illustrations and worn on stage. You could even whip one up with a bed sheet and a couple of pins for a game of Charades.

Some time ago, while writing an article on the appearances of the characters in *The Lord of the Rings* (Martsch), I was struck by the fact that all of Tolkien's beautiful ladies resembled "the lady with the simple gown and white arms." Tolkien, as every would-be illustrator knows (to his teeth-gnashing frus-

Opposite: **"The Princess and the Spiders" by Lancelot Speed. Speed illustrated "The Story of Sigurd" in *The Red Fairy Book*. The picture of the Princess and the spiders is from "The Golden Branch" in *The Red Fairy Book*. The Princess is trying to escape from the Enchanter's hall, but her way is blocked by spiders' webs.**

tration!) does not provide much physical description for his characters. He gives wonderful descriptions of nature. He does an excellent job of creating personality through words and actions (think of Ioreth or Lobelia Sackville-Baggins)—without saying a word about what the person looks like. For hobbit women we have no descriptions or drawings at all.

Tolkien himself was aware of this lack, for he wrote:

> I do not know the detail of clothing. I visualize with great clarity and detail scenery and "natural" objects, but not artefacts....
>
> I have no doubt that in the area envisaged by my story (which is large) the "dress" of various peoples, Men and others, was much diversified in the Third Age, according to climate, and inherited custom. As was our world, even if we only consider Europe and the Mediterranean and the very near "East" (or South).... The Rohirrim were not "mediaeval," in our sense. The styles of the Bayeux Tapestry (made in England) fit them well enough, if one remembers that the kind of tennis-nets [the] soldiers seem to have on are only a clumsy conventional sign for chain-mail of small rings [*Letters* 280–1].

The styles of the Bayeux Tapestry may fit the men (at least in terms of armor and weapons), but what of the women? As noted above, Tolkien never described hobbit women. But he did describe other ladies of great beauty: Goldberry, Arwen, Galadriel, and Éowyn. Usually the description occurs at or near the first encounter with the character.

Goldberry, the first to be encountered in the narrative, also has the most detailed description. She was the first in composition (written c. August 1938),[6] and the only one of these four ladies who existed prior to *The Lord of the Rings*. Goldberry first appeared in print in the poem "The Adventures of Tom Bombadil" published in *The Oxford Magazine* in 1934.[7] The poem had been composed by 1931, and stories about Tom Bombadil were told in the Tolkien household in the late 1920s. (This makes Goldberry a contemporary of *The Hobbit*.) In origin Goldberry is clearly a water-nymph, of a type well-known in English folklore. Her appearance was established in the poem: yellow hair, worn long; a gown of green or silver-green; a garland of flag-lilies (yellow iris) and forget-me-nots worn at her wedding; a close association with green reeds.

In the chapter "In the House of Tom Bombadil" Tolkien merely elaborated on the description in his poem:

> In a chair ... sat a woman. Her long yellow hair rippled down her shoulders; her gown was green, green as young reeds, shot with silver like beads of dew; and

Opposite: **"Men turned and looked" by Lancelot Speed, from** *Eric Brighteyes*. **"Men turned and looked" illustrates a Viking story set in Iceland: the occasion is a wedding which is about to turn into a brawl. The men wear the Victorian conception of Viking dress; the women, the "simple gown with white arms."**

her belt was of gold, shaped like a chain of flag-lilies set with the pale-blue eyes of forget-me-nots [*FR* I, vii, 134].

Then Tolkien adds one telling detail: "… and closing the door she turned her back to it, with her *white arms* spread out across it" (*FR* I, vii, 134; my emphasis).

When he decided that the hobbits would stay at Tom Bombadil's house a second day, and that it would be a day of rain, he gave Goldberry a second costume: "she was clothed all in silver with a white girdle, and her shoes were like fishes' mail" (143). Goldberry is the only lady to be described as wearing two gowns of different colors.

Goldberry still retains her close association with water, and her clothing reflects the moods of the river.

The next lady we meet is Arwen, one of the two most beautiful women in Middle-earth. Arwen was the last of the ladies in composition (late summer—fall 1946). She first appeared in the story (under the name "Finduilas") as the maker of Aragorn's banner carried at the Battle of the Pelennor Fields (*War* 370).[8] Perhaps this explains her relatively small role in the story. Frodo describes Arwen at Elrond's feast:

> In the middle of the table … there was a chair under a canopy, and there sat a lady fair to look upon … Young she was and yet not so. The braids of her dark hair were touched by no frost; her white arms and clear face were flawless and smooth … Above her brow her head was covered with a cap of silver lace netted with small gems, glittering white; but her soft grey raiment had no ornament save a girdle of leaves wrought in silver [*FR* II, i, 239].

This is the only physical description of Arwen in the entire narrative. We are told that she wore "stars on her brow" when she rode to Minas Tirith (*RK* VI, v, 251); and that later she wore around her neck "a white gem like a star … hanging upon a silver chain" which she gave to Frodo (*RK* VI, vi, 253), but this is all.

The only other description of Arwen is in "The Tale of Aragorn and Arwen" in Appendix A, which may have been composed around the time *The Lord of the Rings* was accepted for publication, if not earlier.[9] It occurs when young Aragorn catches his first sight of Arwen walking in Elrond's garden:

> For Aragorn had been singing a part of the Lay of Lúthien which tells of the meeting of Lúthien and Beren … And behold! there Lúthien walked before his eyes in Rivendell, clad in a mantle of silver and blue, fair as the twilight in Elven-home; her dark hair strayed in a sudden wind, and her brows were bound with gems like stars [*RK* Appendix A, 338].

Compare when Beren first saw Lúthien, as described in *The Silmarillion*:

Blue was her raiment as the unclouded heaven, but her eyes were grey as the starlit evening; her mantle was sewn with golden flowers, but her hair was dark as the shadows of twilight [*S* 165].

The other great beauty of Middle-earth is the Elven lady Galadriel, the Lady of Lórien. Galadriel was created *ab initio* during the writing of the Lothlórien chapters, c. August 1940 (*Treason* 217). Following *The Lord of the Rings* Tolkien wrote much (and sometimes contradictory) information about Galadriel as he tried to find her place in his *legendarium*.[10] But he added very little physical detail, save to glorify her hair and to say that she had been athletic in her youth.

Galadriel is tall, slender, with golden hair; and at every occurrence is said to be wearing white. The most detailed description comes in her meeting with Frodo, at her Mirror:

She lifted up her white arms, and spread out her hands towards the East in a gesture of rejection and denial. Eärendil, the Evening Star ... shown clear above.... Its rays glanced upon a ring about her finger; it glittered like polished gold overlaid with silver light, and a white stone in it twinkled ...

[Frodo offers her the Ring]: She stood before Frodo seeming now tall beyond measurement, and beautiful beyond enduring, terrible and worshipful. Then she let her hand fall, and the light faded, and suddenly she laughed again, and lo! she was shrunken: a slender elf-woman, clad in simple white ... [*FR* II, vii, 380–1].

At the farewell meeting, Galadriel wore a "circlet of golden flowers" in her hair (*FR* II, viii, 388). To honor Gimli's request, she "unbraided one of her long tresses, and cut off three golden hairs, and laid them in Gimli's hand" (392).

And she was again "robed all in glimmering white" when she and Elrond passed through the Shire on their way to the Grey Havens (*RK* VI, ix, 308). Since Tolkien refers to Éowyn's mantle as a "robe" (see below), this might have been a white mantle, also.

We come at last to Éowyn. Of the four ladies, she has the most costume changes. The Rohan chapters also have the most complex history of composition.[11] As of the first writing (winter 1941–42), Éowyn and Aragorn would fall in love and marry, or else she would ride openly "as Amazon" to battle and die defending or avenging King Théoden (*Treason* 437, 448). When, after a long hiatus, Tolkien returned to Book V in the late summer of 1946, the story underwent a complex series of revisions and rearrangements (including the invention of Arwen) until it achieved its final form. But the love of Éowyn for Aragorn, and some of the description of their first meeting (*Treason* 445), was retained.

Like Galadriel, Éowyn is tall, slender, golden-haired, and (when not in armor) always clad in white. She is also the only one of the ladies not specified as having "white arms," perhaps due to her athleticism. Éowyn is unique among the ladies in often being described in terms of metaphor: she is compared to a cold pale spring, to steel, to a frozen or white lily, et cetera.

We first see her standing behind King Théoden's throne. As she leaves, she turns and looks back: "Very fair was her face, and her long hair was like a river of gold. Slender and tall she was in her white robe girt with silver ..." (*TT* III, vi, 119).

When Aragorn departs for Helm's Deep, he looks back to see Éowyn standing before the doors of the house: "She was clad now in mail and shone like silver in the sun" (*TT* III, vi, 128). At Dunharrow Éowyn rides forth to greet Théoden:

> As they drew near Merry saw that the rider was a woman with long braided hair gleaming in the twilight, yet she wore a helm and was clad to the waist like a warrior and girded with a sword [*RK* V, iii, 68].

At the Houses of Healing, when Éowyn again assumes women's dress, she is "clad all in white" (*RK* VI, v, 239). Faramir gives her the mantle which had been made for his mother: "a great blue mantle the colour of deep summer-night, and it was set with silver stars about hem and throat" (*RK* VI, v, 239).

There is one other beautiful lady who is not a character in *The Lord of the Rings*; a lady from the past, like Lúthien. This is how the elf-maid Nimrodel is described in Legolas' song:

> Her mantle white was hemmed with gold,
> Her shoes of silver-grey.
> A star was bound upon her brows,
> ....
> Her hair was long, her limbs were white ... [*FR* II, vi, 354].

To sum up, all of our beautiful ladies share many qualities in common with the nineteenth century "lady with the simple gown and white arms":

They are slender (Goldberry, Galadriel, Éowyn); have long hair, either worn in braids (Arwen, Galadriel, Éowyn) or worn long (Goldberry, Éowyn, Nimrodel); wear simple raiment (Arwen, Galadriel), of light color: white (Galadriel, Éowyn), silver or grey (Arwen, Goldberry), and bound with a belt or girdle (Goldberry, Arwen, Éowyn); have white arms (Goldberry, Arwen, Galadriel, Nimrodel). Goldberry alone wears a bright color (green), and Lúthien wore sky blue. (Two other ladies in *The Silmarillion*—Aredhel and Níniel—also wore white.) Mantle styles seem unchanged through the ages: blue (Arwen, Éowyn), or white (Nimrodel, possibly Galadriel), decorated with gold or silver (Éowyn, Lúthien, Nimrodel, and maybe Arwen). Although none of the ladies' gowns are specified as sleeveless, all the references to "white arms" suggest that the arms are exposed.

Of course, all of our beautiful ladies may have been following the current fashion in Middle-earth! But then why did Tolkien select this particular style? Particularly as this style seems to cut across temporal and cultural boundaries, as it were.

Probably most readers, if asked to describe the style of clothing worn in Middle-earth (apart from hobbit lands) would answer "medieval." Certainly the armament of the Bayeux Tapestry (or the late Anglo-Saxon—early Norman period) approximates that of *The Lord of the Rings*. But not so the ladies' dress. For one thing, medieval women did not usually display white arms.[12] As Tolkien was expert in Early and Middle English, he probably knew this.

But Tolkien was not writing a historical novel, he was writing a fantasy. There's a lot more of the fairy-tale in *The Lord of the Rings* than most fans would care to admit.[13] Although Tolkien drew on European cultures to provide the background (and languages) for his creation, he did so selectively. When pressed to describe his beautiful ladies, he fell back on—not the medieval dress of his professional study, nor the styles contemporary with the writing of *The Lord of the Rings*—but the "lady with the simple gown and white arms" from the book illustrations of his childhood.

Can we prove that Tolkien derived his descriptions from book illustrations? No. We can only note their similarity. But we do know that a picture supplied the visual "Origin of Gandalf." And, by studying Tolkien's art, we can demonstrate that he was aware of illustrations. Tolkien had artistic talent, but no formal art training. However, he did learn to use pen-and-ink and water-color, and he had a strong sense of design. Some of his early drawings can be dated on the basis of style alone, which suggests that he (or his mentor[s]) was observing contemporary illustration. And in the late 1930s, when creating his own pictures for *The Hobbit*, he used published book illustrations for guidance. Some of these illustrations have been identified.[14] Interestingly, in *The Hobbit* Tolkien drew upon archaeological research both for his descriptions and for his pictures of Beorn's Hall and of Laketown (and for the cave paintings in his "Father Christmas Letter" of 1932). But his pictures of people in *The Hobbit* seem to derive from other sources: Gandalf is from *Der Berggeist*, the hobbits and dwarves wear nineteenth century European male dress, and his elves look like Victorian elves and gnomes, right down to the tips of their pointy-toed shoes. So it is entirely possible that Tolkien remembered nineteenth century illustrations when he needed to describe the ladies in *The Lord of the Rings*.

John Ronald Reuel Tolkien read books and magazines in his youth and manhood. Many of these nineteenth and early twentieth century books were illustrated. We know that later in life Tolkien turned to book illustration for guidance in his own art. And that in one instance his inspiration for the appearance of a character derived from a picture. So it is not unreasonable to assume that illustrations in the books which he read might have influenced the descriptions in his stories. I have chosen to examine the beautiful ladies in *The Lord of the Rings* to demonstrate their affinity to a popular type in nineteenth century illustration, which I have styled "the lady with the simple gown and white arms." Doubtless other similarities could be found. When we study late nineteenth and early twentieth century literature for influences on Tolkien's *legendarium*, we need to look at the illustrations which accompanied the original text, for they may have served as influences, too.

NOTES

1. *The Red Fairy Book* was second in a series of twelve colored *Fairy Books* edited by Andrew Lang, which were published between 1889 and 1910. They contained not only fairy stories but also condensed versions of myths and legends, and tales from other lands. John Ronald Reuel Tolkien read them all. All were illustrated, as were many other books and magazines at the time, both for children and for grown-ups. J.R.R. Tolkien grew up in the Golden Age of Book Illustration.

Tolkien thought the tale of Sigurd in *The Red Fairy Book* was "the best story he had ever read" (Carpenter 22). In his essay "On Fairy-stories" Tolkien describes his favorite childhood stories: "best of all [was] the nameless North of Sigurd of the Völsungs, and the prince of all dragons.... I desired dragons with a profound desire" (*TOF* 55).

2. For example, Dale Nelson's essays in *Encyclopedia* and *Beyond Bree*; Maggie Burns' essays in *Mallorn*; and Dimitra Fimi's *Tolkien, Race and Cultural History*.

3. Tolkien had carefully preserved a postcard of the painting *Der Berggeist* ("The Mountain Spirit") by Josef Madlener, in a folder marked "Origin of Gandalf" (Carpenter 51). For a reproduction and discussion of this painting see Anderson, *Hobbit*, 36–9, Plate 5.

4. And of Speed's illustrations for other works. Compare the illustrations by H.J. Ford and G.P. Jacomb-Hood in *The Blue Fairy Book* (the first in the series), which show more ethnic variety.

5. For *The Red Fairy Book*, see Note 1. In his notes for his *Beowulf* lecture, Tolkien wrote, "Eric BrightEyes (R. Haggard) is as good as most sagas and as heroic" (*Beowulf and the Critics* 426; cited in *Tales Before Tolkien* 430). My thanks to Douglas Anderson; and to Dale Nelson, who remarked, "The late Benedikt Benedikz, who knew Tolkien, told me about his large collection of Haggard romances."

6. The Tom Bombadil episode was written in the "two or three days" preceding August 31, 1938 (*Shadow* 110).

7. *The Oxford Magazine* 52.13 (15 February 1934): 464–5. For a history of the poem, see *Guide* 23–5.

8. Tolkien seems to have begun rewriting Book V in August or September 1946 (*Letters* 117, 118, *War* 274). The chronology of the composition of Book V onward is set forth in "The chronology of writing" (*Sauron* 12–13), and in *Chronology* 305–8.

9. For "The Tale of Aragorn and Arwen," see *Peoples* 262–3, *Chronology* 389.

10. "Lothlórien" and "The Mirror of Galadriel" chapters were written on "'August 1940' examination script" (*Treason* 217). Much of the additional writing on Galadriel is contained in *Unfinished Tales*, "The History of Galadriel and Celeborn."

11. The chapters on Rohan were written in three phases: first, the end of Book III and outlines, in the winter and spring of 1941–2 (*Treason* 379, 390, 423). This includes Aragorn's first meeting with Éowyn, in "The King of the Golden Hall" (*Treason* 445, 448, *Chronology*

252–3). Second, an abortive start to Book V in October 1944, with outlines for the story to come (*War* 233–4, *Chronology* 279–81). And third, Book V, with many variations, in the late summer and fall of 1946 (Note 8, above).

   12. Arwen's dress is arguably the most "medieval" of all the ladies'. Writing in 1967–9, Tolkien described Arwen's jeweled lace cap as a "tressure," worn by the Eldar and women of high rank among the Rangers. Christopher Tolkien added that "*Tressure*, a net for confining the hair, is a word of medieval English which my father had used in his translation of *Sir Gawain and the Green Knight* (stanza 69)" ("The Rivers and Beacon-hills ..." 11–12, emphasis in the original; *Companion* 205). Tolkien created Arwen about the same time as he was preparing to teach a course on *Sir Gawain*, c. August–October 1946 (*Chronology* 305–8, 309).

   13. Cf. *Tolkien, Race and Cultural History*. Fimi's premise is that Tolkien's *legendarium* developed from Victorian fairy stories.

   14. See Hammond and Scull, *J.R.R. Tolkien: Artist & Illustrator*, esp. Chapter 4, "The Hobbit."

Works Cited

Anderson, Douglas A., ed. *Tales Before Tolkien: The Roots of Modern Fantasy.* New York: Del Rey/Ballantine Books, 2003.

Fimi, Dimitra. *Tolkien, Race and Cultural History: From Fairies to Hobbits.* New York: Palgrave Macmillan, 2010.

Haggard, H. Rider. *Eric Brighteyes*, with Numerous Illustrations by Lancelot Speed. London: Longmans, Green and Co., 1891.

Hammond, Wayne G., and Christina Scull. *J.R.R. Tolkien: Artist & Illustrator.* Boston and New York: Houghton Mifflin, 1995, 2000.

Lang, Andrew, ed. *The Red Fairy Book*, with Numerous Illustrations by H.J. Ford and Lancelot Speed. London: Longmans, Green, 1890. Facsimile ed. Mineola, NY: Dover, 1966.

Martsch, Nancy. "Hair: or What Did the Fellowship Look Like?" *Beyond Bree* June 1993: 3–5 [Newsletter of the J.R.R. Tolkien Special Interest Group of American Mensa].

_____. "What Did They Look Like? Part II: The Ladies," *Beyond Bree* July 1993: 4–5.

Shippey, Tom. "An Encyclopedia of Ignorance." *Mallorn* 45 (Spring 2008): 3–5. [Journal of the Tolkien Society]

Tolkien, J.R.R. *Beowulf and the Critics.* Ed. Michael D. C. Drout. Tempe, AZ: Arizona Center for Medieval and Renaissance Studies, 2002.

_____. "The Rivers and Beacon-hills of Gondor." *Vinyar Tengwar* 42 (July 2001): 5–31. [Journal of the Elvish Linguistic Fellowship]

Appendix: Why did the "lady with the simple gown and white arms" become so popular?

   One can only speculate as to why "the lady with the simple gown and white arms" became a popular representation in fantastic and legendary tales. The nineteenth century was a time of rising nationalism in Europe, and with it an interest in archaeology and early literature, especially that of the North. It was also a time of Romanticism in the arts, of the growth of the novel, theatre and opera. Hence the desire to depict Europe's legendary (and fantastic) past. Unfortunately the peoples of Northern Europe—unlike the Greeks and the

Romans—left comparatively few images of themselves. So popular imagination filled in the gap. Fimi suggests that "the costumes of Wagner's operas, especially of *Der Ring des Nibelungen*, played an important role in standardizing the image of the Viking deities or heroes ..." (172).

Photography may also have played a role. Although photography was invented in the late 1820s, the ability to reproduce photographs in print lagged far behind. This meant that pictures of actual artifacts (including illuminated manuscripts) were reproduced as drawings. Reproduction of photographs in monochrome came later. Modern readers may not realize this, but really good color reproduction did not become commonplace until the latter part of the twentieth century. A reader today has a better opportunity to learn what early Europe actually looked like—from books, not the Internet!—than a reader of Tolkien's day.

Whether the inability to reproduce and widely circulate photographs of actual historical artifacts was a factor in creating the distorted public image of the legendary past I do not know. Certainly limited access to accurate information may have made people more willing to accept inaccuracy in "historical" illustrations. On the other hand, people have always viewed the past through the eyes of the present: a good story (with good-looking gals!) usually trumps historical accuracy. We still use the stereotype of the Viking with the horned helmet (think of Hagar the Horrible in the comic strip) even though we know it's inaccurate. But "the lady with the simple gown" has gone out of fashion along with her white arms.

Places Where the Stars Are Strange: Fantasy and Utopia in Tolkien's Middle-earth

ROBERT T. TALLY, JR.

1. Introduction

In the opening lines of *J.R.R. Tolkien: Author of the Century*, T.A. Shippey observes that "the dominant literary mode of the twentieth century has been the fantastic," and—after listing such writers as H.G. Wells, George Orwell, William Golding, Kurt Vonnegut, Ursula Le Guin, and Thomas Pynchon—Shippey notes that, "[b]y the end of the century, even authors deeply committed to the realist novel have often found themselves unable to resist the gravitational pull of the fantastic as a literary mode" (vii–viii). The rise of fantasy as a genre, surely the most popular genre of literature today, is itself one of the significant features of twentieth-century literary history, on par with (and, perhaps, not unrelated to) the development of modernism in the late-nineteenth and early-twentieth century. But beyond the question of genre or subgenre, the fantastic as a discourse or mode permeates "high" literature as well as "low." The modernism of W.B. Yeats or James Joyce finds itself infused with Celtic, Greek, or medieval mythology, just as the advent of magical realism in Gabriel García Marquez or Julio Cortázar has uncovered the interrelations of the fantastic and the realistic in everyday life, and the postmodern extravagancies of a John Barth or Georges Perec disclose that the lines between imaginary and real are at best oscillatory, provisional, and uncertain. All of these, and many more, partake of the fantastic, sometimes in more or less obvious ways. As Kathryn Hume has made clear in her magnificent *Fantasy and*

Mimesis: Responses to Reality in Western Literature, the fantastic and the imitative or realistic modes "seem more usefully viewed as the twin impulses behind the creation of literature" (195). In any event, the overlapping territories of fantasy and mimesis are significant features of the literary and critical landscape of our time.

The somewhat defensive tone of Shippey's arguments, as well as the implied defensiveness in Hume's, appears a bit justified when confronting critics who would insist upon more clearly mimetic or realistic literature. However, some of the harshest critics of fantasy are not so much the proponents of a sober realism as they are readers whose own preferred forms of creating imaginary worlds are set in opposition to Tolkien's mythmaking and mapping of Middle-earth, not to mention the many and varied successors to Tolkienian fantasy. In particular, I am thinking of the distinction frequently made between fantasy and utopia. Champions of the latter, as a discourse or a genre, often resist and even condemn fantasy as a retrograde, immature, or unworthy approach to the otherworldly. Utopia, which had appeared to be a quintessentially modern genre and discourse, has reasserted itself in recent decades. I myself have argued for the persistence of utopia in postmodernity, and I find that the utopian impulse may have found its moment in the era of globalization.[1] But I dispute the idea that fantasy and utopia are incompatible or opposed, a notion that permeates the discussions of these ostensibly related discourses. In this essay, I wish to examine the utopian critique of fantasy, specifically with regard to Tolkien's imaginary world (or "Other-world": see *TOF* 55), and I want to take up the challenge of our age's greatest utopian critic, Fredric Jameson, who has provided one of the most authoritative critical voices in distinguishing utopia from fantasy. I argue that the fantastic world of Middle-earth is not so neatly defined as some anti-fantasy critics would have it, and that Jameson's own critique, which appears in the context of his analysis of science fiction as the genre most suited to the utopian impulse, mistakes its opponent and thereby overlooks the utopian function and potential of fantasy.

In their imaginative visions of alternative social, cultural, or historical formations, fantasy and utopia share generic aims and effects, but they are frequently set in opposition, often on political grounds. For example, in his landmark treatise on utopian discourse, *Archaeologies of the Future*, Jameson speaks of a "great schism" between fantasy and science fiction. Here Jameson follows Darko Suvin in seeing utopia as a "sociopolitical subgenre of science fiction" (Suvin 61). Fantasy is thought to be anti-utopian in the sense that it is escapist or that it withdraws from the "real world," rather than projecting meaningful alternatives to our present "real world" problems as utopia, or even dystopia, is supposed to do. Jameson is not alone in treating fantasy as an escapist, indeed reactionary, genre: a genre that presents a lost world of magic, a world of clear-cut morality, a world that is preferable to our own, but also unavailable to us except as "fantasy." Indeed, Jameson's discussion of this great schism is largely meant to define utopia in such a way that it can no longer be tainted by fantasy; he even introduces his discussion by saying, "We must now lay this misunderstanding to rest" (*Archaeologies* 56). In Jameson's analysis, science fiction (or utopia) offers the possibility of imagining a radical alternative to the present order by allowing us to think its limits, rather than presenting a distant otherworldly realm which has no bearing on the actually existing conditions of our lives, or worse, which tacitly supports the status quo. For Jameson, severing utopian discourse from the follies of fantasy is a crucial step in establishing the necessity of utopianism for the project of comprehending our present, world-historical condition. Of course, one might declare that this difference in view is largely unremarkable, as Tolkien's many supporters are in no way threatened by the critique of one or more literary theorists. Nevertheless, Jameson is perhaps the most significant utopian thinker of our time, and I do believe it is important to address his objections to fantasy as a genre or a discursive practice. As I will discuss further below, I question whether Tolkienian fantasy really is antithetical to the utopian project, and I find that the fantastic mode offers productive areas for literary and political criticism of the world as we experience it in the here and now. Indeed, by looking at Tolkien's Middle-earth, perhaps the archetypal and paradigmatic fantasy world, I intend to show that even Tolkien's fantasy operates with a utopian and critical force to energize the reader's engagement with this world ... and with its possible alternatives.

Following Jameson's analysis of the great schism between science fiction and fantasy in *Archaeologies of the Future*, I will focus on three elements that are thought to distinguish the genres—or, as I prefer to consider them, the discursive practices or modes—of fantasy or utopia. The first and most general element is the *fantasy world* itself. In fantasy, so the anti-fantasy argument goes, this world is unrelated to and incommensurable with our own "real world." One might also characterize this fault line here as that between *escape* and *extrapolation*, insofar as fantasy is viewed as a mode of escaping from the "real world" in which we live, whereas utopia or science fiction attempts to extend various aspects of our "real world" to their logical conclusions. In fairness, Tolkien himself comes to the defense of the "escapist" impulse (*TOF* 69–75), but as we shall see, he disavows the usually negative valences associated with the term. The second element is the prevalence of *magic*, especially as distinguished from *technology*, in fantasy. Fantasy is thus understood as invoking an irrational, metaphysical, or non-cognitive substitute for science that "magically" avoids the material or logistical problems that would normally take place within the fantasy world. From this perspective, the technological or mechanical details of utopian or science-fictional schemes are preferable, since these aspects more closely relate to our own, again, "real world" experience. The third element is the perceived predominance of *ethics* or an ethical system, especially understood as a stable *good-versus-evil* binarism, in fantasy. This is contrasted with the more nebulous morality (or amorality) of the science-fictional world; or, to put it more pointedly, this distinction is ultimately revealed to be that between ethics and politics, where the former insists upon a once-and-for-all judgment of what is or is not "good," and the latter acknowledges the contested terrain upon which humans struggle to make a life worth living. In Jameson's view, for instance, Fantasy with a capital *F* ultimately suppresses or turns its back on the political sphere. Clearly, I believe that the political remains not only possible, but necessary and active, in the practice of fantasy, and that the utopia-versus-fantasy arguments are misplaced.[2] Indeed, these three elements turn out to be red herrings: the utopian fantastic in Tolkien's Middle-earth combines, but also troubles, these notions.

2. "The World as It Appears under the Sun"

Among those critics skeptical of fantasy, utopia in science fiction offers the possibility of imagining a radical alternative to the present order, rather than a distant otherworldly realm that cannot affect the actually existing conditions of our lives. For example, Jameson draws on the rather anti-fantasy arguments in Suvin's trailblazing study, the *Metamorphoses of Science Fiction*, in which science fiction or utopia is understood to be a genre of "cognitive estrangement" (4). For Suvin, fantasy is not "cognitive" but "metaphysical," employing myth or religion or magic in the place of rational thought. At a superficial level, Tolkien's "mythophilia" and his own religious beliefs lend themselves to Suvin's argument, but the reality of Tolkienian fantasy is more complex than the anti-fantastic utopian critics would have us believe.

In truth, Tolkien's Middle-earth would seem an archetypical example of a fantastic realm, with its elves, orcs, trolls, wizards, and dragons. Furthermore, Tolkien's own distinction between fairy-stories and traveler's narratives might be viewed as confirmation of his distaste for traditional utopian literature. We recall that utopia often appears in the form of the travel narrative, and even Thomas More's *Utopia* takes on the form of a second-hand reporting of a traveler's tale; Raphael Hythlodaeus—his very name suggests that he is a "dispenser of nonsense"—encountered the island nation while taking part in one of Amerigo Vespucci's voyages. But Tolkien's commitment to the creation, or "sub-creation," of a world apart does not necessarily mean that Tolkien turns away from an engagement with the "real" world. The imaginary projection of an alternate reality combines the fantastic and the utopian in Middle-earth, where the integrated or closed *Lebenstotalität* (as Georg Lukács refers to the world of the epic)[3] figures forth a kind of truth not seen in more crudely allegorical narratives. As Tolkien himself notes, "creative Fantasy is founded upon the hard recognition that things are so in the world as it appears under the sun; on a recognition of fact, but not a slavery to it" (*TOF* 65).

The view of the fantasy world as wholly unrelated to our own underlies a key objection to the genre, especially on the part of more politically minded critics. That is, so the story goes, where science fiction offers images of an alternative reality through cognitive estrangement, its world is still an extrapolation of our own real world. To cite the most familiar version of this, the science-fictional world is a look into our future, where certain contemporary problems, like poverty, nuclear weapons, overpopulation, and so forth, are extended to what seems their logical consequences. So, for instance, in a world of growing and rampant overpopulation and consequent food shortages or famines, of course we would find that "Soylent Green is made out of people!" (as immortalized by Charlton Heston's *cri-de-coeur* in that film's final scene). In contrast to this science-fictional world, according to the argument of fantasy's detractors, fantasy either creates a wholly unreal, Never-Never-Land completely unconnected to the world in which we live, or it creates a simplistic and romantic vision of our past that is somehow preferable to our present condition. In both cases, the political message is deemed inappropriate to effecting real social change in the here-and-now. That is, the unreal world is merely an escape into utter "fantasy," a realm of the impossible; or, perhaps worse, in presenting an idealization of the past, fantasy becomes a reactionary nostalgia. For example, this is a large part of Michael Moorcock's critique of Tolkien (and, more so, of Tolkien's epigones): "Since the beginnings of the Industrial Revolution, at least, people have been yearning for an ideal rural world they believe to have vanished—yearning for a mythical state of innocence .... This refusal to face or derive any pleasure from the realities of urban industrial life, this longing to possess, again, the infant's eye view of the countryside, is a fundamental theme in popular English literature" (126).

In Tolkien's Middle-earth, there certainly seem to be elements of both escapism and nostalgia. Tolkien concedes that escapism may be a goal of fantasy, but he disputes the assumption that escape is a bad thing, as when he argues that the "misusers" of the word have confused "the Escape of the Prisoner with the Flight of the Deserter": "Why should a man be scorned if, finding himself in prison, he tries to get out and go home? Or if, when he cannot do so, he thinks and talks about other topics than jailers and prison-walls? The world outside has not become less real because the prisoner cannot see it" (*TOF* 69). Middle-earth is not our world, nor is it even our past world. Yet the otherworldly domain, while independent of our real world, is not altogether incommensurable with our own. As Tolkien notes in "On Fairy-stories," fairy tales are not so much stories about "fairies or elves" but about the Perilous Realm itself: "*Faërie* contains many things besides elves and fays, and besides dwarfs, witches, trolls, giants, or dragons: it holds the seas, the sun, the moon, the sky; and the earth, and all things that are in it: tree and bird, water and stone, wine and bread, and ourselves, mortal men, when we are enchanted" (*TOF* 32, emphasis in original). That is, although this otherworld is clearly not the same as our world, it is not altogether an escape from our world either. The place where we exist (when enchanted) is also a vision of our world that, like the classical utopias and even more like the speculative fiction of modern utopian literature, encourages us to imagine alternatives to our own condition, while actively exploring what might be called "real-world" problems through this imaginative activity of fantasy.

The title of my essay obliquely refers to the overall point about fantasy worlds, as I believe Tolkien's view of Middle-earth as a world very much like, but not crudely homologous to, our own is figured forth in the idea of "places where the stars are strange." As fans and scholars of *The Lord of the Rings* will recognize, the phrase comes from Aragorn's speech during the Council of Elrond, in which he mildly rebukes Boromir, who had just complained of his long journey, by noting just how far and wide he himself had traveled over the years. Indeed, if one regards the map while reading this passage, one discovers that Aragorn had sojourned to its outer limits. As Aragorn puts it: "I have had a hard life and a long; and the leagues that lie between here and Gondor are a small part in the count of my journeys. I have crossed many mountains and many rivers, and trodden many plains, even into the far countries of Rhûn and Harad where the stars are strange" (*FR* II, ii, 261). As beautiful or poetic as this image of lands "where the stars are strange" is, Aragorn's comment might be reasonably viewed as stating a mere matter of fact: to wit, we can discern that he had travelled to regions which lie south of the equator, where he could perhaps view Cetus, the Southern Cross, and other constellations not always visible in the Northern Hemisphere. And this is partly my point. Although we ought never simply graft Tolkien's Middle-earth onto a map of "our" world,[4] Tolkien is nevertheless still speaking of our world, albeit figuratively and in such a way as to maintain the internal coherence and "totality" of his own imaginary geography. Aragorn's journeys take place in a fantasy world, but as readers of this fantasy, we still "know" it to be akin to our own, at least as much so as the worlds of utopian or science-fictional literature.[5]

This is not at all to say that the fantasy world of Middle-earth *is* our real world. Tolkien plainly states that the fantasy world is an "Other-world," and that "Fantasy" itself is "the making or glimpsing of Other-worlds" (*TOF* 55). And, although Suvin quotes this as a sign of Tolkien's escapism, Tolkien's view that "Fairy-stories were plainly not primarily concerned with possibility, but with desirability" is actually closer to Jameson's idea of "the desire called Utopia" than we typically imagine (*TOF* 55). In any event, Tolkien's youthful desire to know a world of magic, dragons, and what not seems to me quite similar to the desire for a world of spaceships and time-travel. (Indeed, Jameson has suggested that the dragon is fantasy's equivalent or analogue of science fiction's spaceship [*Archaeologies* 63].) It really seems that the *enchantment* of such worlds, rather than the otherworldliness of them, is what really disturbs certain utopian critics. But, as Tolkien indicates in several places, the very idea of "magic," so intimately tied to the "sword-and-sorcery" form of fantasy that he helped to launch, is much closer to machinery, technology, and science than is generally supposed.

3. Reflections on Magic

In his well-known letter to Milton Waldman, which has been reprinted as a preface to the Second Edition of *The Silmarillion*, Tolkien essentially identifies what is called "Magic" with what he calls "the Machine." In Tolkien's view, both have the same function, both are means to the same end, and both are catalysts "for making the will more quickly effective" (*Letters* 145). Or, to put it more accurately, "magic" and "the machine" are really two names for the same thing. As Tolkien states, in using the term "the Machine (or Magic), … I intend all use of external plans or devices (apparatus) instead of the development of the inherent inner powers or talents—or even the use of these talents with the corrupted motive of dominating: bulldozing the real world, or coercing other wills. The Machine is our more obvious modern form though more closely related to Magic than is usually recognized" (145–6).

Interestingly enough, for a corpus that so influenced the sword-and-sorcery sub-genre, Tolkien's writings include very little actual magic. Magic would seem to be the particular province of wizards, but even the named wizards in Tolkien's world but rarely perform magical acts. In *The Hobbit*, Gandalf—who is, of course, known to hobbits for his impressive fireworks displays—uses a sort of weaponized fireworks on goblins and wolves, as the pine-cones ignited with magical fire and tossed from the treetops suggest an early use of hand-grenades and incendiary bombs. In *The Lord of the Rings*, Gandalf utters spells, famously in contesting with the Balrog in Moria, and the Balrog apparently utters some curses of its own, and Gandalf continues to wield fire. But in both *The Hobbit* and *The Lord of the Rings*, Gandalf is perhaps handier with the sword than with the wand or spell. Contrasted with his many epigones, such as the celebrated Albus Dumbledore, Gandalf scarcely does magic at all ... but for another kind of "magic," to which I will return shortly.

By way of illustration, let us look at one particular example of magic in *The Lord of the Rings*: the Mirror of Galadriel. It is a memorable scene, and, by virtue of its framing, it may operate as a meditation on the nature of "magic" itself. We recall that the scene begins with Sam and Frodo remarking upon the omnipresence of "Elf-magic" in Lothlórien. "You can see and feel it everywhere," says Frodo, but Sam notes that, unlike Gandalf with his showy fireworks displays, "you can't see nobody working it.... I'd dearly love to see some Elf-magic, Mr. Frodo!" (*FR* II, vii, 376). Galadriel uses just this term to entice Sam to look in the mirror, although she mildly rebukes the hobbits for confusing "Elf-magic" with "the deceits of the Enemy": "this is what your folk would call magic, I believe; though I do not understand clearly what they mean; they seem to use the same word of the deceits of the Enemy. But this, if you will, is the magic of Galadriel. Did you not say that you wished to see Elf-magic?" Yet Galadriel has already indicated the ambiguousness of this particular magic, noting that she is able to "command the Mirror" to reveal many things, often showing "to some ... what they desire to see." But, she goes on, it is more "profitable" to allow the Mirror to show what it will, even though— whether it displays visions of the past, present, or future—"even the wisest cannot always tell" (*FR* II, vii, 377).

This is clearly a dangerous bit of magic, as Galadriel specifically counsels when Sam becomes agitated and alarmed at the Mirror's vision. "Remember that the Mirror shows many things, and not all have yet come to pass. Some never come to be, unless those that behold the visions turn aside from their path to prevent them. The Mirror is dangerous as a guide to deeds" (*FR* II, vii, 378). Most famously, after Frodo has seen his own perplexing visions in the Mirror, he offers the One Ring to Galadriel, who—like Gandalf earlier in the Shire, but even more vehemently—admits that she is sorely tempted, but then passes the test. The wielder of this Elf-magic has survived the "deceits of the Enemy." Hence, the hobbits were not entirely wrong to characterize Elf-magic and the magic of Sauron with the same word. Much of Galadriel's own magical actions involves forms of potential deceit, as the ambiguities of the Mirror suggest. Before she passes her own test, she quite pointedly tests the members of the Fellowship, causing them to see "visions" (whether "deceitful" or not is another question); these visions cause particular pain to Boromir and to Frodo. Indeed, the mirror itself, not Galadriel's magic mirror but our own quotidian one, is perhaps an apt figure for the ambiguities of magic in Tolkien's Middle-earth. A mirror presents a false image, that is, a reflection of the "real world," that may or may not be useful; it might be an accurate representation of the look of things, but the image is also a distortion. Certainly the mirrors can be used to trick the eye just as easily as to satisfy it. The scene in which the hobbits encounter "Elf-magic" in the Mirror of Galadriel reveals a deep ambiguity about magic in Tolkien's world, and this ambiguous stance is not really much different from the concerns over technology in the worlds of science fiction.

Although Tolkien wishes to distinguish the so-called "magic" of the elves from the magic or machinery of others, this distinction does not really hold. As we have just seen, the Mirror of Galadriel is a not wholly reliable or salutary form of magic, but this is not atypical. Other examples in *The Lord of the Rings* include the *palantíri*, whose manifest usefulness is revealed to cause far greater dangers to those, like Saruman or Denethor, who employ them, and of course the *rings* themselves, which ultimately are shown to cause harm, even the "Three Rings for the Elven-kings," as Galadriel notes sadly. While Tom Bombadil and the elves use a type of homeopathic or nature-based "magic" (speaking to trees, for example, or commanding the river to flood), the agents of evil, as they are imagined, use a more artificial or technological form, as with the One Ring or even bombs, such as Saruman contrives for blowing a hole in Helm's Deep. But again, for all of the magical power of the White Wizard and the "Necromancer" Sauron, very little actual magic is wielded. Indeed, for the most part, as Tolkien's letter to Waldman had indicated, the real force of this "black" magic lies in its influence or domination over other wills; that is, the function of magic or machinery for its user is primarily to impose one's will upon orcs, trolls, and corruptible men. However, in a more positive sense, this is also the power wielded by a Gandalf or a Galadriel, although we would prefer to think of theirs as the power of inspiration—for instance, in kindling men's hearts—rather than domination ... the results, however, are similar. Indeed, once it is known that Gandalf himself is wearing "the Third Ring, Narya the Great," it becomes apparent that his real magical power is the ability to "rekindle hearts in a world that grows chill" (*RK* VI, ix, 310, and Appendix B, 366). Like Galadriel, who does not claim to offer counsel, but who clearly offers some anyway, Gandalf's greatest magic is in motivating and guiding others, a more beneficent, but not dissimilar, form of "making the will more quickly effective."

The difference, for Tolkien, comes down to the intent of the magic user and the effect of the magic used, it seems. The fundamental issue is Art itself, which Tolkien characterizes as "sub-creation," since what Tolkien calls the "real primary world" of creation has only one Creator, and its relation to the "primary world." In a reflection on the natural desire for art, for sub-creation, Tolkien considers the origins of "the Machine (or Magic)," as he explains in the letter to Waldman.

> This desire [to create Art] is at once wedded to a passionate love of the real primary world, and hence filled with the sense of mortality, and yet unsatisfied by it. It has various opportunities of "Fall." It may become possessive, clinging to the things made as "its own," the sub-creator wishes to be Lord and God of his private creation. He will rebel against the laws of the Creator—especially against mortality. Both of these (alone or together) will lead to a desire for Power, for making the will more quickly effective,—and so to the Machine (or Magic) [*Letters* 145].

Hence, art itself, when combined with the usual sin of pride, quickly leads to power and the use of "un-natural" devices. However, in attempting to distinguish the "good" magic of the elves from this baleful form, Tolkien avers that "its object is Art not Power, sub-creation not domination and tyrannous reforming of Creation." But, as the entire tragic history of *The Silmarillion* recounts, the problem is "that this frightful evil can and does arise from an apparently good root, the desire to benefit the world and others—speedily and according to the benefactor's own plans—is a recurrent motive" (*Letters* 146).

Thus magic, which is supposed to infuse the fantasy world, is really related to the broader question of ethics. In other words, the distinction between magic and technology dissolves in Tolkien's world—and, more generally, in fantasy at large—as they become names for the same thing: means of enhancing the aesthetic ability of the artist or sub-creator. Perhaps this is why so many would-be Saurons or Gandalfs appear as hybrids of the magician and the scientist, like Faust, Frankenstein, Ahab, and so on. What counts, then, is not the mythological versus the cognitive estrangements in the world, but the ethical approach to being in the world. This is the seemingly inevitable problem of good versus evil.

4. Fantasy Beyond Good and Evil

The anti-fantasy arguments of those favoring science fiction or utopia frequently cite the simplistic ethical system that undergirds the fantastic realm. That is, to use Jameson's words here, one of the "structural characteristics of fantasy which contrast sharply with SF and which can serve as *differentiae specificae* for this genre" is "the organization of fantasy around the ethical binary of good and evil," in addition to "the fundamental role it assigns to magic" (*Archaeologies* 58). Some of Tolkien's detractors cite this seemingly simplistic, good-versus-evil ethical code as a primary objection to the fantasy world of Middle-earth. It is not just that Tolkien seems to have adopted a strictly Manichean worldview, at least in their view of it, but that his world also establishes once and forever just who is good (elves, for instance, or noble men and well-bred hobbits) and who is evil (Sauron above all, but then the various monsters like orcs, trolls, dragons, and so on). From this ethics, a reactionary politics must inevitably emerge. For instance (in what I take to be a serious misreading, by the way), Moorcock objects that "*The Lord of the Rings* is a pernicious confirmation of the values of a morally bankrupt middle-class.... If the Shire is a suburban garden, Sauron and his henchmen are that old bourgeois bugaboo, the Mob—mindless football supporters throwing their beer-bottles over the fence—the worst aspects of modern urban society represented as the whole by a fearful, backward-yearning class for whom 'good taste' is synonymous with 'restraint' (pastel colours, murmured protest) and 'civilized' behaviour means 'conventional behaviour in all circumstances'" (125).

This view of Tolkien's world cannot long withstand scrutiny, and a careful consideration of Tolkien's texts reveals a far more nuanced ethical framework, whatever Tolkien's own personal religious or moral tenets. Shippey has quite rightly undercut Edwin Muir's notion that *The Lord of the Rings* contains a simplistic happy ending in which "The good boys, having fought a deadly battle, emerge at the end of it well, triumphant and happy, as boys would naturally expect to do." As any serious reader would recognize, the ending not nearly so simple: Frodo is literally and figuratively scarred for life (Shippey calls him a "burnt-out case" [*Author* 148]).[6] Théoden's prophetic words—"much that was fair and wonderful shall pass for ever out of Middle-earth"—come true (*TT* III, viii, 155), Elrond's and Galadriel's powers wane, and so forth. Far from presenting a neat victory for good over evil, Tolkien introduces us to Galadriel's poignant concept of the "long defeat." Indeed, as the magic of Galadriel's Mirror or of Denethor's *palantír* suggests, the basic morality of things is not so clear cut in Tolkien's world. Whatever Tolkien's own view on the matter, the ethical framework of his Middle-earth cannot be reduced to a good-versus-evil caricature.

As I have pointed out in "Let Us Now Praise Famous Orcs," the representatives of so-called "evil" in Tolkien's world are far more complex and ambiguous than generally supposed. The problem of any inherent orcish evil troubled Tolkien, and he felt that their mere existence meant that they could not be beyond redemption. But then, this must be the case with all "evil" beings in this world, right? Indeed, so many of the "evil ones"—such as Sauron, Saruman, and even the great original Satan-figure, Melkor or Morgoth—are really the Fallen, figures of pity rather than pure hatred. Gollum, of course, is the very avatar of this concept of pitiable "evil." Similarly with the Ringwraiths and Denethor and Fëanor and so on, each of whom commits horrific acts but who are also the victims of some greater "evil," like pride or hopelessness. Furthermore, as Tolkien had indicated in his letter to Waldman, in almost every case, this so-called evil emerges out of a desire to do good. (Morgoth would seem to be the exception, as noted by Tolkien, but I think a case could be made for even his greater moral ambiguity.) This is of course why both Gandalf and Galadriel decline Frodo's offer of the Ring. As Gandalf puts it, the Ring would corrupt him precisely because of his "pity for weakness and the desire of strength to do good" (*FR* I, ii, 71). But, as Tolkien makes clear in his identification of Magic with the Machine, all the Ring really does is enhance the inherent power of the user. Thus, Tolkien suggests, the very desire to do good is at the root of all evil.

Tolkien is no moral relativist, but he does invite the possibility of a kind of Nietzschean perspectivism which would undermine the simplistic, binary ethical model attributed to him. Famously, in *The Two Towers*, Sam sees the slain Harad soldier, and wonders "what the man's name was and where he came from; and if he was really evil of heart, or what lies or threats had led him on the long march from his home; and if he would not really rather have stayed there in peace" (*TT* IV, iv, 269). Of course, Sam—who frequently longs for home and peace—never asks what possible "lies and threats" have led him so far from the Shire, but his sympathy for the enemy soldiers suggests a far more interesting ethical framework than most give Tolkien credit for maintaining.

Shippey has made much of how evil in Tolkien is characterized by the ambiguous figure of "the Shadow" (see, e.g., *Author* 128–29). A shadow is, of course, simultaneously a presence and an absence, existing and nonexistent at the same time, much like the reflections in Galadriel's mirror. It seems to me that this evocative figure is well suited to the depiction of evil in Tolkien's world, since it both is and is not present, and when visible, it is largely seen in its effects; moreover, those effects may not be recognizable or able to be evaluated until much later. The "ruse of history" does not spare Middle-earth, and Jameson's view of the dialectical reversal might also bear on the events in this imaginary place. Tolkien's contention that "evil" arises largely out of a desire to do good—that the human, all-too-human desire for sub-creation, for Art itself, is what makes possible, if not *inevitable*, the Fall—seems applicable to this world.

In the end, the ethical framework of Tolkien's Middle-earth is much more complex, even muddied, than either his detractors or his champions frequently believe. Tolkien's apparently idealized elves turn out to have much to find fault with, and even in their most noble images, they do not always stand for what is good, as seen most clearly in *The Silmarillion*. Hobbits and dwarves are somewhat more nuanced, which also makes them more interesting, and men are far more complex in their tendencies toward good or evil or that which lies beyond good and evil. The fact is, as the angelic (Maia) Gandalf indicates at the very outset of the adventure, the ethical argument should not require either some adherence to an abstract and unchanging ideal or the repulsion of an ever-nefarious evil, but rather it must involve the basic ways we comport ourselves in our world. Echoing a sentiment felt by everyone at some point, or rather at many points, in his or her life, Frodo wishes this "evil" had not arisen in his own lifetime, and Gandalf replies, "So do I ... and so do all who live to see such times. But that is not for them to decide. All we have to decide is what to do with the time that is given us" (*FR* I, ii, 60).

The wisdom here lies partly in a recognition of the degree to which all we are ever doing is muddling through. We are undoubtedly doing our best with the materials at hand in the time available, but nothing can prove to us in this time and place that we are doing some transcendent "good." Indeed, even the good we feel pretty sure we are doing will have consequences that are to our minds baleful, as when Galadriel notes that the destruction of the One Ring will inevitably lead to the disintegration of Lothlórien and of elven culture more generally. The end of Sauron, which is followed a bit later by the end of Saruman, is not at all the Hollywood happy ending some would suppose. The catastrophic transformation of Middle-earth resembles, dare I say, the more *realistic* vision of a world altered by the forces of history.[7] As with real history, in Gandalf's words, "even the very wise cannot see all ends" (*FR* I, ii, 69). Hence, the apparent "good-versus-evil" worldview gives way to a more nuanced and more realistic ethics, one which shares a great deal with the aims, if not always the methods, of politics, insofar as the political realm is always understood to be a site of contest, compromise, second-looks, and reevaluation. This too helps in transforming the image of the real world by establishing an imaginary space in which to envision our own world in a new light.

5. Conclusion

Just as the simplistic good-versus-evil binary is not an apt model for Tolkien's ethics in Middle-earth, so too it seems that the *fantasy-versus-utopia* opposition does not hold. The misplaced preposition misleadingly opposes two discursive formations whose defining territories often overlap. The real value of utopia lies not in its presentation of a blueprint for an ideal society, but in the ways that it enables us to imagine radical alternatives to the present society. In other words, utopia is a critical practice, and I agree with China Miéville, who sees utopia or science fiction as a subset of fantasy[8]; hence, fantasy is also a critical practice. In a world made mystified and false by ideology and alienation, the fantastic might actually be a better way to gain access to the "real" world, which can no longer be simply read off the page of realistic fiction.

The interrelations of fantasy and utopia in Tolkien's world serve to establish a sense of radical difference from our own everyday world which is nevertheless also a ground upon which we may reflect upon real-world conditions. One might even note how much the reverse might also be true: that is, how realism partakes of fantasy, as in the marvelous anecdote of the "MOOR EEF-FOC" (also cited by Tolkien) which, according to G.K. Chesterton, reveals "that elvish kind of realism Dickens adopted everywhere."[9] In this case, even the distinction between fantasy and realism might be blurred, since both modes interact in various ways to open up our perspectives on our world, including of course the world made visible through acts of the imagination. As Eric Rabkin summarizes it,

> Fantasy represents a basic mode of human knowing; its polar opposite is Reality. Reality is that collection of perspectives and expectations that we learn in order to survive in the here and now. But the here and now becomes tomorrow; a child grows, a culture develops, a person dreams. In every area of human thought, civilization has evolved a functioning reality, but the universe has suffered no reality to maintain itself unchanged. The glory of man is that he is not bound by reality. Man travels in fantastic worlds [227].

In the end, the real question is not whether a sober realism, a critical utopianism, or a creative fantasy offers the best mode in which to engage artistically with the world, but rather how we are to engage at all. Otherworldliness may indeed be the best way of seeing our own world with fresh eyes, and, in an age which seems to have forgotten how to think critically, historically, or speculatively, the sort of literary work accomplished by a Tolkien in Middle-earth—be it labeled fantasy, utopia, or other—is all the more necessary. As Shippey notes well, the opposition to fantasy often corresponds to the poverty of one's imagination. Speaking of Nokes (a character in Tolkien's *Smith of Wootton Major*), Shippey writes: "He has only a weak ... notion of fantasy himself, but assumes that this is all there can ever be; and since he is well aware of the feebleness of his own imagination, he assumes all images of the fantastic, of Faerie, must be feeble too" (*Author* 299). Ironically, perhaps, Jameson has said something similar about our own postmodern condition, in which for many it is easier to envision the end of the world than an end to the present economic system: "perhaps that is due to some weakness in our imaginations" (*Seeds* xii). With strengthened imaginations, the utopian impulse may indeed find realization in the form of fantasy, and we may again look upon our own world with fresh eyes, having visited places where the stars are strange.

NOTES

1. See my "Radical Alternatives: The Persistence of Utopia in the Postmodern."
2. Here it should be acknowledged that there are in fact many practitioners and theorists

of fantasy who do not nicely fit into these stereotypes, and one could easily list many liberal, left-wing, or Marxist fantasists, from Mervyn Peake to China Miéville, Alan Moore to Neil Gaiman, and so on. Indeed, Miéville has noted a certain rapprochement between Marxism and fantasy, visible in the special issue of *Historical Materialism* devoted to the subject (see note 8, below). See also Marc Bould and China Miéville's edited collection, *Red Planets: Marxism and Science Fiction*. In an afterword to this volume, Miéville notes that many Marxist critics remain skeptical of fantasy and committed to science-fiction or utopia, largely because of the "ideology of cognition" established by Suvin, Jameson, and others, and that these critics have ignored the revolutionary potential of the fantastic. As Miéville concludes, "*Red Planets* we have. We should not neglect the red dragons" (245).

3. See Georg Lukács, *Theory of the Novel*.

4. Hence, I am not speaking of the "real world" history and geography that Brian Bates has explored in his *The Real Middle-earth*.

5. It is perhaps worth noting that Shippey, quite rightly, has identified Tolkien's "cartographic plot" as the basis for *The Lord of the Rings*, especially insofar as this work is made far more complex—far more "real"—than its predecessor *The Hobbit*. Establishing an imaginary geography is thus crucial to the tale that grew in the telling. See *Road* 94–134.

6. Shippey quotes Muir's review, "A Boy's World," *Observer* (November 27, 1955), 11.

7. Thoroughly analyzing the notes, drafts, and other unpublished writings (some of which are available in *The History of Middle-earth* volumes), Dimitra Fimi has argued that Tolkien's shift from the materials that became *The Silmarillion* to *The Hobbit* represented a movement from myth to history; see her excellent *Tolkien, Race and Cultural History*.

8. See China Miéville, "Editorial Introduction," *Symposium: Marxism and Fantasy*.

9. According to Chesterton, a young Charles Dickens discovered these magical words by seeing the sign "Coffee Room" from the other side of a glass door. Chesterton concludes that "it is the masterpiece of the good realistic principle—the principle that the most fantastic of all is often the precise fact" (47–48). Tolkien cites this Chestertonian fantasy in "On Fairy-stories," but finds this sort of fantasy, one which observes "the queerness of things that have become trite, when they are seen suddenly from a new angle," is rather limited when compared to truly creative fantasy (*TOF* 68).

WORKS CITED

Bates, Brian. *The Real Middle-earth: Exploring the Magic and Mystery of the Middle Ages, J.R.R. Tolkien, and "The Lord of the Rings."* New York: Palgrave Macmillan, 2003.

Bould, Marc, and China Miéville, eds. *Red Planets: Marxism and Science Fiction.* Middletown, CT: Wesleyan University Press, 2009.

Chesterton, G.K. *Charles Dickens: A Critical Study.* New York: Dodd Mead, 1906.

Fimi, Dimitra. *Tolkien, Race and Cultural History: From Fairies to Hobbits.* New York: Palgrave Macmillan, 2010.

Hume, Kathryn. *Fantasy and Mimesis: Responses to Reality in Western Literature.* New York: Methuen, 1984.

Jameson, Fredric. *Archaeologies of the Future: The Desire Called Utopia and Other Science Fictions.* London: Verso, 2005.

_____. *The Seeds of Time.* New York: Columbia University Press, 1994.

Lukács, Georg. *Theory of the Novel.* Tr. Anna Bostock. Cambridge: MIT Press, 1971.

Miéville, China. "Editorial Introduction." *Symposium: Marxism and Fantasy. Historical Materialism* 10.4 (2002): 42–43

Moorcock, Michael. *Wizardry and Wild Romance: A Study of Epic Fantasy.* London: Victor Gollancz, 1987.

Rabkin, Eric S. *The Fantastic in Literature.* Princeton: Princeton University Press, 1976.

Suvin, Darko. *Metamorphoses of Science Fiction: On the Poetics and History of a Literary Genre.* New Haven: Yale University Press, 1979.

Tally, Robert T., Jr. "Let Us Now Praise Famous Orcs: Simple Humanity in Tolkien's Inhuman Creatures." *Mythlore* 29:1/2 (#111/112) (Fall/Winter 2010): 17–28.

_____. "Radical Alternatives: The Persistence of Utopia in the Postmodern." *New Essays on the Frankfurt School of Critical Theory.* Ed. Alfred Drake. Newcastle-upon-Tyne: Cambridge Scholars, 2010. 109–123.

Middle-earth and the Waste Land: Greenwood, Apocalypse, and Post-War Resolution

E.L. RISDEN

"There were giants on the earth in those days."—Genesis 6.4

Despite the Inklings' distrust of T.S. Eliot and his methods, we may draw some productive direct comparisons between Tolkien's *The Silmarillion* (plus parts of *The Lord of the Rings* and *The Hobbit*) and Eliot's *The Waste Land*. Those divergent works exhibit rather extraordinary parallel concerns with the landscapes of "end-times" in personal, social, and cosmic terms. Significant commonalities emerge through various lenses—for instance, through extreme landscapes, concerns with hidden brutalities, and culturally precipitous moments. Together they create an intertextual sense of ambivalence buffered by differently but exquisitely textured confrontations with resolution. As Tom Shippey has noted in *J.R.R. Tolkien: Author of the Century*, Eliot observed of Modernism that it allowed a writer to replace narrative method with "mythical method," and a concern with myth had provided the "whole drive of Tolkien's work" (313). Both *The Waste Land* and Tolkien's fiction find their particularity in non-realistic approaches to fully realistic feelings and ideas—and in the writers' responses to post-war devastation both physical, in the landscape of Europe, and emotional, in the suffering of nations worldwide. Their authors grapple with loss on a grand as well as on a personal scale. For this discussion I will attend, of course, to both Tolkien's and Eliot's texts, but I'll direct my course particularly by means of Professor Shippey's notable commentary on Tolkien (such as his ideas of evil). Tolkien's use of both private and mythical landscape and Eliot's unfolding of both blasted and enervated human topography invoke similar themes through different literary modes and means. Both writers foreground the private and public creation of language and landscape to address post-war issues of loss, responsibility, and power.

As Shippey clarifies, many of the post–World War I generation of writers "saw in humanity a basic urge to destruction" and expressed quite clearly that "people could never be trusted, least of all if they expressed a wish for the betterment of humanity" (116–17). Moreover, as C.S. Lewis's *Perelandra* demonstrated (in response to the Romantic view of Satan as a tragic figure in *Paradise Lost*), "there was nothing at all grand, dignified and tragic about evil, which was instead tedious, sordid and squalid" (159). In *The Return of the King*, when Denethor in his disease foresees the end of the civilized world in a great fire, its ashes blown away by wind, his vision parallels a nuclear apocalypse, but that vision is also tempered by Frodo's assertion that the great stories never end, though the individual people in them do (173, 153). We can resist evil through courage and with the help of luck, by means of the native virtue we can stir up. Tolkien would foreground—as would Eliot in his later work— that the world was made by a force for and of good. We must also persistently resist despair and even weariness: Shippey calls attention to the "French *défaitisme*, a word which came into being about 1918 to express the war-weariness of the Allies, the feeling ... that the sacrifices already made should now be abandoned for an inconclusive peace" (149)—Frodo is finally worn down by the Ring, but Sam must not be, and we must not be, since we, the audience, have little choice but to see problems through to their end. The Hobbits must "scour" the industrializing Shire before they can attempt to put the War of the Ring behind them. Readers of *The Lord of the Rings* had World War II behind them, but the Cold War before them. The great epic ideas, such as the need for steadfast courage that we find in *Beowulf,* don't relieve a people, an age, the earth of the necessity or fear of an ending; they do, though, allow a means of choice by which we may most likely persist through difficult and even horrifying times, best show kindness and compassion, and leave something behind that may prove worthwhile for ages to come. Tolkien and Eliot seem in *The Waste Land* and *The Lord of the Rings* both to have reached that conclusion, whether tentatively or with spiritual resolve.

Eliot's poem, which appeared in 1922, resolves into five sections: (1) "The Burial of the Dead"; (2) "A Game of Chess"; (3) "The Fire Sermon"; (4) "Death by Water"; (5) "What the Thunder Said." Burying the dead, a complicated matter after the devastation of a generation that occurred in World War I, begins in the poem with an image of spring lilacs rising from desiccated land. But the fragile image appears in the "cruelest month" of April: the dead are not so much the fallen soldiers as the displacement, decadence, and phony spiritualism that preceded the war, their memory as fragile and intoxicating as flowers, and Spring will not, should not, renew them: a lost world needs something more tangible and dependable to grasp. The chess game alludes to a distraction from a Renaissance play by Thomas Middleton: a seduction takes place offstage while the game occurs onstage. But conversation, music, parties, and drinking can't fully distract the memory of the dreadful losses of the war, which came about through a seduction by violence, the madness of a pre–World-War-I generation that feared it wouldn't have the chance for glory in war. Both before and after the war, the Waste Land remains barely below the flimsy cultural cover that attempts to hide it. Part three alludes to Gautama Siddhartha's famous, concentrated homily on the destructive passions of the flesh, with the rape of Philomela, the continuing poverty of the slums, and the sickly fog of the "Unreal City" sifting up through the cacophonous gloom—even confessions of the war's horrors can't stop the City's remnant burning. "Death by Water," the brief fourth section, encourages compassion and meditation on the transience of life. It may refer to Noah's Flood or to the bitter, poisonous waters of Revelation 8:11, but it suggests more a baptism than another death: after the war we must cleanse and rebuild, regardless of how painful the process. "What the Thunder Said," the concluding section, refers to a prophetic utterance in the Book of Revelation that the Bible does not share: "Do not write what the Thunder said," the voice warns in 10:4. But Eliot's thunder calls us to give, sympathize, and exhibit self-control: the individual non-participants must find some way to respond to the horrors of the war that circulate constantly in their midst. *Shantih*, the call for peace that concludes the poem, may comprise simply an ironic, powerless refrain, or it may suggest that true peace comes only from recognition, compassion, purgation, and the will to persist anew.

The polyphonic uncertainty of the poem provides both its beauty and its difficulty, but it leads us either way to a similar point: when we come to an end, we must make an end—not avoid and distract, but bury our dead, create a compassionate peace, do our penance, find new ways to understand and improve our lot, and listen for the warnings that would keep us from repeating our errors. Eliot's Europe missed that last message, and they drew the rest of the world with them into another even more devastating conflict. Tolkien knew, too, as he showed in *The Silmarillion*, that evil and war persist: some people want them, and some may not seek them but can't resist them. The immense loss of World War I did not teach us the necessity of responsibility or the dangers of power.

For Eliot, growth, with its trees, flowers, variegation, greenery—the restorative Garden—and accompanying spiritual regeneration, doesn't return until 1930's *Ash-Wednesday*: a specifically religious as well as a personal and cultural rebirth. Russell Kirk remarked that *Ash-Wednesday* "accomplished more to redeem the time—to attract support for a tolerable civil social order, as well as to restore a consciousness of spiritual order—than did everything Eliot wrote for his *Criterion*" [the literary review that Eliot founded in 1922], and it "turned toward Christianity many of the rising generation" (171). "To care and not to care" (from part I of the poem), Audrey Cahill observes, "reflects the heart of the Christian predicament" (82), and Eliot like Tolkien chose decisively to care and to try to change those things that writing can hope to change (perhaps finding difficulty in achieving detachment). Eliot's commitment to Christianity provides him a means to restore psychological as well as social landscape. The war brought death on a grand scale and the end of an age, but faith restored hope for at least a potentially redemptive apocalypse. He writes in section VI of the poem:

> Blessèd sister, holy mother, spirit of the fountain, spirit of the garden,
> Suffer us not to mock ourselves with falsehood
> Teach us to care and not to care
> Teach us to sit still
> Even among these rocks,
> Our peace in His will
> And even among these rocks
> [*Complete Poems* 67].

While, as James Miller points out, Eliot rejected the notion that *The Waste Land* expressed "the disillusion of a generation" and asserted that he "wasn't even bothering whether [he] understood what [he] was saying" (152), Eliot produced more than simply a "personal...'grouse against life'" (*Waste Land* frontispiece). We may call the work both a "work of literary criticism" (Miller ix) and, as with "Prufrock," a voice that came to speak for a generation, its regrets and fears, whether Eliot intended it to do so or not. *Ash-Wednesday* adds a new chorus: affirmation growing out of the desert land. As did *The Lord of the Rings* with its broader fan base, *The Waste Land* embodied a landscape partly visible and partly invisible to the eye. As Michael North observes, "[t]he multiplicity and incompatibility of human points of view were never more unavoidably obvious than in the early twentieth century, when the Great War focused for the first time nearly the whole of human consciousness on a single event, an odious squabble the purpose of which almost no one could enunciate" (15); Eliot exploits that polyvocality to show how and to what extent, as Hamlet would say, the times were out of joint. *Ash-Wednesday* may have assumed finally, in a smaller scale, the position that *The Silmarillion* did for Tolkien: the "work of the heart." As Eliot searched for spiritual resolution, Tolkien exhibits in his mythography the sense that the waste land will persist externally—we can fight it, but in the long run our hope of success comes only internally, particularly in a world before the Incarnation.

For Tolkien also humanity had got itself disjoined from Nature. Both *The Hobbit* and *The Lord of the Rings* foreground the green landscape (both *anti-* and *ante-*waste land), its beauties and dangers and its potential loss (in the war-wrought waste land to come). Tolkien noted that as a boy he loved stories of American Indians because there were "above all, forests in such stories" (*TOF* 55). The forests, along with vibrant towns and spectacularly architectural cities, evidence a sound heart in a living, breathing Age; their destruction, or their replacement by the rise and fall of blasted or infernal landscapes, marks end-times that we may not assume precede new, redemptive ages for Middle-earth and its peoples. Lórien, Fangorn, and even Mirkwood contrast markedly with the pre-apocalyptic Mordor landscape that Sam sees in *The Return of the King*:

> Hard and cruel and bitter was the land that met his gaze. Before his feet the highest ridge of the Ephel Dúath fell steeply in great cliffs down into a dark trough, on the further side of which there rose another ridge, much lower, its edge notched and jagged with crags like fangs that stood out black against the red light behind them.... Far beyond it, but almost straight ahead, across a wide lake of darkness dotted with tiny fires, there was a great and burning glow; and from it rose ... the billowing canopy that roofed in all the accursed land [*RK* VI, i, 175].

Sauron took Mordor—"black land," but suggesting also Old English *morþor*, "murder"—in the Second Age, then reclaimed it in the Third Age. "Of the Rings of Power" in *The Silmarillion* records that when Sauron fell,

> the towers of Barad-dûr crumbled in ruin, and at the rumor of their fall many lands trembled. Thus peace came again, and a new Spring opened on earth; and the Heir of Isildur was crowned King of Gondor and Arnor, and the might of the Dúnedain was lifted up and their glory renewed [304].

The landscape that could have engulfed Middle-earth collapses, but its grounds won't flower soon: evil corrupts the land as it corrupts human hearts, and it leaves behind reminders of ages past—a necessity, given the brevity and inaccuracy of memory alone.

The Silmarillion shares with *The Waste Land* a sense of periodic fragmentation and decay, of dwelling between two worlds, one of energy, desire, and hope, one of failure, destruction, and darkness. Verlyn Flieger describes Tolkien's great myth-creation as "permeated by an air of deepening sorrow, of loss, of estrangement, and ever-widening distance from the light and all that is [*sic*] signifies" (60). In that sense Tolkien appears in the tradition of Milton and Blake, writers who focus on "the meaning and consequences of the Fall"; like them Tolkien establishes an "extended image of light diminished from its primal brilliance, yet still and evermore faintly illuminating the world" (60).

All three exploit thereby a lingering feeling of the *grotesque*, in the Romantic sense of that word, of creatures dwelling in the midst of metamorphosis, changing, becoming, uncertain of their direction or end. Frodo in *The Lord of the Rings*, Flieger adds, "is splintered light, and in his fragmentation he makes obvious the need for that reunion with self, with the world, and with God that Tolkien felt to be joy beyond the walls of the world" (158); not so much joy as relief and resignation conclude *The Lord of the Rings*, and the repetition of the motif of lost ages directs the course of the all the tales of *The Silmarillion*. A sense of loss as powerful as that of Eliot's surreal post–World War I landscape pervades the book, and it has much greater magnitude. Frodo's world, like our post–War age, lay in fragments, and like Humpty Dumpty, we didn't know how to put ourselves, or the World, back together again. Tolkien's notion of "ages" suggests we must put behind us the old fragments: we cannot simply reconstruct—what we have destroyed, tainted with evil, we must leave behind; we must instead build anew with new hopes, new leadership, and new ideas, without forgetting what we have known that was good and true and remains so. The greatest moment of renewal in all of *The Lord of the Rings*—which Peter Jackson transfers as Gandalf's words of hope to Pippin as battle reaches its climax in Minas Tirith—comes at its conclusion, as Frodo sails from the Grey Havens with the elves and Gandalf into the West, where "it seemed to him that as in his dream in the house of Bombadil, the grey rain-curtain turned all to silver glass and was rolled back, and he beheld white shores and beyond them a far green country under a swift sunrise" (*RK* IV, ix, 310). What Frodo finds we but glimpse: a healed landscape of sunshine and greenery where old cares can finally fall away. *The Silmarillion*, in contrast, shows only serial rise and fall, and hope rests finally in the limited and occasional human ability to eschew evil and seek good and in the knowledge of a kind Creator beyond the bounds of the world.

"Ainulindalë" ends with "the first battle of the Valar with Melkor for the dominion of Arda" (*S* 22). "Valaquenta" concludes with the War of Wrath and the defeat of Morgoth; the Valar thrust Morgoth through the Door of Night beyond the world, but "so great was the fury of those adversaries that the northern regions of the western world were rent asunder" (*S* 252), and the shape of the lands changed: Middle-earth's waste land. "Akallabêth" recounts another rise and fall, that of Númenor; when the Númenórean king Ar-Pharazôn sets foot upon the shores of the Blessed Realm, "claiming the land as his own."

> [Then] Manwë upon the Mountain called upon Ilúvatar ... [who] showed forth his power, and he changed the fashion of the world; and a great chasm opened in the sea between Númenor and the Deathless Lands ... [a]nd all the fleets of the Númenóreans were drawn down into the abyss ... and the mortal

warriors that had set foot upon the land of Aman were buried under falling hills
... [and] the land of Aman and Eressëa of the Eldar were taken away and removed
beyond the reach of Men for ever. And Andor, the Land of Gift, Númenor of the
Kings ... was utterly destroyed [*S* 278–9].

The Third Age ends as does the Second, with the destruction of Sauron and
a new Spring for Middle-earth, the course of which lies in the hands of humans,
to preserve or to destroy. Each age recapitulates its apocalyptic motifs and
unfolds its potential waste lands: the unveiling of a time of fall, followed by
hope of renewal and warnings of the responsibilities and dangers that go with
the gifts of land and life.

As Tom Shippey observes in "Tolkien as a Post-War Writer," we can see
Tolkien not just as post–World-War-I writer, but also "in essence as a post–
World-War-II writer," one of that group "whose subjects were war and evil
[and] ... who wrote in non-realistic modes essentially because they felt they
were writing about subjects too great and too general to tie down to particular
and recognisable settings" (235). We can see evil as an "addiction" (228), as,
W.H. Auden added, "defiantly chosen" so that eventually it "can no longer
imagine anything but itself" (qtd. in *Author* 231). While the First World War
led the parties involved in the Second to conceal their brutalities the more
skillfully, the Second vastly extended both the destruction of landscape and
the Landscape of Destruction—any question of whether and to what extent
the world had changed exploded in fire bombs, death camps, and the waste
land of the Nuclear Age. As both world wars appeared to end all wars, they
marked the turn to a new age of mass destruction, industrializing a perverse
desire for lingering lethality. *The Silmarillion* similarly shows a series of pro-
tagonists and antagonists bent, age after age, not only on rule, but also on
destruction. Their desire for vengeance, acquisition, or domination decon-
structs the earth around them, reshaping or eliminating much of what was
beautiful, lasting, and good. And the scope and influence of the book extended
far beyond its original intent; as Shippey points out in *Author of the Century*,
"*The Silmarillion*, centered ... on the sins of possession and mastery and the
desire to exercise skill whatever the consequences, becomes less a mythology
for England and more one for its own time" (260–61)—the book becomes
not just of its time and place, but for its time and world in the time to come.

While Tolkien never fell into cynicism, and while his narrative hardly
shied from the darkness and evil of both internal and external landscapes, and
while the resurrective quality of the greenwood lasts only so long, he located
in Middle-earth's movement from age to age potential for both resolution and
at least occasional comfort. Though the greenwood even as anti–waste land
doesn't always provide a place of "goodness" or safety—Treebeard will not take
kindly to anyone who threatens his forest or who even enters surreptitiously,

and Old Man Willow is dangerous to anyone unwary—it allows natural growth. In the Old Forest, as Marjorie Burns notes (quoting from *The Fellowship of the Ring*), "everything is 'very much more alive'" (85); that eminently living quality empowers the author's hope. Tolkien's sense of Christian optimism—not for this world, but for the world to come—translated in Middle-earth as a renewable landscape with fading, yet remnant and still-powerful greenwood. Eliot, too, recovered from the spiritual dryness of his fragmented waste land to find a garden of spiritual consolation not in a narrative world, but in a refreshing flood of imagistic hope. Tolkien and Eliot both realized that the resolve to replant the waste land must come from within; Eliot took longer than Tolkien to agree on the source of hope, but came more quickly to believe that we could actually do something physically constructive with it. For both writers, so different in thought, method, and sensibilities, the end of an Age, the slow, painful step from the wasteland of World War I and postwar malaise to the briefest respite, filled with its own detachment and woe, unveils neither goodness nor eucatastophe. Instead, what resolution we can find comes in the hope that a person and a people may breathe, look about, and gather strength for the mad gyre that spins itself into the Age ahead. In mutual song, complex and symphonic, though hardly harmonic, the two writers chant for us the same message: find courage, find joy, and pray earnestly, and write what matters.

WORKS CITED

Burns, Marjorie. *Perilous Realms: Celtic and Norse in Tolkien's Middle-earth.* Toronto: University of Toronto Press, 2005.

Cahill, Audrey. *T.S. Eliot and the Human Predicament.* Cape Town: University of Natal Press, 1967.

Eliot, T.S. *The Complete Poems and Plays 1909–1950.* New York: Harcourt, Brace, 1958.

_____. *The Waste Land: A Facsimile and Transcripts of the Original Drafts Including the Annotations of Ezra Pound.* Ed. Valerie Eliot. New York: Harcourt Brace, 1971.

Flieger, Verlyn. *Splintered Light: Logos and Language in Tolkien's World.* 2d ed. Kent, OH: Kent State University Press, 2002.

Kirk, Russell. *Eliot and His Age: T.S. Eliot's Moral Imagination in the Twentieth Century.* New York: Random House, 1971.

Miller, James E., Jr. *T.S. Eliot's Personal Waste Land: Exorcism of the Demons.* University Park: Pennsylvania State University Press, 1977.

North, Michael. *Reading 1922: A Return to the Scene of the Modern.* New York: Oxford University Press, 1999.

Shippey, Tom. "Tolkien as Post-War Writer." *Scholarship & Fantasy: Proceedings of* The Tolkien Phenomenon, *May 1992, Turku, Finland.* Ed. K.J. Battarbee. *Anglicana Turkuensia* 12. Turku: University of Turku (1993): 217–36. [Rpt. *Proceedings of the J.R.R. Tolkien Centenary Conference.* Ed. Patricia Reynolds and Glen H. GoodKnight. *Mallorn* 33 / *Mythlore* 21.2 (# 80) (Winter 1996): 84–93.]

The Jewels, the Stone, the Ring, and the Making of Meaning

Verlyn Flieger

1. Introduction

In 1982 Tom Shippey asked, "What is a Silmaril?" and went on to inquire:

> More acutely, what is the relationship in the story [of Eärendil] between success and failure? Eärendil's star appears to be a victory emblem, "the Flammifer of Westernesse," and yet is associated with loss and homelessness, with the weeping of women on the "Hither Shore" [*Road* orig. edition 146, rev. edition 194].

While Tom's question is specific, highlighting how Tolkien's poetry introduces names without explaining them ("a pattern forever being glimpsed but never quite grasped" *Road* 193), I'd like to expand it to address a larger issue, namely, "What did Tolkien mean the Silmarils to mean?" It is as good a question now as it was thirty years ago, and to my knowledge no one has yet produced a satisfactory answer. Unless Tolkien is being so profoundly pessimistic that most of his readers are reluctant to see it, the jewels' essence as "unsullied light" and their function as the catalyst for great harm seem at cross-purposes. Yet what seems like pessimism may better be explained as Tolkien having taken on more than he could adequately handle, for behind the apparent contradiction there can be discerned a pattern in the making, a design that grew in coherence as the designer's skill improved through practice.

It is obvious to anyone reading *The Silmarillion*, *The Hobbit*, and *The Lord of the Rings*, that in each a particular treasure is the carrier of a familiar

Tolkien theme: the danger of uncontrolled desire, covetousness grown to obsession. Shippey suggests "love of things" as "the besetting sin of modern civilisation," calling it "not quite Avarice and not quite Pride, but somehow attached to both" (*Road* 242). As early as 1981 Randel Helms remarked on the relationship between the Silmarils and the Arkenstone and between both of these and the Ring, and marked the development from earliest to latest. In *Tolkien and the Silmarils* he described *The Lord of the Rings* as "*The Hobbit* writ large" (77), and *The Hobbit* as "*The Silmarillion* writ small" (80). Helm's comparison touched on, but did not explore in any depth, the relative value and function of the three artifacts in their respective stories. Douglas Anderson's *Annotated Hobbit* dealt at length with that book's chief artifact, the Arkenstone, and cited the etymology and usage of the word *arkenstone/ eorclanstān* in other works as possible indicators of its position and purpose in Tolkien's story (Anderson 293–4). John Rateliff devoted extensive coverage to the relationship between the Silmarils and the Arkenstone in his two-volume *History of The Hobbit*. Tom Shippey notes apparent anomalies in Tolkien's treatment over time of the Silmarils and the Ring (*Road* 293–4). No one, as far as I am aware, has devoted attention to the relative success in its particular work of each artifact in comparison to the others.

While the Silmarils, the Arkenstone, and the Ring provide a range of lessons on the danger of possessiveness, Tolkien's earliest attempt, the Silmarils, is the least satisfactory: there is a disconcerting incongruity between the light they house and the effect they have. Their light is positive; their effect—on everyone but Beren and Lúthien and their descendants—is insidious and morally destructive. Tolkien's last effort, however, the Ring of Power, more successfully coordinates medium and message. The Ring is evil, and its effect—on everyone but Faramir—is insidious and morally destructive. The problematic gap is closed and the message is clear. The odd man out in this sequence is the Arkenstone. Neither good nor evil, it is poised between the Silmarils and the Ring, reminiscent of both but less than either. Unlike the other treasures, the Arkenstone has no indwelling nature, no symbolic significance, yet it displays characteristics that tie it to its predecessor and successor.

Discussing Bilbo's "Song of Eärendil" at Rivendell, Shippey points out (as we have seen) that "Eärendil's star [a Silmaril] appears to be a victory-emblem, 'the Flammifer of Westernesse,' *and yet* is associated with loss and homelessness, with the weeping of women" (*Road* 194, my emphasis). Shippey's "and yet" highlights the disconnect—not just in the poem but also in the "Silmarillion" as a whole—between the positive connotations of Light and the negative impact of the Silmarils. In *Arda Reconstructed* Douglas Kane went a bit farther to remark that the "holy jewels ... alone preserved the 'pure' Light, yet also generated so much of the strife described in these tales" (23). Although

Kane did not pursue the implications, his "yet also," like Shippey's "and yet," acknowledged the contradiction between preserving pure light and generating strife that distinguishes the Silmarils from the other artifacts. Tolkien's statement (*Letters* 148) that the events of his *legendarium* were "threaded upon the fate and significance of the *Silmarilli* ('radiance of pure light')," is not much help, for if their fate is clear, their significance is anything but.

The problem is that light, which is generally assumed to be beneficial, comes with significance already attached, as Tolkien well knew. He wrote to Milton Waldman that light "is such a primeval symbol in the nature of the Universe, that it can hardly be analysed" (*Letters* 148n). He also was surely aware that light as a concept carries specific religious, mystical, moral, and intellectual associations stretching from the Book of Genesis to the Gospel of John to the Buddha to Locke and Hume and Voltaire. Yet his portrayal of light in his story is in direct opposition to both the "primeval symbol" and these later associations. One has only to consider the multiple applications of the word "enlightenment" in all its contexts to spot the disjuncture between the Silmarils' inner light and their outer effect. While Tolkien does not refer to his light, whether that of the Lamps, the Trees, or the Silmarils, as "good," preferring words such as "holy," "unsullied," "hallowed," he describes the Light of Valinor as "derived from light before any fall," and as "the light of art undivorced from reason, that sees things ... and 'says that they are good'—as beautiful" (*Letters* 148n). If the light of the Silmarils is so holy, why do they have such a negative impact? Medium and message are inconsistent with one another.

The obvious contrast is the Ring, where medium and message are consistent with each other, not least because the quality of the treasure is markedly different. The Ring contains Power, not Light. Power attracts, and the power of the Ring attracts Saruman, Boromir, Denethor, Galadriel, Grishnákh, Gollum, even Sam Gamgee. We know why Sauron made the One Ring—to "rule them all," which is also why other people want it. On the other hand, we don't know why Fëanor made the Silmarils, and as far as we know, neither does he. Is it heretical to suggest that maybe Tolkien didn't know either? The narrative only says that Fëanor was "filled with a new thought" (*S* 67), but what that thought was is never explained. Unlike the Ring, the Silmarils confer no special benefit on their possessor, in fact quite the opposite. Contrary to their nature they do not enlighten; they endarken. They awaken possessiveness in Fëanor, covetousness in Morgoth, the impulse to murder in Thingol, and are the direct cause of the death of Maedhros and perpetual self-exile of Maglor. A side-effect but worth noticing is the departure of Melian from Doriath and Middle-earth. That's a lot of harm to be caused by light.

To address, if not solve, this conundrum I'll examine the role of each treasure in its own story by posing three questions—what? how? and why?

2. The Silmarils

Let us go beyond Shippey's question of "What is a Silmaril?" to explore the larger issue of "What are they supposed to mean?" As unique artifacts with significance beyond themselves, they invite comparison with similar objects in myth and literature, most notably the Sampo of the Finnish *Kalevala* and the Grail of Arthurian romance. In *Kalevala* the Sampo is an irreplaceable and mysterious object of enormous value, though never defined or described. It is forged by a craftsman but apparently can only be made once, and while many ideas of its nature have been offered—it is a mill, it is a pillar, it is a treasure-chest, it is the world tree—no single one has prevailed. Whatever it is, it brings wealth and prosperity to its possessor. Louhi, Mistress of the North, first commissions the Sampo, and then locks it in a mountain and refuses to share with the heroes Väinämöinen, Ilmarinen, and Lemminkäinen, who retaliate by stealing it. In the ensuing tug of war the Sampo is lost—broken up and drowned in the sea.

Similarities to the Silmarils are obvious and I am not the first to point them out.[1] As with the Sampo, the fate of the Silmarils is clear but their significance is ill-defined. The medium (light) is not congruent with the message (greed and possessiveness). Like Louhi with the Sampo, Fëanor keeps the Silmarils "locked in the deep chambers of his hoard" (*S* 69). Like the Sampo, they are stolen, first all of them by Morgoth and then later one by Beren. Originally a cluster of three, they are, like the Sampo though more metaphorically, broken up and scattered before reaching their "long homes" in earth, sea, and sky.

Similarities to the Grail are also obvious. The Grail is the symbolic center of the Arthurian story, as are the Silmarils in Tolkien's. Both have an obvious mystical dimension. Both are called "holy." Both are the objects of a life-changing quest. The Grail Quest is the search for transcendent spirituality, as the quest for the Silmarils is the effort to regain lost Light. The ultimate symbol of sacrifice and redemption, the Grail is the cup of Christ's blood at the Last Supper and its receptacle when he bleeds on the Cross. The Silmarils also are containers, not of blood, but light, housing the last of the "unsullied" light from Aman, the "blessed land." Yet where the blood-filled Holy Grail brings healing and transcendence, and the mysterious Sampo brings prosperity, the light-filled "holy jewels" bring misfortune, injury, pain, and death. The closer you look the harder it becomes to reconcile the Silmarils' nature with their role in the story.

This may be because the tale grew in the telling, for both the story and the Silmarils changed over the twenty or so years of their development. In their earliest appearance in the 1918 *Book of Lost Tales*, they are not what they later become, unique and the last of the light. They are simply part of a larger bout of Noldorian gem-making that includes crystal and amber and chrysoprase and topaz and garnets and rubies, emeralds, sapphires, amethysts, moonstones, beryls and onyx and agate and opals and diamonds. Challenged to make something fairer (the only motive we are ever given), Fëanor creates a new gem made of "the sheen of pearls and the faint half-colours of opals" bathed in the "radiant dew" of Silpion and a "single tiny drop" of the light of Laurelin (*Lost Tales I* 128). Pleased with his handiwork, he makes two more. All three are stolen by Melko together with a "treasury of gems" and an apparently unrelated herd of horses (145).

Days later in an unrelated incident the Two Trees are killed, suggesting that at this stage the jewels and the Trees were not thematically linked. Christopher Tolkien comments:

> The primary motive in the later story of Melkor's desire for the Silmarils ... is here represented only by a lust for the gems of the Noldoli in general: it is indeed a remarkable feature of the original mythology that though the Silmarils were present they were of such relatively small importance [156].

This "remarkable feature" may have prompted Shippey's comment that "it is possible to feel ... that Tolkien did not know what he was doing" (*Road* 294) and his further comment that "Tolkien's own efforts to say what *The Silmarillion* was 'about' were never completely illuminating" (243). We may suspect a pun in Shippey's well-chosen adjective.

Subsequent versions of their story increase the significance of the Silmarils. They next appear in a late[2] revision of the 1917 "The Tale of Tinúviel," where the Crown of Melko and the setting of the Silmarils therein first appear (*Lost Tales II* 53). Tinúviel's father Tinwelint (not yet Thingol) asks Beren (here no Man but an Elf) to bring him a Silmaril from Melko's crown (13). The jewel now has a "holy magic" attributable to its making in Valinor "before evil came there" (34), and has acquired supernatural, moral, and spiritual value. The Silmarils are also mentioned in a fragment tentatively dated by Christopher to early 1925 (*Lays* 131) where they are

... the Three ...	thrice-enchanted
globes of crystal	by gleam undying
illumined, lit	

[*Lays* 134].

Christopher writes, "It is clear that the Silmarils had already gained greatly in significance since the earliest period of the mythology" (138).

In all these versions the constants are their beauty, desirability, and theft by Melko/Melkor. The variables are the amount of light they contain, the source or sources of that light, and the exact nature of their holiness, whether (as in early versions) simply through association with Valinor, or because (as in *The Silmarillion*) the gems are "hallowed" by Varda (*S* 67).

How do they work? Another good question. Mostly, they warp people's lives, which is not what you would expect of hallowed light. Fëanor is the prime example. That light should drive its preserver into his own darkness seems a paradox too far, matched by the irony that without him the light would be irretrievably lost.[3] Moreover, their effect varies from psychological (corrupting Fëanor and Thingol) to physical (burning Morgoth, Carcharoth, Maedhros, and Maglor), with Beren, Lúthien, and Eärendil the exceptions to both. We might assume that the one Silmaril burns Morgoth and Carcharoth, and the remaining two burn Maedhros and Maglor, because in each case the possession is wrongful, as if light misappropriated turns to heat. Fair enough. But by that token the Silmaril for which he barters his daughter should also burn Thingol, whose possession is no more rightful than the others'. Yet it doesn't, though his motive and murderous scheme for getting it hardly qualify him as a worthy recipient. That same Silmaril, stolen by Beren, bequeathed to Eärendil and borne aloft into the night sky as he voyages through the heavens, becomes the Evening/Morning Star. It is thus visible but unattainable, and as Shippey observes (see above) it is associated not with illumination but with loss and homelessness, with the weeping of women. If there is a message here, it is mixed.

There is one place where the message is not mixed, where Tolkien is in full command of his material and his Light behaves like light, not dark. This is in *The Lord of the Rings*. Here Eärendil's Silmaril is neither an object nor a trophy, but a beacon, a Light when all other lights go out, in the phial Galadriel gives to Frodo. When he advances down the Tunnel in Cirith Ungol holding aloft the phial, Light does precisely what light actually does do—defeat darkness. Light does it again when Sam uses the phial against Shelob. It is noteworthy that both instances occur in Ungol, "unlight," that is to say, dark. A third time the Light is used, again by Sam, to break the will of the Watchers at Cirith Ungol, blazing to "grace with splendour his faithful brown hobbithand" (*RK* VI, iii, 191), an echo of Beren's hand holding the Silmaril. What has made this treatment different from its predecessors? My answer is "time and experience." On the basis of the paper, Christopher Tolkien dates Tolkien's drafts of the Company's farewell to Lórien and Galadriel's gift of the phial only to sometime after 1940. However, he dates the Cirith Ungol chapter to May 1944. It is hard not to suppose that, perhaps through parallel experience in handling the Ring, Tolkien had learned how to make medium and message work together to support his theme.

Which leads to my next question. *Why* are the Silmarils there?

The answer is mixed. They contribute materially to plot, but less clearly, perhaps less effectively, to theme. There has to be a fulcrum for the plot and the Silmarils are it. In this respect, they function as traditional fairy tale treasures and occupy a traditional role in the story. It's clear from the early drafts that as the mythology developed their importance grew and light became a central concept. The shift of vehicle from Trees to Jewels allows for more action, for while the Trees' Light shines impartially on and for all Valinor, the Jewels' Light can be and is coveted, possessed, hoarded, hidden, stolen, and transported. The problem is that their nature and their role as possessed items are at odds, and seem confusingly to combat rather than support one another, as light becomes both the reason for and the price of war in Middle-earth. Again I will ask: what is the message here? Is Tolkien's world not ready for the Light?

That the message is not clear (see Shippey's comments above) may be a function of the discrepancy between the height of Tolkien's ambition, the intractability of his material, and the limitations of his skill at the time. Like many poets, his reach exceeded his grasp. He aimed lower with the Arkenstone.

3. The Arkenstone

The Arkenstone both does and does not share salient characteristics with the treasures that bracket it, the Silmarils before and the Ring after its invention. Like them it is beautiful, desirable, and the catalyst for a lot of trouble. Unlike them it has no inherent characteristic such as holiness or power, and confers nothing on its possessor. Moreover, it inhabits a fundamentally different work and world from the other two treasures. While *The Hobbit* has tangential ties to the "Silmarillion" and more obvious ones to *The Lord of the Rings*, it is still a lesser work than either, a children's story set in a fairy tale world, not a mythology or an epic romance in an invented cosmos. There is no agenda behind the Arkenstone's role in the story, so the answer to my three questions is easier. As to *what*: it is a stone dug out of the mountain, shaped and polished by the Dwarves. It is an heirloom passed down from Dwarf father to Dwarf son. It becomes a coveted treasure, but with no indwelling capacities associated with light, dark, good, evil, or any other concept. No meaning beyond its beauty is suggested. Thus it can more easily fulfill the modest expectations Tolkien builds into *The Hobbit*, a far less ambitious effort in both intention and execution than the "Silmarillion" or *The Lord of the Rings*.

Like the Silmarils, the Arkenstone went through changes before settling into its identity as Thorin's much-desired heirloom. Initially unnamed, it acquired credentials as the Gem of Girion given by the King of Dale to the dwarves of the Lonely Mountain. This was later changed to the Arkenstone of Thrain found by the dwarves in the heart of the mountain. Even then, however, its function was contrary to its eventual position as the most desirable object, for at this early stage it was meant to be Bilbo's fourteenth share, small and portable enough to carry in his pocket. Unlike the Silmarils, the Arkenstone is a secondary ingredient in its story, an add-on on to a plot expanding beyond its original parameters. Its most direct precursor is not any artifact from the depths of myth, but the nineteenth-century novelist Wilkie Collins' Moonstone in the novel of the same name, a jewel whose theft followed by its pursuit and subsequent recovery by its rightful hereditary possessors are the burden of what is usually conceded to be the first English detective novel. Collins's description of the Moonstone as shining "out of the depths of its own brightness," with a light "that streamed from it ... like the light of the harvest-moon" (Collins 61) is not unlike Tolkien's descriptions of both the Arkenstone and the Silmarils, and one is tempted to look no further for Tolkien's most immediate inspiration.

This immediate influence aside, it is as if material left over from the "Silmarillion" was recycled into *The Hobbit*, but without the extra significance. John Rateliff has argued that there was some connection in Tolkien's mind between the two, never fully defined but most clearly shown in their descriptions and the way details about one bled over into descriptions of the other.[4] Nevertheless, fully defined or not, the ghost of the Silmarils still haunts the stone. It is a "great white gem" (*H* XII, 243) and a "great jewel" (XIII, 249); it has its own "inner light" (249) yet also changes external light into "sparks of white radiance" (249). The overlap is no surprise when we recall that Tolkien worked simultaneously on both stories, putting aside the "Silmarillion" only when *The Hobbit* went into production. Tolkien also used a form of the word Arkenstone in the Old English version of the Annals of Valinor to refer to "þá Silmarillas, þæt wæron Eorclanstánas" ("the Silmarils, that were precious/holy stones"), where the word element *eorclan* can mean both "precious" and "holy" (Anderson 294; Rateliff 604, 605). The presence of the word *precious* in this context is hard to ignore.

How does it work? Or more precisely, what does it do? This is easy to answer, because unlike the other artifacts the Arkenstone doesn't *do* anything. It is a patient, not an agent. The Silmarils can burn and the Ring ensnares and corrupts its possessor, but the Arkenstone has no active ingredient.

So *why* is it in the story? Its chief function seems to be to reveal character. Though its late introduction seems almost an afterthought, once it is there, like both Silmarils and Ring, it appeals to the inherent flaws in human nature. It makes Thorin crafty, devious, and not above a crooked deal, and it turns Bilbo into a real thief. "Now I am a burglar indeed!" he says as he shuts his eyes and pockets the Arkenstone (*H* XIII, 249). And when the hurly-burly's done, and the battle's lost and won, he tells himself, "You are a fool, Bilbo Baggins, and you made a great mess of that business with the stone" (XVIII, 301). At least he knows it. Fëanor never attains this self-knowledge, and for a fuller exploration of the idea we will have to wait for the fall and redemption of Boromir.

But Bilbo's fall[5] and subsequent self-knowledge are sidebars to the story proper. They do not affect the plot. Nor does the Arkenstone. We are led to expect that as a bargaining piece between Bard and Thorin it will avert a battle, and thus Bilbo's theft, though still a moral lapse, will be justified after the fact. But the bargain, though struck, is never concluded. Thorin delays payment, and the Dwarves' attack to recapture the stone is aborted by the arrival of Bolg and the goblins. This forces the former foes to unite against a common enemy, and precipitates the Battle of Five Armies in which the Arkenstone plays no part.

In sum, the Arkenstone is both less meaningful and less plot-integrated than the Silmarils or the Ring. Its role in the story, while consistent with its own nature as a beautiful object to be admired and coveted, is devoid of any greater significance. For these very reasons it works better than the Silmarils. Moreover, it marks a kind of hesitation between the early Silmarils and Tolkien's later and more fully realized Ring of Power.

4. The Ring

The answer to the *what* question is harder to pin down with the Ring than with the other two, partly because like the Silmarils and the Arkenstone, the Ring also went through changes before settling into its role as an instrument of power. Shippey points out a "naïve note" in *The Return of the Shadow* stating that the Ring is "not very dangerous, when used for good purpose" (*Road* 293, *Shadow* 42). In light of its subsequent nature and function, "naïve" seems too mild a word. The practical answer to the what question is that the Ring is a container.[6] It houses Sauron's power in an object outside his body (see *Letters* 153, 279), like the soul of the demon Kastchei in the Russian fairy tale.

But like the equally obvious answer for the Grail or the Silmarils, this doesn't capture its real significance, which is as a power, not a receptacle. Tolkien himself, in a letter to Rhona Beare, cautioned, "You cannot press the One Ring too hard, for it is of course a mythical feature." He went on, "If I were to 'philosophize' this myth, or at least the Ring of Sauron, I should say it was a mythical way of representing the truth that *potency* (or perhaps rather *potentiality*) if it is to be exercised, and produce results, has to be externalized" (*Letters* 279, emphasis in original). The word "mythical" here seems to betoken a non-realistic treatment weighted with symbolic meaning. Tolkien's "philosophizing" is on the mark, for attempts to "push the Ring too hard" simply show how difficult it is to define. For all Gandalf's description of its purpose, the greatest effect of the Ring, the power to "rule them all" that it gives its possessor, is barely illustrated.

How does it work? Aside from invisibility (the least of its attributes), the function of the Ring is shown through characters' response to the *idea* of it far more than by its own action. Only three times in the story do we see it do what it's advertised as doing. Each time it is Frodo (not desirous of power) who does not "rule them all," but only Gollum. The first time is in the Emyn Muil where the Ring is the guarantee for Gollum's promise not to run away. "Swear by it, if you will" (*TT* IV, i, 225) Frodo tells him, and Gollum swears. The second is at the Forbidden Pool when Frodo uses the Ring to bring Gollum to Faramir: "'Come!' ... 'Precious will be angry'" (*TT* IV, vi, 296). And Gollum comes, carrying a half-eaten fish. The last is on the path below the Cracks of Doom when Frodo, clutching the Ring as a "wheel of fire," banishes Gollum. "Begone, and trouble me no more!" (*RK* VI, iii, 221)[7] and Gollum goes, though not for long.

So *why* is it there? It is in the story because it *is* the story. The power of the Ring and the corrupting effect of that power are what the story is about. But its effect appears only gradually. Bilbo's belligerence toward Gandalf after the Party, and his reluctance to relinquish it, are the first illustrations. Frodo's subsequent temptation to use it at the first appearance of a Black Rider is ambiguous; is he succumbing to a natural impulse to hide or is the Ring itself compelling his behavior? The question is not answered, as Tolkien moves the Rider on before Frodo can take any action.

Early drafts had Frodo next put on the Ring at Farmer Maggot's in a comic episode of disappearing beer, greatly expanded in a later version (*Shadow* 96–7, 292–4). This was scrapped in favor of the more pointed later scene in the house of Tom Bombadil when Frodo puts it on but stays visible to Tom while becoming invisible to Sam, Merry, and Pippin. Tom himself has just put on the Ring and has *not* disappeared. This defines the nature of the Ring in a way that the scene with Farmer Maggot could not. The Ring works on humanity's desire to dominate. Unlike Maggot, Tom is a personified force of nature, not a conventional human being, and thus has no such desire. Power has no effect on him. And not much on Frodo at this point.

The next episode is at the barrow, where Frodo's courage and loyalty, not his susceptibility to the Ring, are tested. The Ring here is less a compulsion than a practical means of escape. Frodo's temptation is not yielding to the

Ring, it is abandoning his comrades. Both the situation and Frodo's victory over himself are clear. In contrast, his action at The Prancing Pony is loaded with ambiguity. During his encore of "The Man in the Moon," Frodo has his hand in his pocket. In his final disastrous caper, he falls, and his finger and the Ring connect. However, whether this is due to the Ring itself or is mere accident (the uncertainty here is deliberate), the result is minimal. He disappears, but suffers no further consequence than being revealed to the squint-eyed Southerner.

Not until the incident at Weathertop do we see fully how and on what the Ring works—on the human psyche. Wearing the Ring on Weathertop, Frodo is invisible to Sam but visible to the Riders (and they to him), for unlike in Tom's house and at Bree, here the Ring alters his perception. It makes the real world shadowy, the shadow world sharp and clear. It takes Frodo into the dark psychological world of which it is at once the embodiment, the instrument, and the gateway. It is no accident that Sam hears his master's voice coming from "under the earth" (*FR* I, xii, 209), for Frodo has entered the underworld of human nature.

Both this experience and the additional effect of the wound from the Morgul-knife permanently alter Frodo. Descriptions of his condition during the journey to the Ford show that though he has taken off the Ring, he is still in the shadow-world. His perception is so altered that the actual world around him loses substance. "The trees and rocks about him seemed shadowy and dim" (215); "every now and again a mist seemed to obscure his sight" (216–7); "the mist before his eyes ... darkened, and he felt that a shadow was coming between him and the faces of his friends" (222); "during the day things about him faded to shadows of ghostly grey. He almost welcomed the coming of night, for then the world seemed less pale and empty" (224). In the final confrontation at the Ford he can, as he could on Weathertop, see the Black Riders clearly, and as on Weathertop they can see him. No longer wearing the Ring, he is still half in the Ringwraiths' world.

At Rivendell, Bilbo's request to see the Ring triggers in Frodo a similar response, making him see Bilbo as a grasping creature with bony hands reaching for his treasure. It is a projection of his own inner darkness, his own desire. The image tells us about Frodo, not Bilbo, whose reaction when he sees Frodo's face is to say, "I understand now ... Put it away! I am sorry" (*FR* II, i, 244). What Bilbo understands will be clear only after the entrance of Gollum into the story, when we begin to see the terrible transformation which this episode foreshadows. It is in Moria, where he first becomes aware of Gollum, that Frodo can see further into the dark than his companions.

The next significant incident is between Frodo and Boromir on Amon Hen. This relates less to Frodo's previous experience with the Ring than to

Bilbo's with the Arkenstone. In each case a character rationalizes his desire as his "right," Bilbo as his fourteenth share; Boromir as a Númenórean. Both characters "fall," Bilbo metaphorically, Boromir both literally, as his foot catches on a stone, and metaphorically as he hits bottom in his surrender to temptation. Bilbo's self-recognition in *The Hobbit*, that he is capable of theft, that he is "a burglar indeed" foreshadows Boromir's more fully integrated fall and self-realization—"What have I said? ... What have I done? ... A madness took me, but it has passed" (*FR* II, x, 416). Boromir's self-knowledge, his confession and apology to Aragorn, echo Thorin Oakenshield's farewell to Bilbo, about valuing food and cheer above "hoarded gold" (*H* XVIII, 301).

Subsequent chapters in Book IV and the beginning of Book VI focus on Frodo's continuing struggle against the Ring. Tolkien does not tell us, he has Frodo tell us, through his many references to being in the dark, or the dark entering his heart, through his rage at Sam in the Tower of Cirith Ungol. And through his remorse afterward. His "What have I said? ... What have I done?" echoes Boromir on Amon Hen, but what Boromir calls "madness," Frodo recognizes as "the horrible power of the Ring" (*RK* VI, i, 188). Nearing Mount Doom, he tells Sam, "I am almost in its power now ... and if you tried to take it I should go mad" (*RK* VI, iii, 214). His self-knowledge has a higher price than Boromir's, whose madness passes, leaving him whole, while Frodo's possesses him, leaving him broken. It is the measure of Tolkien's skill that the moment at the Cracks of Doom when Frodo claims the Ring stuns first-time readers, yet is fully consistent with everything we have been told about it.

To conclude, there are not just differences among the artifacts, there is marked improvement and refinement over time in Tolkien's handing of vehicle and theme. He is least successful with the Silmarils, whose role in the story is counter to their essential nature. They may be light, but they generate more heat than illumination. He is less ambitious, therefore more successful in his treatment of the Arkenstone. The story is a fairy tale, not an epic, the stakes are lower, and the Arkenstone itself is just a stone with no symbolism attached. Ultimately, it is less a prize than a memorial, buried with Thorin. Finally, Tolkien is most successful in both intent and execution with the Ring of Power, which acts in accord with its own nature and is consistent with its story in a way the Silmarils do not and are not.

In short, Tom's question was not just a good one, it was the right one, and he was right to ask it. The Silmarils are not a perfect representation of what I believe Tolkien was trying to accomplish. Like the tale itself, his ability to corral his material and harness it to his design grew in the telling. Over thirty years he taught himself how to coordinate vehicle and theme and to make them work for each other, for him, and for his audience.

NOTES

1. See Jonathan B. Himes, "What J.R.R. Tolkien Really Did with the Sampo?"

2. The date would place it before the 1918 appearance already discussed, except that the 1917 text exists only in an ink-over-pencil palimpsest which Christopher places as "one of the latest elements in the composition of the *Lost Tales*" (*Lost Tales* I 204), probably before the c. 1925 *Lay of Leithian*.

3. A passage in *Unfinished Tales* alludes to Fëanor's request for a "tress" of Galadriel's silver-gold hair, whose "gold was touched by some memory of the starlike silver of her mother," and that "the Eldar said that the light of the Two Trees, Laurelin and Telperion, had been snared in her tresses" (*UT* 230). The passage suggests that this saying first gave Fëanor the idea of "imprisoning and blending" the two lights that "later took shape in his hands as the Silmarils" (230), a surprising complication to an already-complicated concept of the connection between light and desire. Christopher dates the passage to "certainly" after the publication of *The Road Goes Ever On* (229).

4. For more on this interesting speculation see "The Arkenstone as Silmaril" in *The History of The Hobbit, Part Two: Return to Bag-End*, 603–9.

5. The ground for this has been prepared by Bilbo's theft of the Ring (at least from Gollum's point of view) and his weeks of pilfering the larder in the Wood-elves' caves (for which he later apologizes to the Wood-elf King himself).

6. Wagner's *Ring of the Nibelung* is the comparison most often made, but the epitome of the search for Tolkien's possible sources is David Day's popularizing *Tolkien's Ring*, which ransacks literature for any and all mentions of magic rings however near to or far from Tolkien's Ring of Power they may be.

7. There is some debate as to whether the voice that speaks out of the wheel of fire is the voice of Frodo or that of the Ring itself. I propose that at this point in Frodo's long surrender there is very little difference between the two.

WORKS CITED

Collins, Wilkie. *The Moonstone*. New York: The Heritage Press, 1959.

Day, David. *Tolkien's Ring*. London: HarperCollins, 1994.

Helms, Randel. *Tolkien and the Silmarils*. Boston: Houghton Mifflin, 1981.

Himes, Jonathan B. "What J.R.R. Tolkien Really Did with the Sampo?" *Mythlore* 22.4 (#86) (Spring 2000): 69–85.

Kane, Douglas Charles. *Arda Reconstructed: The Creation of the Published* Silmarillion. Bethlehem: Lehigh University Press, 2009.

Rateliff, John D. *The History of The Hobbit*. 2 vols. Boston: Houghton Mifflin, 2007.

Shippey, Tom. *The Road to Middle-earth*. 1st ed. London: Allen & Unwin, 1982.

Tolkien and Apposition

LESLIE STRATYNER

In 1982, long before *Tolkien Studies* and the renaissance in academic interest spurred by Peter Jackson's movie versions of *The Lord of the Rings*, Thomas Shippey made what is perhaps the most provocative point about the influence of *Beowulf* on Tolkien. In *The Road to Middle-earth* he suggests a reading of "*Beowulf*: The Monsters and the Critics" proves Tolkien was so enamored of and attuned to the poem that Tolkien believed "that no one, friends or descendants or maybe even contemporaries, had understood *Beowulf* except Tolkien…. Tolkien felt more than continuity with the *Beowulf*-poet, he felt a virtual identity of motive and of technique" (47). Nearly two decades later, in "Tolkien and the *Beowulf*-Poet," Shippey's belief in this virtual identity leads him to ask: "Did Tolkien ever wonder whether he might possibly be the *Beowulf*-poet reincarnated?" (1). For various reasons, Shippey posits that the answer is "no," yet in this essay Shippey also asserts that the connection between Tolkien and the *Beowulf*-poet goes beyond merely "a certain sympathy, a fellow feeling, between Tolkien and the poet" (6). Shippey's insights in that regard touch on larger, thematic issues such as the "virtuous pagans" that inhabit both *Beowulf* and Middle-earth, but he also points out that

> while Tolkien read *Beowulf* very carefully, he did not read it like a literary critic, but like a philologist. His insights tended to be drawn from tiny details, often very technical ones [13].

For a variety of reasons transparent to any Anglo-Saxonist (which would of course include Shippey), this makes perfect sense. And if Shippey is right, close inspection of Tolkien's work will show that his use of elements such as Anglo-Saxon words and word origins and the incorporation of the Riders of Rohan into the narrative (elements which Shippey has pointed out as well) are only the most superficially obvious of connections. Close inspection will show that *The Hobbit* and *The Lord of the Rings* are informed not only ornamentally, through the mere borrowings of words, but at the very deepest levels, by Tolkien's understanding of Anglo-Saxon poetic structures and technique, of the bone and sinew of how the poetry itself was built.

It is that bone and sinew I wish to explore, specifically the technique known as apposition, what Fred Robinson (quoting Klaeber) recognizes as "the very soul of the Old English poetical style" (3). Robinson develops this most famously in Beowulf *and the Appositive Style*. Indeed, in this regard Robinson is also building on Tolkien's groundbreaking work on the poem, for in his lecture "Beowulf: The Monsters and the Critics," Tolkien himself asserted that "[The poem] is essentially a balance, an opposition of ends and beginnings. In its simplest terms it is a contrasted description of two moments in a great life" (*MC* 28).

Though much of his argument is devoted to the question of grammatical apposition, Robinson does devote some attention to the appositive style as used in the creation of character, citing that "[a] favorite means of characterization in *Beowulf* is the drawing of parallel portraits so that the juxtaposed descriptions imply through similarity or contrast the essential qualities of a character" (21–22). Robinson cites the appositional pairing of the characters of Modthryth and Hygelac's wife Hygd as an example. The *Beowulf*-poet defines Hygd's character via an appositive pairing with Modthryth, a badly-behaved queen who had men throttled just for looking at her. She was a "queen of the folk," or "folces cwēn" but her crimes were terrible (*Beowulf* line 1932; all translations are mine). Queen Hygd, in stark contrast, performs her duties admirably, and the *Beowulf*-poet describes her as wise, honored, well spoken, and a giver of gifts. She does not misuse her power.

As one would expect, Beowulf is himself defined appositively as well, many times throughout the poem. After the hero kills Grendel, the *scop*, or bard, composes a song of Beowulf's praise, contextualizing his accomplishment within that of another acknowledged and legendary hero: Sigemund. The appositive style in this case elevates Beowulf's status to that of the great warrior before him, and the tale of Sigemund's victory over a dragon also foreshadows Beowulf's similar fight with another dragon at the end of the poem.

Likewise Beowulf's character is faceted via the *scop* through the apposition of his feats against those of a particularly nasty king named Heremod, who slaughtered his men and kept all the treasure for himself. Hrothgar later tells Beowulf specifically that from Heremod's bad example he can learn the nobler virtues of men. Via apposition with Heremod, the evil Danish king who murders the companions of his own table (*Beowulf* 1713), Beowulf's greatness, his level-headedness, his generosity, and his kindness are all shown as if in relief.

Thus, within *Beowulf*, the use of the appositive style defines the characters not just in terms of their own actions, but within the panorama of human experience and possibility, good and bad, providing the kind of textured reference that paradoxically both delineates a man like Beowulf and subsumes him. He is never just himself. He is always himself in relation to heroic history. And always, always, the appositive style, especially with regard to the creation of character, underscores the fragile nature of any victory, and of human striving in general. We see how terribly difficult it is to become a Sigemund or a Beowulf, and how terribly easy it is, once that status is attained, to transform into a Heremod, or a Modthryth.

Hrothgar's great speech to Beowulf just before the hero returns to Sweden underscores that the gravest danger to heroes isn't dragons or monster-men with a taste for human flesh, but a hero's refusal to remember that he is mortal, and as such "his selfa ne mæg / his unsnyttrum ende geþencean" or "he cannot in his foolishness think of an end" (1733b–1734). He who acts without remembering this becomes arrogant, and there is where the trouble begins. It is apposition that exposes the spectrum of possibility inherent in all human action, good and bad, within *Beowulf*.

Though doubtless many are oblivious to the origins of the appositive style, Tolkien's use of it seems immediately obvious to anyone aware of the technique. As Marjorie Burns observes, "[m]ost of Tolkien's key characters have their shadow side" (128). Tolkien actively employs apposition in the creation of most, if not all of his important characters. Some obvious instances include Théoden and Denethor, Saruman and Gandalf, Sauron and Frodo, and the nine Walkers and the nine Ringwraiths. And that is just a beginning.

Yet perhaps the most extended and significant appositive comparison is that of Bilbo and Gollum. The essential qualities of each that emerge as a result of this comparison transform both hobbits into far more complicated individuals, plot aside, than they would have been had they never faced each other to begin with, or had Tolkien not made use of the appositive style.

Because, of course, Gollum is in fact a hobbit. Even before Gandalf specifically pronounces Gollum "of hobbit-kind" (*FR* I, ii, 62) it's obvious that Tolkien intends us to see Gollum and Bilbo as distant kin. From their first meeting great care is taken to characterize Bilbo and Gollum appositively, indeed using what Robinson terms "juxtaposed description" in which Gollum and Bilbo's "essential qualities" are contrasted. The two are more similar than dissimilar, and Bilbo's first great challenge, in fact in retrospect his greatest challenge, is to transcend a foe who is, in essence, *himself*, or a self he has the potential of becoming. And the consequences aren't merely relevant to his life; it later becomes clear that the entire fate of the War of the Ring hinges upon the choices Bilbo makes by the dark pool under the Misty Mountains.

From the beginning Tolkien constructs explicit similarities between the two creatures. Their kinship is initially underscored in *The Hobbit* by a riddle game. Gollum is the one who suggests it, probably because "Asking them, and sometimes guessing them, had been the only game he had ever played with other funny creatures sitting in their holes in the long, long ago" (*H* V, 84). Commenting later to Frodo on this episode in *The Fellowship of the Ring*, Gandalf tells him that "There was a great deal in the background of their minds and memories that was very similar. They understood one another remarkably well, very much better than a hobbit would understand, say, a Dwarf, or an Orc, or even an Elf" (*FR* I, ii, 63–64).

We must note that the inclusion of the riddle game itself is a testament to Tolkien's knowledge and respect for this particular brand of intellectual game, which is rooted in antiquity in the riddles of Symphosius, and in Tolkien's own area of particular expertise: Old English poetry, which includes the riddles of the *Exeter Book*. The riddle game in *The Hobbit* is serious business, "sacred and of immense antiquity, and even wicked creatures were afraid to cheat when they played at it" (*H* V, 90).

But while both Bilbo and Gollum each understand the unwritten rules of the riddle game (as well as Bilbo's final failure to come up with a genuine riddle, when he resorts to asking a question about what he has in his pockets), each character tells vastly different sorts of riddles. Tolkien's use of the riddle game itself foregrounds his intention for us to view his characters appositively. And it is here that we can see most clearly the nature of apposition itself with regard to character, because apposites are not opposites. Gollum is not Bilbo's opposite. He is not "opposed to" or completely different from Bilbo. He is *apposite*, meaning we are supposed to view the two characters as side-by-side.

The existence of the riddle game proves that Tolkien intends to fashion Bilbo and Gollum as appositives, but it is the content of the riddles themselves that illuminates their respective characters, because, while they both understand the riddle game, and in a very real sense understand each other, the riddles that each tells are a reflection of their true natures. The riddles themselves are heart of the appositive characterization. Bilbo's riddles are about teeth, sun on the daisies, eggs, and a man eating fish at a table and giving the bones to his cat. The answers to Gollum's riddles are mountain, wind, dark, fish, and time. Gollum's riddle of fish imagines a creature "Alive without breath, / As cold as death" (*H* V, 87). Bilbo's riddle of fish is much more convivial, of a man sitting at a table and eating, and sharing his dinner with the cat. Gollum imagines darkness. Bilbo imagines sun on the daisies. Thus we can see that Gollum's riddles reflect Gollum himself, a creature molded by murder, dark, loneliness, and an endless stretch of wearying, destructive time. Bilbo's riddles, about things like sun, flowers, teeth, eggs, reveal him to be a creature of much more genial appetites.

What is the point of this appositive likeness in Tolkien's work? As in *Beowulf*, in part it provides us with the ominous hint of danger to each character should they become corrupted. Just as Beowulf is potentially in danger of becoming the kind of king that hoards gold and murders his thanes, Bilbo, for example, could easily become the kind of hobbit that slinks under a dark mountain instead of a living in a bright hobbit-hole. Gollum is Bilbo's obvious appositive presence, exposing the terrible possibility of what might happen to Bilbo, much as the repeated mention of Heremod offers a whisper of a threat as to what Beowulf could become if he doesn't stay on the right road. Apposition facets the virtue of Bilbo's character in comparison with Gollum in the same exact way that it facets the virtue of Beowulf's character in comparison with Heremod.

And Bilbo becoming Gollum, or Gollum's equivalent, is a most definite possibility. It is far, far after his acquisition of the Ring that the danger to Bilbo becomes completely apparent. Before he leaves the Shire for good, Gandalf pressures him to give up the ring that he found under the Misty Mountains so long ago, trying to persuade him that it's in his own best interests to do so.

Bilbo is not convinced easily. "It is mine, I tell you. My own. My precious. Yes, my precious," Bilbo says, whereupon Gandalf tells him, "It has been called that before ... but not by you" (*FR* I, i, 42). And it is at this point that Bilbo, like Gollum before him, turns violent, perhaps even with murderous intent, and "His hand strayed to the hilt of his small sword" (42).

Had Bilbo retained the Ring, had Gandalf not been able to help him give it up, doubtless eventually he would have become a creature much like Gollum, if not caught by the enemy first. He would not have seen Frodo, Gandalf, or elves again, or Rivendell. His journey from Hobbiton after the long-expected party would have been very different, yet no doubt akin to what happened to Sméagol after he took the Ring.

Yet we also see the virtue of Bilbo's character in comparison with Gollum's in *The Hobbit*. Gollum is utterly wretched, most especially because it's obvious that he hasn't lived in a cave for all of his life. He's not a goblin. He wasn't born to live in darkness. He's a hobbit. He remembers sunlight, and daisies. He remembers his grandmother. And when Bilbo makes the most important decision of his life, when he chooses not to kill Gollum, we see that Bilbo has an understanding of the creature born out of a shared kinship and comprehension of Gollum's deprivation:

> He was miserable, alone, lost. A sudden understanding, a pity mixed with horror, welled up in Bilbo's heart: a glimpse of endless unmarked days without light or hope of betterment, hard stone, cold fish, sneaking and whispering [*H* V, 97].

It is only later that we find out Gollum's "ownership" of the Ring began with an exact inverse parallel to Bilbo's. Gollum began his ownership of the Ring by *taking* the life of Déagol, a friend who intended him no harm. Bilbo's began by *sparing* the life of Gollum, an enemy who wished to murder him. The appositive characterization has given us a moment that defines the magnitude of Bilbo's spirit, at the same time as it defines the threat of Bilbo turning into a creature such as the one he pities.

In *The Hobbit*, as in *Beowulf*, the hero's greatness, his level-headedness, his generosity, and his kindness are all shown as if in relief beside the appositive character that defines him. But the use of apposition also exposes the foes, by delineating the magnitude of the tragedies of Gollum and Heremod as well. The archetypal "bad king," Heremod doesn't just *behave* badly; he himself is unhappy. His bloody acts against his own men, his holding of treasure, don't provide him any pleasure. He doesn't die glutted with evil glee at his own deeds; Heremod "oþ þæt hē āna hwearf, / mǣre þēode mondrēamum from ... drēamlēas gebād, / þæt hē þæs gewinnes" "turned alone, that great prince, from the happiness of men ... he lived deprived of joys, suffered because of what he had done to his people" (*Beowulf* 1714b-1715, 1720b-1722a).

With the exception of the term "great prince," these words could be used to describe Gollum. In *Beowulf*, it's obvious that Heremod's tragedy is magnified because of appositive characterization with the title character. But just so, in *The Hobbit* and *The Lord of the Rings*, is Gollum's tragedy magnified because of the appositive characterization with Bilbo.

It is in *The Two Towers* that this is brought to fruition, because it is here that Gollum's tragedy is explored in the greatest detail. Even here Gollum is not completely ruined. Though he spends the rest of his life attempting to recover his "stolen" Ring, the fact that he does not possess it anymore allows some semblance of his old self to return. His role as guide to Mordor for Frodo and Sam provides him with some degree of friendship and companionship as well, though he wages a constant battle with himself and his desire for the Ring. For it isn't just Frodo's will and his status as Ringbearer that master Gollum (though they are certainly a factor), it is Gollum's growing affection for his "master," whom he has promised to help. Gollum's love for Frodo, his gratitude for his trust and companionship, is at one point at least as strong as his twisted love for the Ring.

His desire to regain his "precious" drives him to make a devil's bargain with Shelob, the massive, ancient, and very hungry spider to which he leads the hapless hobbits as a kind of offering. Much as he felt guilt over the murder of Déagol, Gollum feels considerable guilt over his plans to reclaim the Ring, which he hopes he will recover when it is cast aside after Frodo has been killed. Though he had promised not to harm Frodo, Gollum keeps to the letter of this vow by attempting to lead Frodo to his death, but not actually doing the deed himself (and of course, Gollum never promised not to harm Sam, whom he tries to murder in Shelob's Lair). Gollum's guilt is plain when he returns from worshipping Shelob and securing his scheme, as Frodo and Sam are resting on the stairs of Cirith Ungol:

> Gollum looked at them. A strange expression passed over his lean hungry face. The gleam faded from his eyes, and they went dim and grey, old and tired. A spasm of pain seemed to twist him, and he turned away, peering back towards the pass, shaking his head, as if engaged in some interior debate. Then he came back, and slowly putting out a trembling hand, very cautiously he touched Frodo's knee—but almost the touch was a caress. For a fleeting moment, could one of the sleepers have seen him, they would have thought that they beheld an old weary hobbit, shrunken by the years that had carried him far beyond his time, beyond friends and kin, and the fields and streams of youth, an old starved pitiable thing [*TT* IV, vii, 324].

This is one of the most profound moments in the trilogy, which could not have been accomplished if Tolkien had created Gollum as, say, an orc, or a ruined ent, elf, or dwarf. Gollum's tragedy depends on the appositional relationship developed with Bilbo in *The Hobbit*.

Chance suggests that "[p]erhaps Tolkien manifests the civilization and humanization (hobbitization?) of Gollum in order to make more horrible Gollum's final treachery ... to allow to be killed what he most loves next to the Precious" (78), and that is certainly true. But this incident also serves as another display of the terrible, oft-repeating tragedy of Gollum's existence: he is essentially a fratricide. He kills Déagol, attempts to kill Bilbo, and then likewise arranges for the death of Frodo and then attempts outright to kill Sam. Thus despite the core of "hobbitishness" that remains with him, despite his ability to love and feel friendship and longing and pain, like Heremod he is plagued with unhappiness. This is the most tragic moment in a long past filled with tragic moments, because it is here that Gollum came, according to Tolkien, "within a hair of repentance—but for one rough word from Sam" (*Letters* 110). In that moment upon the stairs, the possibility of Gollum becoming whole again, becoming Sméagol the hobbit again, is just as real as the possibility of Bilbo becoming Gollum at the beginning of *The Fellowship of the Ring*.

It is not necessary to know *Beowulf* to appreciate *The Lord of the Rings*. It is not even necessary to know that Tolkien was an Anglo-Saxonist. Chances are that many, if not most, of the people who voted for *The Lord of the Rings* as the best book of the 20th century know neither (*Author* xx–xxi). But without an understanding and incorporation of issues such as Anglo-Saxon poetic technique the work remains underappreciated, and by scholars, undervalued.

In his two-page, rather tossed-off, introduction to his edited anthology of Tolkien criticism, Harold Bloom writes that he is "not able to understand how a skilled and mature reader can absorb about fifteen hundred pages of this quaint stuff" (2). "Absorb" has a negative connotation, as if the book itself is unpalatable; even Bloom would have to agree that many "skilled and mature" readers find the book endlessly engaging. No, what Bloom cannot imagine is why a skilled and mature reader would in fact not only "absorb" but *revere* and *admire* this "quaint stuff." But though Bloom uses the word "quaint" to imply *The Lord of the Rings* is fussy and old-fashioned, the word also has a related meaning: ancient, and archaic. I would suggest that it is precisely in the utilization of such "ancient" and "archaic" techniques, such "quaint" methods as apposition that the work not only establishes its charm, but also its power, and its resonance.

Shippey would doubtless agree, as he himself writes that "one of the grandeurs of philology has always been the way in which tiny details can open up great vistas of suggestion and, furthermore, find a natural connection between ancient and modern, and even with the facts of one's own life" ("Tolkien and the *Beowulf*-Poet" 13).

Works Cited

Beowulf and The Fight at Finnsburg. Ed. Fr. Klaeber. 3rd ed. Lexington, MA: Heath, 1950.

Bloom, Harold. Introduction. *Modern Critical Interpretations: J.R.R. Tolkien's The Lord of the Rings.* Ed. Harold Bloom. Philadelphia: Chelsea House, 2000.

Burns, Marjorie. "Doubles." *Encyclopedia* 127–128.

Chance, Jane. The Lord of the Rings: *The Mythology of Power.* New York: Twayne, 1992.

The Exeter Book. Ed. George Philip Krapp and Elliot Van Kirk Dobbie. New York: Columbia University Press, 1936.

Robinson, Fred C. Beowulf *and the Appositive Style.* Knoxville: University of Tennessee Press, 1985.

Shippey, Tom. "Tolkien and the *Beowulf*-Poet." *Roots* 1–18.

III. "Philological Inquiries"

Keeping Counsel: Advice in Tolkien's Fiction

John R. Holmes

When I first moved from the status of graduate student to full-time professor, the prospect of each new academic task seemed exhilarating—except for the thought of student advising. The scenario I dreaded was facing the headstrong eighteen-year-old—Derek, for instance—who just knew he wanted these five or six courses, even though none of them would advance his major (or his *major du jour*, as Derek, though only a sophomore, was now on his seventh). I was sure I would have to figure out how to steer him toward something that would help him graduate. Of course, I needn't have worried. The hypothetical Derek never materialized. My real-life problem was the Cindy. Cindy came to me with a blank schedule form and simply said, "Tell me what to take." Never mind that I had never met this young woman in my life, knew nothing about her abilities, aspirations, likes, or dislikes: I was supposed to choose a future for her. And that has been the story of my advising career for a quarter century: an army of Cindies, but not a single Derek.

That moment was an epiphany not only as an advisor, but as a reader of Tolkien. Until the day I stared at Cindy's blank schedule, I could never understand—not even after reading Shippey—a cryptic hobbit *gnomon* cited by Frodo in the third chapter of *The Fellowship of the Ring*: "*Go not to the Elves for counsel, for they will say both no and yes*" (*FR* I, iii, 93). Or rather, I *mis*-understood it, for at that time I was as sure of the rightness of my superficial reading of *The Lord of the Rings* as Derek was sure that only those five or six courses could guarantee his happiness for the rest of his life. I read it as another of the many examples of hobbit ethnocentrism in *The Lord of the Rings*: to a hobbit, Elvish advice always sounded like politicians talking out of both sides of their mouths. And now, decades later, I don't think that reading was wrong, just incomplete. What I really needed to work out was Gildor's answer.

Advice or counsel in Tolkien represents a form of semantic displacement, a linguistic phenomenon that takes many forms in *The Lord of the Rings*. Linguist Leonard Bloomfield first spoke of displacement in language in 1933. At about the same time, Alfred Korzybski (his first name proclaiming him another elf-advisee, as we shall see below) was reducing the notion of semantic displacement to its negative form, his famous dictum "The Map is not the Territory." In Tolkien's fiction, however, it is easy to see how positive forms of linguistic displacement—that is, using the "map" (words) to displace the "territory" (objective reality, the *Ding-an-Sich*) are crucial for fantasy. When Aragorn sings of Beren and Lúthien, or when Gandalf reads the ancient manuscripts of Isildur, they bring the wisdom of ancient folk into the present. Prophecy reverses the process (or at least reverses its vector), bringing the future into the present. When a prophecy is fulfilled, the present of its realization is connected back to the past of its utterance. Particularly valuable to Hobbits is their love of what the ancient Greeks called *gnomic* poetry, bits of folk wisdom reduced to proverbs, handed down across generations.

If *gnomoi* represent semantic displacement from past to present—ancient folk sayings representing an ancestor's counsel to later generations—then just plain everyday advice is semantic displacement from present to future. Advice is always directed toward the future, even if it is stated in present terms, and includes the present. We can advise our friends to do something now and in the future, but we cannot advise them to do something in the past. It is true that we can say "You should have done this," or "You should never have done that," but the sense of such an admonition is still subjunctive, and not really pointing to the past—indeed, it could implicitly be read as "if this situation arises again, you should do *X*."

Our best-known cultural tool for semantic displacement from the past to the present is a form of magic now so common that is no longer (more's the pity) recognized as magic. It is known by a modern English descendent of the *-ræd* radical in *Ælfræd* and *Scippigræd*:[1] the verb *to read*. Whatever wisdom we glean from Professor Shippey, we owe as well to those even greater wizards, the poorly-rewarded *istari* who in our youth taught us to siphon counsel from markings on a page. In a simpler age and place—such as the Little Kingdom of Tolkien's Farmer Giles—the magic of reading was rare enough to be appreciated. Then the discipline was not termed "reading" but "grammar," and its status as magic, as Shippey has advised us, is seen in the etymologically related *glamour* and *grimoire* (*Road* 51–54). In Tolkien's *Farmer Giles of Ham*, the parson was capable of the semantic displacement toward the future (prophecy) precisely because he was a "grammarian"—that is, he could read. "He was a grammarian," Farmer Giles's narrator tells us, "and could doubtless see further into the future than others" (48). "Parson" and "grammarian" would be near-synonyms anyway, in the same way that to Chaucer *clerkish* could mean either "religious" or "intellectual," and even today *clerical* can refer either to something ecclesial or something involving writing or ciphering. A few pages later the parson-grammarian again cites his grammarian powers of prophecy: he hands Giles rope that he knows the farmer will need, "unless my foresight deceives me" (55). The *Scippigræd* will recognize a doublet of that scene in *The Lord of the Rings* when the elves offer Sam the very item he was kicking himself for not bringing: a rope (*FR* II, viii, 387). And that instance of the elves' forward thinking brings us back to their aversion to advice.

It may be the inherent future-orientation of advice that accounts for a curious reluctance of Tolkien's elves, a reluctance noticed by the other races in Middle-earth, to advise the shorter-lived races. It is embedded in Frodo's proverb, already cited: "*Go not to the Elves for counsel, for they will say both no and yes.*" Far from taking offense, the elf to whom Frodo pointedly directs the remark, Gildor, laughs and explains: "Elves seldom give unguarded advice, for advice is a dangerous gift, even from the wise to the wise, and all courses may run ill" (*FR* I, iii, 93). *All courses may run ill.* This is the wisdom of an immortal race, and a race that has, therefore, more insight into the future than mortal races have—or at least, can take a longer view. In fact, the grammatical subtlety of Gildor's sentence obscures the relationship between "advice is a dangerous gift," and "all courses may run ill." A brief analysis of this sentence might elucidate the Elvish attitude toward advice. Or it may simply be that, because I aspire to be *Scippigræd,* I really just want to analyze the sentence for its own sake. Note at this point how characteristic it is of the *Scippigræd* to answer a problem of interpretation with philological analysis.

In the history of most languages, coordination and subordination are late developments. Any semantic connection between sentences in the earlier stages of a language is accomplished by parataxis, simple juxtaposition of sentences or clauses. Where the modern speaker would say, "I was late because I overslept" (subordination), the ancient speaker might say, "I was late. I overslept" (parataxis). The older, paratactic expression can still convey the connection between the lateness and the oversleeping, but the connection is more subtle than in the subordinated expression; it demands more interaction with the listener to convey that connection. Even coordinate expressions are sometimes paratactic in languages like Old English and Old Norse. Whereas we might say, "I am Thorrstein, and he is Bjorn," a saga writer might say, "I am Thorrstein. He is Bjorn."

Both modern English structures, subordination and coordination, appear in Gildor's sentence: modern grammarians would call it a compound-complex sentence. The first two clauses are linked by subordination: "Elves seldom give unguarded advice" (main, independent clause), "for advice is a dangerous gift, even from the wise to the wise" (subordinate clause, with a parenthetical phrase tacked on).

Already I am on dangerous ground with grammarians, for what I have just identified (and imitated in this clause) as a subordinate clause most grammarians would consider coordinated, of equal weight with the first clause. That most venerable of prescriptive grammarians, H.W. Fowler, in his entry on "for" in *A Dictionary of Modern English Usage* is unequivocal in declaring *for* "a coordinating conjunction, i.e., one that connects two independent sentences," and insisting that it is *not* "like *since* & *because*, a subordinating conjunction that joins a mere clause to a sentence" (186). Yet surely the semantic force of *for* is precisely like that of *since* or *because* in this sentence. Why does *for* seem so like a causal subordinator if it is, as Fowler asserted, a coordinator?

It is in the Old English ancestor of the construction that the answer can be seen. *For* as a conjunction of causality is vestigial in modern English for Old English prepositional phrases like *for þām þe*, "for the reason that." In the twelfth century writers began eliding such phrases until *for* became the semantic equivalent of *because* even in expressions which today would not admit *for*, as in Emilia's observation in *Othello*: "They are not ever jealous for the cause, / But jealous for they are jealous" (III. iv).

So if the reader will indulge me in considering Tolkien's second clause subordinate, we may proceed. The second clause, that advice is dangerous, is (the grammar implies) the *reason* elves seldom give it. But that explanation itself begs explanation (why is advice dangerous?), so Gildor amplifies, this time by coordination. It is in the last clause that the subtlety lies. For the modern grammarian and stylist would not have used coordination in this instance. The twenty-first-century freshman English instructor, in fact, might be tempted to "correct" Professor Tolkien's grammar on this point. "Improper coordination" would be the marginal comment, and the suggested correction might be "Advice is a dangerous gift *because* all courses may run ill." The modern grammarian tells us that "and" should not be used for subordination. But the modern grammarian is wrong.

In the days when parataxis was king in Old English syntax, our sturdy and flexible "and" was quite an efficient subordinator, as it still is in all colloquial English, and in a special way in Irish English. It could be adversative, as Wulfstan demonstrated in his famous *Sermo Lupi ad Anglos* (1014):

> Among heathen people one dare not withhold little nor much that is ordained for the pagan gods' worship; and we withhold everywhere God's dues all too often.

On hæþenum þeodum ne dear man forhealdan lytel ne micel þæs þe gelagod is
to gedwolgoda weorðunge; *and* we forhealdað æghwær Godes gerihte ealles to
gelome.

Here we would expect after the first clause an adversative, "and yet." The "and"
in Modern English does not usually perform the adversative function, as it
does here in Old English, though it easily could do so by a slight adjustment
in tone, as we often do conversationally: "You never come to class, and you
expect an *A*?" Even though it is unexpressed, the "yet" can be heard by the
Scippigræd between "and" and "you expect." We can feel, even in translation,
the adversative force of the "and" in the Wulfstan passage: clearly it is the
hinge pin between the clauses, contrasting the pagan's fidelity to false gods
with the backsliding English Christian's *in*fidelity to the true God.

Similarly, modern Irish English uses *and* as a subordinating conjunction
as we would use *because* or *since*. In the opening scene of J.M. Synge's 1907
Irish classic *The Playboy of the Western World*, Pegeen Flaherty tells her fiancé
Shawn Keogh that her father is coming. Shawn replies, "I didn't see him on
the road." Pegeen retorts, "How would you see him, and it dark night this half
hour gone by?" Clearly there is an intended semantic connection (causal)
between the first clause, "How could you see him?" and the second, "[since]
it has been dark for half an hour now." Later in the same play Honor Blake
tells Christy Mahon, "[Y]ou should have a thin stomach on you, and you that
length walking the world." Twenty-first century British or American English
would express the same sense by turning the "and" to "if," making an adverbial
clause. In both sentences from early twentieth-century Irish English, the word
and works just fine as a subordinator.

But the real subtlety of Tolkien's construction of Gildor's sentence mirth-
fully assessing the Elvish taboo against advice is, as is often the case with
Tolkien's supposed archaisms, a Miltonic awareness of the tension between
modern and archaic meanings. Tolkien scholars (the *Scippigræd*) most often
cite the dialectic between ancient and modern in Tolkien's prose in terms of
single words, which Tolkien will use with overlapping modern and etymological senses. In the most familiar examples, Tolkien describes a *reek* in Mordor
with overtones of its original sense of "smoke" or "exhalation"; the word *doom*,
even as a proper noun in Mt. Doom, or as an onomatopoeic sound effect of
an orcish booming in the mines of Moria, recalls both the modern sense of "a
bad end" and the more neutral etymological sense of "judgment," either good
or bad. Yet Tolkien is capable of balancing ancient and modern on the syntactic
level as well, a subtlety to which critics who speak slightingly of Tolkien's supposed "archaic diction" are demonstrably deaf. In the line quoted from Gildor
(at the risk of over-analyzing a single sentence), Tolkien blends a very modern
subordination (with "for") with an older parataxis (with "and"), creating an

ambiguity in the latter. That is, read with the ancient syntactic sensibilities which could detect a causal connection in a simple "and," Gildor's statement is a justification of Elvish caution; read with modern word-sense alone, it is simply an additional comment—perhaps even a change of subject. If we read with modern syntactical tools alone, we often miss very simple narrative points in Tolkien. But if we read the way Shippey taught us, we do not.

To a student of Old English history and literature, the Elvish reluctance to advise mortals carries a smack of irony, since the most famous name in the Anglo-Saxon annals is Alfred (*ælf-ræd*, "advised by elves"). So despite the reluctance of Third-Age elves like Gildor, the elves of AD 849, the year Alfred was christened, were apparently not above offering advice. The preponderance of the *–red* suffix in Old English onomastics speaks to the centrality of counsel or advice in the culture. In the *Anglo-Saxon Chronicles* alone we find Aldred, Alhred, Bealdred, Burgred, Cenred, Ceolred, Cuthred, Eadred, Ealdred, Ethelred, Forthred, Heardred, Osred, Sefred, Selred, Thored, Wihtred, and Wulfred (a compound duplicated by the Norse name *Radhulf*, which survives as *Ralph*). Naming is perhaps the greatest protective magic a parent has, so no loving mother or father would seal a child with a name ending in *–red* if it were not a good thing.

The verb *to read* is not the only modern survival of the Germanic root. The modern German cognate never lost its connotation of "advice," *Rath*, which also gives us the compound *Rathaus*, "City Hall" (where advice is certainly dispensed, if seldom by elves), and beneath the city hall the *Rathskeller* (where beer is dispensed, along with better advice). Shakespeareans know that the English cognate *rede* survived into Elizabethan times, as when Ophelia warns Laertes not to be like the hypocrite preacher who "recks not his own rede"—doesn't practice what he preaches (*Hamlet* I. iii). "Rede" is one of the many archaisms Tolkien favors in his *Legend of Sigurd and Gudrún*, where the word appears five times. In *The Lord of the Rings* Legolas uses the word to voice what sounds very like a *gnomon* running counter to Gildor's: "Rede oft is found at the rising of the Sun" (*TT* III, ii, 31). In current English, *reading* is not the only form of advice from the past: gnomic advice is sometimes memorized in cryptic form that needs to be unraveled, a *riddle* (Old English *rædl*, from the same root). Even before his first Tolkien book, Professor Shippey's scholarship has advised his readers of the role of Old English riddles as wisdom literature in *Poems of Wisdom and Learning in Old English* (1976).

Ancient usage of the root, whether Old English *ræd* or Old Norse *ráð*, seems uninstructive on any negative connotations of advice. And if we go back past the Germanic branch of the Indo-European development of the word, it doesn't even seem to mean "advice" at all. Sanskrit *radh* means "to succeed, to accomplish." But another Sanskrit word that does mean "advice" offers additional insight into the nature of counsel. The word is, as Max Müller pointed out a little more than a century ago, *mantra*. In Western usage we usually think of a "mantra" as a chanted sound capable of effecting spiritual transformation, but originally mantras could be written as well. But whether written or spoken (or thought), mantras can indeed convey, like reading, advice from the past (particularly Vedic texts). Now, as *Scippigræd*, we know Max Müller mainly as the author of a *gnomon* with which Tolkien took exception in "On Fairy-stories" (namely, "Mythology is a disease of language" [*TOF* 41]). But in a posthumously-published article entitled "How to Work," Müller ends up on the same page as Tolkien in an article that appeared half a century later.

What Müller and Tolkien independently agree on has to do with the etymology not of the Old English word for advice, *ræd*, but the modern English word, "advice." The word was not around in Alfred's time: the earliest OED citation is dated 1297. But its spelling affords a clue which etymological dictionaries missed, but both Müller in 1900 and Tolkien in 1951 noted. The dictionaries—Tolkien cited specifically the "R.E.W.," Wilhelm Meyer-Lübke's *Romanisches Etymologisches Wörterbuch*—theorized a Latin *ad-visum* (or in Tolkien's case *ante-visum*). The trouble with this notion is that the "d" in English "advice" is unhistorical. The spelling we learned when those ancient wizards taught us to read is what is known as an "etymological respelling," a linguistic phenomenon that occurred with the introduction of the printing press in England. This spelling, in fact, was devised by the first English printer, William Caxton.

The earliest spelling of the word was "avis," as it was spelled in the Norman French it came from. Robert of Gloucester has the earliest appearance of the word in *Metrical Chronicles*, his verse history of England covering Arthurian times (based largely on Geoffrey of Monmouth):

> His *conseil* he tok þo, how he myȝt make þere
> Some werk, in honowr of hem, þat euer in mynde were.
> þe erchbischop of Walis seide ys *auis*
> "Sire," he seide, "gef þer ys any mon so wys,
> That beste *red* þe can *rede*, Merlyn þat ys."
>
> [His counsel he took then, how he might make there
> Some work, in honor of them, that ever were in mind.
> The Archbishop of Wales said his advice.
> "Sire," he said, "if there is any man so wise,
> That can give thee the best advice, it is Merlin"] [144–5, my italics].

Whatever this is as poetry, this first appearance of *advice* as a noun is valuable advice on "advice," containing in the space of five lines three synonyms for the word: *conseil, auis,* and *red(e)*. (The same work offers the first known instance of the verb *advise* as well: "he avisede þe ost suiþe wel" ["he advised the host very well"], 558.)

But then Caxton, the first of a group of well-meaning classicists who would meddle with our spelling, stepped in. Caxton, thinking, as Meyer-Lübke did for a Spanish word four centuries later, that the word must stem from Latin *advisum*, added the "d," and so we're stuck with it (like the *p* in *receipt* and the *b* in *debt*). But Caxton was wrong. Müller suggested that the Old French *avis* was related to the phrase for the future, *l'avenir*, "that which is to come" (to come = *venir*)—perhaps a calque of the German word for future, *Zukunft*, etymologically "to come" (Müller 295; Shippey advised us on calques in *Road* 102).

Tolkien's entry into the debate was actually with a different but related word, Old Spanish *anviso* or *anbiso*. In his 1951 lecture for the *Congrès International de Philolgie Moderne*, "Middle English 'Losenger,'" Tolkien rejects a theoretical Latin *ante visum* as an etymon for the two Spanish words for reasons similar to Müller's for *advisum*: (1) it is unattested, and (2) other etymons are more logical—including an attested Old English cognate.

> In the same way, observing the Old Spanish word, *anviso, ambiso* "wise, prudent," I should be inclined to reject the etymology of R.E.W. *antevisum*: not so much because that compound did not exist, and had it existed should have meant "*foreseen*" or "seen in front," but because in the area of Indo-European languages concerned the *active* sense of this participial formation is characteristic (a special mark) of the Germanic, not of the Italic or Celtic branches. The exact counterpart is, moreover, actually recorded in Anglo-Saxon *andwīs* "wise, clever" [69–70].

If, then, the etymological meaning of *advice* has to do with the future, Gildor's reluctance to look into the future (*a-vis*), for those who have less of the future than he, is an act of charity.

But that is surely not the last word on advice in *The Lord of the Rings*, even from elves. In fact, when Sam is remembering the exchange with Gildor, two chapters later, he remembers it as Gildor *giving* advice. "[Y]ou did ought to take the Elves' advice," he admonished Frodo. "Gildor said you should take them as was willing, and you can't deny it" (*FR* I, v, 116). The hobbits readily take advice, and call it advice, from Tom Bombadil (*FR* I, vii, 144; *FR* I, viii, 159), Strider (*FR* I, x, 175), Elrond (according to Pippin, *FR* II, iv, 311), and always, countless times, from Gandalf. From these figures of authority, advice is welcome, but even they are curiously backward in offering it. Gandalf prefaces his warning to Frodo about using the Ring with "if you take my advice" (*FR* I, i, 49), and to Bilbo on letting it go with "[i]f you need my advice any longer" (*FR* II, ii, 283). From a character we would never describe as humble, we find an attitude toward advice that looks curiously like humility.

In fact, in the characters who offer advice in the novel, Tolkien builds an inverse relationship between real authority and willingness to dispense counsel.

It is the paradox alluded to at the start of this essay: the wisest, who are most qualified to give advice, are often also the most reluctant. The four characters mentioned—Tom Bombadil, Strider, Elrond, and Gandalf—are the most qualified to offer advice, and the humblest in doing so. Conversely, there are various degrees of pride in three characters who offer advice unasked. The first is Farmer Maggot. As likable as Maggot is, his parochialism is a form of pride. When he tells Frodo, "I'm glad that you've had the sense to come back to Buckland. My advice is: stay there! And don't get mixed up with these outlandish folk," we know he means to keep Frodo safe (*FR* I, iv, 104). But there is a limitation to his advice that Gildor's generalization acknowledged. "[A]dvice is a dangerous gift, even from the wise to the wise" (*FR* I, iii, 93). As wise as Maggot is in his smaller world, he does not have the scope of a Strider or a Gandalf, or he would realize that traffic with "outlandish folk" is good for Frodo.

In the spectrum of pride after Maggot's parochialism, the gradient is steeper when we come to Boromir. His first unbidden advice is quite practical, and heeded: as the company prepared to cross the Redhorn Pass in "The Ring Goes South," Boromir suggests loading up on firewood. This first advice is offered with an effacement not quite as broad as Gandalf's—"I will add a word of advice, if I may" (*FR* II, iii, 301). The wording suggests officiousness ("I will") masquerading as deference ("if I may"). Boromir's second counsel to the company is worded more strongly, but still with vestigial pretense of deference. In "Farewell to Lórien," when Celeborn—the one person in the scene most qualified to advise—asks which shore the Company should take (the question itself conveying an unwillingness to suggest), Boromir is quick to declare, "'If my advice is heeded, it will be the western shore," to which he feels the need to observe, "But I am not the leader of the Company"—clearly he thinks he should be (*FR* II, viii, 383). The company's lack of response to Boromir ("The others said nothing") is eloquent. The thirst for lordship that will lead to his betrayal makes Boromir's counsel of dubious value.

Third and finally, after Boromir, the danger of unasked advice escalates to Saruman. In the white wizard's faux-wise counsel to Gandalf we see the fulfillment of Gildor's prophetic caveat, "advice is a dangerous gift, even from the wise to the wise," for that is just what Saruman's rede to Gandalf is. Like Boromir, Saruman bridles when his counsel is snubbed, so he projects his own pride onto Gandalf. "You are proud and do not love advice, having indeed a store of your own wisdom" (*TT* III, x, 186). Saruman's rebuke recalls a "well-known Sanskrit verse" quoted by Müller (though he neglects to cite a source):

Who are blind? Those who do not see the other world.
Who are deaf? Those who do not hear good advice [291].

The *Scippigræd* could add a third line: "Who cannot taste? Those who are not counseled by Tom." The punch line for a fourth, "Who cannot smell?" I shall leave to the reader's own advices.

NOTE

1. Those counseled by Tom Shippey, as "Alfred" is "elf-counseled"; see the companion piece "Counseling the *Scippigræd*" elsewhere in this volume, for a fuller discussion. [Eds.]

WORKS CITED

Bloomfield, Leonard. *Language*. New York: H. Holt, 1933.

Fowler, H.W. *A Dictionary of Modern English Usage*. New York: Oxford University Press, 1950.

Korzybski, Alfred. *Science and Sanity*. Lancaster, PA: The International Non-Aristotelian Library Publishing Company, 1933.

Meyer-Lübke, W[ilhelm]. *Romanisches Etymologisches Wörterbuch*. Heidelberg: Carl Winters Universitätsbuchhandlung, 1911.

Müller, F[riedrich] Max. "How to Work." *Last Essays, First Series*. London: Longmans, Green, 1901. 291–297.

Pietsch, K. "Spanish Etymologies." *Modern Philology* 7 (1909): 49–60.

Robert of Gloucester. *Robert of Gloucester's Chronicle. Transcrib'd and now first publish'd, from a MS. in the Harleyan Library by Thomas Hearne, M.A.* Oxford: Printed at the Theatre, 1724.

Shakespeare, William. *Shakespeare: The Complete Works*. Ed. G.B. Harrison. New York: Harcourt, Brace & World, 1968.

Shippey, Tom. *Poems of Wisdom and Learning in Old English*. Cambridge: D.S. Brewer, 1976.

Synge, J.M. *The Playboy of the Western World. The Complete Plays of John M. Synge*. New York: Vintage Books, 1960. 5–80.

Tolkien, J.R.R. *Farmer Giles of Ham*. Boston: Houghton Mifflin, 1999.

_____. "Middle English 'Losenger': Sketch of an etymological and semantic enquiry." *Essais de Philologie Moderne* (1951): 63–76.

Tolkien's Wraiths, Rings and Dragons: An Exercise in Literary Linguistics

JASON FISHER

> "If we seek to recapture what they had forgotten, and examine each of the original elements in turn, it must be rather for the pleasure of the hunt than in hope of a final kill."
> —J.R.R. Tolkien, "Sigelwara Land" (II 95)

1. Introductory Remarks: Literary Linguistics and Creation from Philology

Tolkien once wrote that "The Tree of Tales ... is closely connected with the philologists' study of the tangled skein of Language" (*TOF* 39), suggesting an intimate and complex symbiosis between creation and philology—and pioneering an entirely novel critical methodology. A few years before making this statement,[1] Tolkien himself undertook one of the first combined literary and philological examinations of a literary work in his 1934 essay, "Chaucer as a Philologist: *The Reeve's Tale*."[2] Two years later, he afforded *Beowulf* a similar kind of treatment. During roughly the same period, his own creative writings began to exhibit a maturing and purposeful influence from his academic training in philology, honed in the years leading up to *The Hobbit* by his work on the *Oxford English Dictionary*, his glossary for Kenneth Sisam's *Fourteenth Century Verse and Prose*, and his and E.V. Gordon's edition of *Sir Gawain and the Green Knight*.

97

   Some years later, the same hermeneutic lens would be aptly turned on Tolkien's own fiction. In a 1979 essay (an essay which "set the rocket off," at least for me), Tom Shippey termed this unique generative methodology "creation *from* philology,"[3] and it is this approach to "reconcil[ing] the two sides of Tolkien" (Godden 492)—Lit. and Lang., so-called by Tolkien himself[4]— that will encompass the discussion to follow. Specifically, what I would like to do is to present a series of linguistic roots, then trace out a ramifying tree of interrelated words and meanings in many of the languages of Tolkien's expertise, connecting them to the ever enlarging scope of Middle-earth. For the sake of brevity, I will focus primarily on *The Lord of the Rings*; however, the theoretical approach needs no such limitation, and similar exercises in literary linguistics might be expanded into all corners of Tolkien's *legendarium*. But instead of attempting such a broad exploration here, I will discuss the etymologies of and relationships between a more limited gamut of words: *wraith, writhe, ring, willow, worm*—and a few others. As I proceed, I will attempt to show how Tolkien assembled explanatory narratives out of what began as purely philological ruminations, and how, as a narrative coalesced, he would follow it from word to word like a trail of breadcrumbs. But unlike the breadcrumbs in the traditional *märchen* of Hansel and Gretel, I hope to show that much of this trail may still be followed today.

   While several of Tolkien's inventions through philology are now well known, almost to the point of banality,[5] many other points of contact between linguistic theory and literary praxis have remained largely unexplored. To unearth these connections, we need to delve deeper than the primarily thematic and literary studies to date, examining sources in their original languages and consulting philological reference works to which Tolkien himself would have turned. In the end, I hope that what we find—the fruit of the Tree of Tales, as it were—is compelling enough to overcome the charge of mere coincidence. To some degree, of course, we can never be certain. Tolkien himself left behind mixed messages on the search for sources—encouraging it on some occasions,[6] criticizing it on others[7]—however, no caveat from the author has ever been forceful enough to stop the hunt. C.S. Lewis once wrote: "The philologist's dream is to diagrammatise all the meanings of a word so as to have a perfect semantic tree of it; every twig traced to its branch, every branch traced back to the trunk. That this can seldom, if ever, be perfectly achieved does not matter much; all studies end in doubts" (*Studies in Words* 9). This, *mutatis mutandis*, is precisely what I hope to accomplish here, and my results will no doubt be as imperfect as Lewis predicts. But if I need still further justification to proceed, then let me turn to the words of Malcolm Godden, who currently holds the same academic chair at Pembroke College that Tolkien once occupied.[8] He wrote: "It is clear that the scholarly implications of names, languages, allusions, and quotations form a very real part of the pleasure and substance of [*The Lord of the Rings*] and that one of the most useful things that Tolkien-criticism can do is to explain them" (493).[9]

2. Rooting Among Old Words: From Wraiths to Rings

All stories begin with words. George Steiner explains that "[w]hen using a word we wake into resonance, as it were, its entire previous history. A text is embedded in specific historical time; it has what linguists call a diachronic structure [that is, a structure changing over time]. To read fully is to restore all that one can of the immediacies of value and intent in which speech actually occurs" (qtd. in Turner, 132). And so, Edmund Wilson's denigrating dismissal of *The Lord of the Rings* as merely "a philological curiosity" ("Ooh, Those Awful Orcs!") is to me precisely one of its greatest strengths. To take this position is no doubt to announce myself as one of Tolkien's "infatuated admirers" (loc. cit.), but this is a risk I am willing to take.

Tom Shippey has argued for decades, and quite convincingly, that Tolkien's preoccupation with philological cruces invariably set his imagination going. We see Tolkien engaged in just this sort of "etymological puzzle," confronting "elements forgotten or obscured" ("Sigelwara Land" 192) again and again, as in the essay on Chaucer, mentioned already, as well as in another major essay of the same decade, "Sigelwara Land"—and in many smaller papers before and after. Indeed, most of Tolkien's academic work falls into this category. But as it turns out, so does his fiction. "Tolkien," Shippey tells us, "feels that words have a life of their own, which continues irrespective of rough treatment from time and careless speakers" ("Creation from Philology" 301), and where "ancient knowledge begins to turn into new creation" (293).

I noted above that some of these cases are well known by this time—for example, the genesis of the Elves, Ents, Orcs, and even the Hobbits.[10] I would like to begin this essay with another case, that of Sauron's most terrible servants, the nine Ringwraiths. In the absence of any direct depiction of Sauron—who works much better as a presence, felt and feared, but never actually seen—evil in Middle-earth is most effectively embodied in the Nazgûl, or Ringwraiths. Tolkien himself called them "very alarming" (an understatement!), and he blamed their invention on "readers young and old who clamoured for 'more about the Necromancer'" (*Letters* 42). The Ringwraiths are usually seen robed in black, faces hidden (in fact, invisible), sowing the seeds of terror and despair wherever they go. So powerful is this image that it is has now become a commonplace in fantasy literature—one recalls Grimnir in Alan Garner's *Weird-*

stone of Brisingamen (1960), and the Dementors in J.K. Rowling's *Harry Potter* novels (1997–2007), to give just two examples.

But Tolkien didn't invent the word *wraith*. It was in use much earlier by many of Tolkien's intellectual forebears, including Jacob Grimm, Sir Walter Scott, Alfred Lord Tennyson, Andrew Lang, William Morris, and George MacDonald.[11] So what is a wraith, actually? The usual sense is of some sort of specter, ghost, apparition, or often, a premonitory omen of death. This is how it has been *used*, but what does the word actually *mean*, and how did these different senses develop? For the best sense of *that*, we would ordinarily turn to the word's etymology. But, to paraphrase Tolkien, "[i]n this case you will turn to the *Oxford English Dictionary* in vain" (*TOF* 28). There, while we do learn that the word made its first appearance in English in a 16th-century translation of *The Aeneid*,[12] the OED offers only an unhelpful note on the etymology, calling it "[Of obscure origin]."[13]

But this won't do at all, so let us dig a little deeper. In his influential *Etymological Dictionary of the English Language*, Walter William Skeat conjectures that the word might be of Scandinavian origin, not Scottish as the OED supposes, but he does not have a great deal to back up the notion. His best suggestion is to connect it to Old Norse *vörðr*, meaning a "warden or guardian" (720). Skeat also quotes John Jamieson's earlier *Etymological Dictionary of the Scottish Language*, a work Tolkien knew ("Philology" 27), in which one of the suggested meanings for wraith is a "guardian *angel*" (Jamieson, [n.p.], emphasis added). But of course, this would not have made for a very frightening adversary in *The Lord of the Rings*, so let us forget putting a nimbus over Tolkien's wraiths and get back to the nimbus of possible etymologies surrounding the word itself.

Expanding the search, we find that in his *Glossary of North Country Words* John Trotter Brockett connects *wraith* to a northern dialectal word, *waff*, meaning "an apparition in the exact resemblance of a person, supposed to be seen just before or soon after death" (200–1, 202).[14] He guesses the word may be linked to *waft*, no doubt envisioning an airy apparition wafting along in a gentle breeze on the moors of the North Country. I may be alone in this, but I find that image somewhat redolent of the Barrow Downs.

Poking around in various other etymological dictionaries of the period, we find other suggestions, some good, some not so good—including Old English *weard*, *ward*, "a warden or guardian" (the cognate of Skeat's Old Norse suggestion, *vörðr*); Old Gaelic *breith* (aspirated form, *bhreith*), meaning "doom, judgment"; and even Modern English *wrath*, *wroth* (from Old English *wráð*), suggesting a wraith might be a particularly *wrathful* spirit.

Any one of these suggestions is a possibility, but Tolkien likely had a different etymology in mind.[15] As Shippey has pointed out, Tolkien arguably thought *wraith* might have developed from the verb *writhe* "to twist or struggle, as in pain," with an archaic past participle, *writhen* (from Middle English *writhen*, in turn from Old English *wriðen*, meaning "twisted, bent, writhed, or tortured").[16] Citing Richard Blackwelder's *Thesaurus*, Shippey notes that Tolkien used this obscure participial form twice in *The Lord of the Rings* ("History in Words" 32; it's actually three times—Dr. Blackwelder missed one[17]). In any case, the idea here is that a wraith was something twisted, contorted, bent out of its proper original shape, or turned aside from its proper path— in the case of the Nazgûl, by temptation, greed, and evil (*Road* 148–50). This would, in fact, cousin the word to *wrath*, *wroth*, which has a literal meaning closer to "twisted by rage" than is usually remembered. Its Old English form was *wráð*, derived from Primitive Germanic **wraithaz*. Now *that* is beginning to look familiar!

Other interesting and probably related cognates include the Gothic *wraiqs*, meaning "curved, crooked, winding, or twisting," *wraks*, meaning "a persecutor or punishing pursuer," and perhaps *fra-wairþan* "to corrupt." There is also Old Frisian *wreth*, meaning "evil," Old Saxon *wred* and Middle Dutch *wret*, both meaning "cruel"; Old High German *reid* and Old Norse *reiðr*, both meaning "wroth"; and Old Norse *ríða* "to twist, knit, or wind." All of these words appear to have developed from the same Indo-European root, **wreit* "to turn, bend, or wind." Another descendent of this root is Modern English *wreath*, from Old English *wriða* "a band (that is to say, that which is wound around)." This is beginning to sound rather like a *ring*, isn't it? After all, what is a ring but something bent around until it turns back on itself, returning to its beginning? And indeed, in the Old English corpus, *wriða* is sometimes used for "ring" (as in the homilies of Ælfric).

Since I am discussing wraiths, it's worth a digression to consider the only one of the Nazgûl given a name by Tolkien. This is Khamûl, the Shadow of the East, and it turns out that his name may reinforce the "bent" etymology of the wraiths. Khamûl only emerges as a distinct character in a collection of background narratives labeled "The Hunt for the Ring," the bulk of which was published in *Unfinished Tales*.[18] Other than his name, movements, and a few character traits, we know very little else about him. And nowhere, to my knowledge, does Tolkien discuss any possible etymology of his name. He seems to be a case of spontaneous invention on Tolkien's part. That being said, we do know that Khamûl was second only to the Witch-king of Angmar in the pecking order of the Ringwraiths. He dwelt for a while at Dol Guldur as Sauron's lieutenant after Sauron had returned to Mordor. It was also Khamûl who spoke so menacingly to the Gaffer on the night the Hobbits finally left Hobbiton. And perhaps most interesting: "Of Khamûl it is said ... that he was the most ready of all the Nazgûl, after the Black Captain himself, to perceive the presence of the Ring, but also the one whose power was most confused and diminished by daylight" (*UT* 352–3n1). Interesting stuff, but small beer on which to base any theories of etymology. Or is it?

There may actually be some philological evidence to bring things back to *wraith* / *writhen*, with a defensible primary-world etymology for Khamûl as "the bent or crooked one." This would, of course, richly echo the etymology of *wraith*. Can it be proven? No, certainly not. The name may in fact be completely arbitrary, chosen solely for its alien sound. But if you will humor me, let's see where further dictionary diving may take us. It turns out there's another Indo-European root of interest; two roots, actually: **kemb*, **kamp*, meaning, once again, "to bend" (Watkins 39, 36). These roots have made their way even into Modern English, for example, in the word *akimbo*. The root is attested in the Latin *camur*, *cămŭrus* "crooked or crumpled," from a past participial form of the Greek *κάμπτω* "to bend, crook, or curve." As old or older, a cognate may be found in Sansrkit: कुब्जा [*kubja*] "crooked," and this word has spread throughout the Indo-Aryan language family, as in Panjabi ਖਮ [*kham*] "crooked."

But even better for students of Tolkien, the root has left a considerable number of Celtic cognates as well. These include such "bent and crooked" words as the Welsh *kam* "crooked" and *kamy* "to bend." Tolkien proved himself well aware of this cluster of Celtic words in the entry he wrote for *cammede* in his 1922 *Middle English Vocabulary* (21). A further sampling demonstrates how widespread the word became: we find it in Old Irish, Scottish Gaelic, Manx, Cornish, and, from the coast of Brittany, Breton and Armoric, with the universal meaning of "crooked," and sometimes with interesting metaphorical variations such as "deformed, evil, or deceitful." I mention these in spite of Tolkien's professed tastes—"I have no liking at all," he said, "for Gaelic from Old Irish downwards, as a language, but it is of course of great historical and philological interest, and I have at various times studied it" (*Letters* 385).

It seems very telling to me that the example he was discussing on the occasion of that statement was *nasg*, the Gaelic word for "ring," an unconscious cognate to his own *nazg* in the Black Speech of Mordor, and obviously the first part of the compound Nazgûl. Tolkien says that the other part, *gûl*, is meant to convey in the Black Speech "any one of the major invisible servants of Sauron dominated entirely by his will" (Nom 762), that is to say, a *wraith*. There's an apparent relationship to Sindarin *gûl*, meaning "magic" (as in, Minas Morgul and Dol Guldur), and this word in turn derives from the root *ñgol*, meaning "wise, wisdom, [to] be wise" (*Lost Road* 377). That root also gives us the word *Noldor*, and I am sure I need not remind readers how the lust for the Silmarils *bent* and *twisted* the fates of Fëanor and all his people. However, it also bears pointing out that *gûl*, Black Speech for *wraith*, is homophonic with the Modern English *ghoul*—derived from Arabic, but very close in its sense to the historical definition of *wraith*. This is surely no accident. And just as Tolkien admits the likelihood that the Gaelic *nasg* "became lodged in some corner of my linguistic memory" (*Letters* 385), so too may have the English *ghoul*.

But returning to the Welsh *kam*, at points of Celtic contact, obviously primarily in the west, the word also made its way into English dialectal usage. Samuel Johnson includes the adjective *kam* "crooked" in his 1755 dictionary, attested by no less a word-hoarder than Shakespeare. Further examples include the Lowland Scotch *camsteerie* "crooked, confused, or unmanageable"; and in Lancashire, we have *cam* as a noun, where it means "a contradiction or crooked argument"; as an adverb, meaning "awry"; and as a verb, where it means "to cross or contradict; to oppose vexatiously; to quarrel"—all from the same Welsh source. Even more specifically localized, we find Southern Lancashire *cammed* and Northern and Eastern Lancashire *caimt* "crooked, bad-tempered, or ill-natured." I especially like these last words, despite Tolkien's normal preferences for the West Midland dialects, because they resonate with the fact that Tolkien served in the Lancashire Fusiliers during World War I, and was stationed in Yorkshire after his return from France, both of which would have exposed him to northern dialect first-hand.[19] All of this boils down to the guess on my part that Khamûl's name may mean "the bent one." Let us not forget that while still in the Shire, Frodo encountered Khamûl himself, and Tolkien writes: "The shadow *bent* to the ground, and then began to crawl towards him" (*FR* I, iii, 88, emphasis added).[20]

I demonstrated above how *wraiths*, for Tolkien, could have been connected to *rings* by common etymology, and how that etymological connection is reflected in the story, indeed in the very compound, *Ringwraith*. I would like to return to this point now. The more common Old English word for *ring* is *hring*, which may have developed from a different Indo-European root **(s)ker*, meaning "to turn, to bend" (Watkins, 78).[21] A prime example may be found in the following lines from *Beowulf*:

> ðá wæs hring-bogan   heorte gefýsed
> sæcce tó séceanne   [2561–2].[22]

Wayne Hammond and Christina Scull tell us that Tolkien translated this: "Now was the heart of the coiling beast stirred to come out to fight" (qtd. in *Artist & Illustrator* 53).[23] Christopher Tolkien reports a slightly different version of the translation made by his father: "The heart of the coiling beast was stirred" (*Pictures* plate 40 [n.p.]). Tolkien would certainly have been aware of the *ring* hidden in the line; it is responsible, in his translation, for the coiling of the dragon. What's more, we can actually *see* what Tolkien himself had in mind here. As it transpires, he took inspiration from these lines for a 1927 painting, which he titled *Hringboga Heorte Gefysed*.[24] That first word, *hring-boga*, deserves a closer look.

The word *hring*, as I have already reported, is "ring," and *boga* gives us the Modern English word "bow," as in "an arch, angle, corner, or something curved." Related is *bogen*, meaning "bowed, bent, gave way," past participle of *búgan* "to bow (down), bend, or swerve." The great Bosworth-Toller[25] diction-ary of Anglo-Saxon glossed the entire compound as "a serpent [from its being bent into coils]" (561). And in this figurative image, there seems to be a clear connection to the *writhen / bent* notion I have taken such pains to point out. Most of the translations of *Beowulf* I have consulted render *hringboga* as "the coiled (one)," "the dragon," "the serpent," or something similar; however, James Harrison and Robert Sharp (two American scholars roughly contemporary with Tolkien's early years) give in their glossary "hring-boga, w.m., *one who bends himself into a ring*: gen. sg. hring-bogan (of the drake, bending himself into a circle)" (*Beowulf* tr. Harrison 256). A few years earlier, James Garnett (also an American) gave the lines a literal treatment which serves to highlight the point: "Then was the *ring-bowed* eager in heart / The contest to seek" (*Beowulf* tr. Garnett 78, emphasis added). It is worth noting that Tolkien also used the word *hringboga* in a fragmentary poem of Attila the Hun in Old English, published only recently as part of *The Legend of Sigurd and Gudrún*. There (374–5), he writes of "[h]ringbogan snicon, / wyrmas gewriðene" ("ser-pents were creeping, coiled snakes"), bringing *hringboga* and *wriðen* together in a single phrase. These lines, of course, bring up dragons as well as rings, but I will come back to this connection a little later.

3. Tracing a Few of the Branches: Wraiths, the Righteous Path, and the Lost Road

For the moment, let's see where are. We now have the idea that a proper etymology of *wraith* ought to include the sense of a being twisted, contorted, and turned toward evil from good. The idea of a thing that turns or twists, furthermore, calls to mind the idea of the One Ring, for which we also found some etymological evidence. So where do we go from here?

Let's return for a moment to Skeat's suggested etymology of *wraith*. As you recall, he proposed the Old Norse *vörðr* "a warden or guardian." In the genitive case, the word is *varðar*, showing a vowel change, and meaning "of the guardian." This form strikes one as bearing a more than superficial resemblance to Varda, the Vala whom the Elves most revere. Tellingly, it is Varda that the Elves (as well as a few others, such as Frodo and Samwise) invoke for protection in some of the few explicit references to the Valar we find in *The Lord of the Rings*. While Quenya "Varda" means, at root, "Exalted," she is, in fact, the Elves' *guardian*, and a real world etymological connection to the Old Norse *vörðr* is therefore a possibility worth considering. It seems even likelier one when we take into account the fact that in Old Norse *vörð* is also a poetic word for "woman" (Zoëga 503).

This could of course be mere coincidence; after all, Tolkien was unconvinced by Skeat's etymology. Still, he would have been aware of it. One might even postulate that Tolkien, with tongue in cheek, was planting fictive seeds that would explain Skeat's quite understandable error. In any event, the resemblance between *vörð(r)*—a guardian woman—and Varda is tantalizing. And all the more so when we remember that the road leading back to her from Middle-earth became *bent* when the shape of the world was changed after the Fall of Númenor.

In *The Lost Road* (and in a further variation, in "The Notion Club Papers"), we find a very curious passage: "Westra lage wegas rehtas, nu isti sa wraithas" (*Lost Road* 43). This is Old English and means "a straight road lay westward, now it is bent."[26] The reference is to the Straight Road by which the Elves sometimes set sail across the great western sea, returning to the Blessed Realm from Middle-earth. How telling that Tolkien would extrapolate (or invent) *wraithas* "bent" to describe how the Straight Road had become lost after the Fall of Númenor. As Tolkien wrote in the "Akallabêth":

> Therefore the loremasters of Men said that a Straight Road must still be, for those that were permitted to find it. And they taught that, while the new world fell away, the old road and the path of the memory of the West still went on, as it were a mighty bridge invisible that passed through the air of breath and of flight (*which were bent now as the world was bent*), and traversed Ilmen which flesh unaided cannot endure, until it came to Tol Eressëa, the Lonely Isle, and maybe even beyond, to Valinor, where the Valar still dwell and watch the unfolding of the story of the world [*S* 281–2, emphasis added].

The idea seems clear: to be bent, twisted, turned, generally from good toward evil—or, if not *toward* evil, then bent or turned *because* of evil—was to be *writhen, wraithas*, or to become a *wraith*. Even the English word *wrong* derives from the same cluster of Indo-European roots. And here is another salient point regarding *writhen*: in his 1922 *Middle English Vocabulary*, Tolkien defines *wryþe(n)* as, first, "to twist; [to] bind"—something the One Ring does—but second, "[to] turn aside (from the just course)" (156).

Tolkien's telling definition of the Middle English verb *wryþe(n)* is based on a usage in *Pearl*, an anonymous fourteenth-century poem of great interest to Tolkien, particularly as an example of the West Midland dialect so important to him both professionally and personally. *Pearl* is found in the same manuscript as *Sir Gawain and the Green Knight*, with two other poems, *Patience* and *Cleanness*, all apparently written by the same poet. *Wryþe* occurs a little less than halfway through the poem, in the following lines (the text quoted here is from Kenneth Sisam's *Fourteenth Century Verse and Prose*, for which Tolkien prepared the Glossary in question):

> I may not traw, so God me spede,
> Þat God wolde wryþe so wrange away; [63].

As most readers will know, Tolkien himself translated *Pearl* into modern verse. How then does he render the word, *wryþe*? Tolkien translates the lines as follows: "I cannot believe, God helping me, / That God so far from right would stray" (*Sir Gawain* 102).

I will not bore you with an exhaustive comparative survey, but I will note that Tolkien's definition of *wryþe(n)* differs from others of the period.[27] Most of the translations before and contemporary with Tolkien's translate the lines much as Tolkien did,[28] so Tolkien's translation isn't as unique as his gloss. And the reason is clear: the connotation comes from the entire phrase, *wyrþe so wrange away*. What is especially interesting is that Tolkien decided to imbue the verb alone with some of the sense conveyed in *Pearl* through these additional words, and it appears he may be unique in this.

The Ringwraiths, then, as well as the Ring itself, right and wrong, and the bent road that no longer leads to Aman (and to Varda)—all come together in a handful of Germanic roots. Further, I would note in passing that Tolkien seems to have borrowed from these same Germanic sources for some of the roots of his own languages. For one example, we find the Quenya *raika*, meaning "crooked, bent, wrong," and the Noldorin *rhoeg*, meaning "wrong." Earlier in Tolkien's language-making, we also have the Gnomish *raig*, meaning "awry, twisted, distorted. perverse. wrong" and *rictha* to "contort. twist. confuse, disarrange, upset" ("Gnomish Lexicon" 64, 65). And cognate to these, the Qenya *riqi-* meaning "wrench, twist," possibly (we may think) related to *rinko*, a "disc, circle, orb" ("Qenya Lexicon" 80). Again, these roughly echo the same cluster of Germanic cognates. Decades before Tolkien would conceive of the Ringwraiths, and yet still strongly redolent of them, he set down the Qenya and Gnomish *rauta-* and *rautha-* to "chase, hunt, pursue" ("Qenya Lexicon" 79; "Gnomish Lexicon" 65). Here, the *meaning* is not the same, but the sense is very suggestive of the behavior of the Ringwraiths. Perhaps I am overreaching here, but who knows how long these words might have lingered in the back of Tolkien's imagination? If words from Primary World languages could linger in his "linguistic memory," one must imagine that words from his own invented languages could do likewise.

Talking of roots, I suppose it's appropriate I make a comment or two on

Old Man Willow, another character who seems to have *wyrþe so wrange away*. Readers will remember the Hobbits' first major adventure in the Old Forest, in which they become lost and drift ever further down into the valley of the Withywindle, "the queerest part of the whole wood—the centre from which all the queerness comes, as it were" (*FR* I, vi, 124). Withywindle, for all the queerness of its name, just means something like *willow-winding*. *Withy*—or *with(e)*—is, in fact, a real but archaic English word for a willow, deriving unchanged (except in spelling) from OE *wiðig*. The word exists across the Germanic spectrum, as well, from ON *við*, *viðja* to OHG *wídá* (Skeat, 715, and others). The word can ultimately be sourced to the Indo-European root **wei*, yet another root meaning "to turn or twist" (Watkins 96). The sense was of a tree with bendable, pliable branches, perhaps twisting in the wind. The word left traces all over the British Isles, in part because the so-called "twisted tree or *with*" was routinely substituted in England for palm branches on Palm Sunday (Moor 489). This, of course, is because the palm is not indigenous to the British Isles. In fact, the English frequently called the feast Willow Sunday.

What of the element—*windle*? I noted a moment ago that it basically means *winding*, and so it does, but there is another archaic word, *windle* (or *windel*), which meant a box or basket made of woven willow branches. The word is etymologically related to the Modern English "to wind." Bosworth attests *windle-tree*, from OE *windel-treow*, as meaning "a tree from which baskets were made, a willow" (463). So when you boil all this down, it becomes quite clear that both elements of Withywindle convey the same sense of bending or twisting, each reinforcing the other. Even more, the Modern English *willow*, which is not a translation of *withy* but rather a synonym of it, also derives from a root meaning "to bend or twist" (Skeat 711). And this is just what Old Man Willow does, isn't it? He himself is certainly twisted at heart, and he literally twists the large root on which Frodo is sitting and dumps him into the river. And moreover, it is not just Old Man Willow doing the twisting, it is the entire Old Forest, bending, twisting, and distorting the hobbits' sense of direction until they're all hopelessly disoriented and lost.

4. A Handful of Withered (?) Leaves[29]: Smaug and Sméagol

Now, ranging further through the tree of "the philologist's dream," I would like to trace out another branch. The same Indo-European root that gives rise to *wraith*, *wrath*, *wroth*, and *writhe* also leads in another direction: to *worm*, in its earlier sense of "dragon." From Primitive Germanic **wurmiz*, we find Gothic *waúrms*, Old English *wyrm*, Middle English *worme*, Old Norse *ormr*, Old High German *wurm*—to which, compare the Latin *vermis* (from which we get the English reflex, *vermin*).[30] How far the mighty dragon has fallen, to be lumped in today with rats and bugs![31]

Worms—that is, dragons—were very important to Tolkien and were a key element in his imagination from childhood.[32] We find them in his fiction as well as in the literature of his scholarly interests, as in the Old English *Beowulf* and the Old Norse *Fáfnismál*. What of that more common word, "dragon?" Its ancestors[33] include Greek δράκων and Latin *drăco*, which were borrowed for Old High German *traccho*, Old Norse *dreki*, Old English *draca*, and (via Old French) Middle English *dragun* (whence also the Modern English *dragoon*). There is even another Modern English cognate (albeit an archaic one), *drake*. But where *worm* comes originally from the sense of "turning, winding," as in Tolkien's 1927 painting, *dragon* comes from an Indo-European root, **derk*, meaning "to see." Thus the dragon is "the seeing one" or the monster with "the evil eye."

In his professional study of *Beowulf*, Tolkien wrote that "*Beowulf*'s dragon ... is not to be blamed for being a dragon, but rather for not being dragon enough, plain pure fairy-story dragon." Instead, its depiction "approaches *draconitas* rather than *draco*" (*MC* 17). Tom Shippey then explains how Tolkien's response to this was to put a real, honest-to-goodness dragon at center stage in his own novel, *The Hobbit* (*Road* 90). Even more interesting is Tolkien's choice of names, Smaug—derived, Tolkien himself says, from **smaug*, the past tense of **smugan*, Primitive Germanic for "to squeeze through a hole" (*Letters* 31). Perhaps even more suggestive, Shippey reminds us that an Old English cognate, *sméogan*, occurs together with a *worm* in an ancient protective spell: "wið sméogan wyrme" "against the penetrating worm" (*Road* 89); it is beside the point that "worm," in this case, may mean not a dragon but an invertebrate parasite thought to cause illness. Along these same lines, Bosworth and Toller also give an explicit compound, *sméa-wyrm* "penetrating worm" (888). And it bears pointing out that *sméocan* "to smoke, reek" is very close to *sméogan*—just as "smoke" is phonologically close to Smaug, who is, after all, a fire-breathing dragon.

I might mention that the other common English words *serpent* and *snake* are not, in spite of their suggestive consonants, directly related to **smugan*. Rather, they come from a pair of Indo-European roots, **serp* and **sneg* both meaning "to crawl, [or] to creep" (Watkins 76, 81), and from which we also derive the word "snail." There may be a loose relationship between the three words, but if so, I have not seen it documented. I *have* wondered whether the Old English *snaca*, meaning "snake," might have been an unconscious source for Tolkien's *snaga*, a Black Speech word said to mean "slave" and used to refer to weaker, smaller orcs, as for example, the goblins in *The Hobbit*. (The Gothic word *snaga* "a garment" is clearly on the wrong track!)

Before leaving Smaug, let us consider the name Tolkien *originally* gave to the dragon in *The Hobbit*. This was Pryftan, something we have known since Humphrey Carpenter's *Tolkien: A Biography* (178). But in all the thirty years since, I cannot recall seeing any discussion of its etymology, not even by John Rateliff, so in this case you will turn to *The History of The Hobbit* in vain.[34] Actually, it's straightforward Welsh, a compound of *prŷf*, which means "worm," and *tân*, meaning "fire"—hence, a fire-breathing dragon. Tolkien would have found both words in William Salesbury's *Dictionary in Englysche and Welshe*,[35] which we know he owned.[36] He would have seen them again in Sir John Morris-Jones's *Elementary Welsh Grammar* (55, 178), which he bought with the proceeds of his Skeat Prize for English at Exeter College in 1914 (*Chronology* 51). Both words are common in the extant corpus of Medieval Welsh literature, and even the compound, *prŷf tân*, occurs in a few places, though there is no direct evidence Tolkien knew this. The compound had a composite meaning of "glow-worm," perhaps suitable as a *euphemism* for a fire-breathing dragon, but in the end, the connotations of the Welsh *prŷf* (including various kinds of insects, as well as small animals such as foxes and badgers) would have been much too twee for "Smaug the Chiefest and Greatest of Calamities" (*H* XII, 234). This would have been rather like the diminution that we saw earlier with *worm*—from "dragon" to "vermin." And so the name Smaug was put in place of Pryftan, a considerable improvement.

All this talk of Smaug naturally leads—philologically—to Sméagol, Gollum's alter ego. Tolkien derived this name from the same root that gave him Smaug, and with the same meaning (Shippey, "Creation from Philology" 301). Like Smaug, Sméagol has wormed his way into rather a small hole in the ground, making him all the more appropriate a foil for Bilbo Baggins, who also lives in a hole. What do Hobbits do, after all, but squeeze—since they tend to be "fat in the stomach"—into small holes? Remember, too, that in the opening passage of *The Hobbit*, the narrator explicitly tells us that "the ends of worms" are not to be found in Bilbo's comfortable hobbit hole. But metaphorically, the end of a Worm is, in fact, in this particular hobbit hole, the end of the worm, Smaug.[37] But coming back to Gollum: readers will recall that he possessed the One Ring for a very long time indeed. It unnaturally preserved his small, mean person—making him still smaller and meaner—for untold years beyond the normal lifespan of his kind. He was, in fact, being *bent* by the Ring. Even literally, he walks bent over, nearly on all fours, with his face practically touching the ground. Sméagol was, in fact, becoming more and more like a *wraith* (*Road* 148–50).

And though I really might write much more, this is probably a good place to stop. Let me offer this, by way of a closing fillip. I am reminded of something Gollum once said (or is reported to have said):

> It would be cool and shady under those mountains. The Sun could not watch me there. The roots of those mountains must be roots indeed; there must be great secrets buried there which have not been discovered since the beginning [*FR* I, ii, 63].

For all his faults, Gollum is something of a philologist.[38] Bent to the ground, searching backwards though history for its roots, hoping to discover a few of those great secrets buried in the vault of time. And wraiths, rings, lost roads, wicked willow trees, Smaug, and even Gollum himself may all have a part to play in revealing those roots. Can we ever be absolutely certain Tolkien had these *particular* roots and their many philological connections in mind? Unless further evidence should come to light, no. At best, I might be right about a few of them. But they all strike me as plausible, many of them *probable*, and I believe I have argued the case in much the same way Tolkien himself would have done and as Tom Shippey often *has* done. In any event, remember C.S. Lewis's observation that it may not matter much in the end: all studies end in doubts. Tolkien himself once admitted the same: "If we seek to recapture what they had forgotten, and examine each of the original elements in turn, it must be rather for the pleasure of the hunt than in hope of a final kill" ("Sigelwara Land" II 95). And so the hunt goes on.

NOTES

1. In his Andrew Lang Lecture at the University of St. Andrews (1939), which would go on to become the landmark essay, "On Fairy-stories" (1947, and subsequently reprinted).

2. This essay has been recently brought back into print in *Tolkien Studies* 5: 109–71. Some might argue that Jacob Grimm and others in the same tradition had laid the groundwork, and while this may be true in a very loose sense, Grimm's work was differently motivated, more concerned with philology than literary merit, and with the promulgation of a German nationalistic agenda.

3. Shippey, "Creation from Philology in *The Lord of the Rings*" (emphasis added). Somewhat surprisingly (to me, at any rate), the term and the methodology behind it have not been taken up by very many others in the scholarly community. Apart from Shippey (and myself), few scholars are pursuing this line. Allan Turner has done so, but more from the angle of translation studies. Mark Hooker falls into the same category. David Lyle Jeffrey has pursued philological studies of Tolkien's words and names; however, his conclusions (to me) represent the kinds of missteps one may take on too careless an investigation into the origins of Tolkien's words and nomenclature.

4. See Tolkien's "Valedictory Address to the University of Oxford," in *The Monsters and the Critics*.

5. For example, see various of Tom Shippey's discussion of these matters—e.g., the discussion of Gandalf in "Tolkien and Iceland: The Philology of Envy" (*Roots* 187–202); of Elves, Orcs, Ents, *inter alia*, in "Creation from Philology"; his discussion of the Old English *orðanc enta geweorc* in the same essay, and so on.

6. For example, in the letter responding to someone calling himself Habit (*Letters* 30–32; omitted from the first edition index) and in letters to Rhona Beare and W.H. Auden.

7. Most famously through the metaphor on "the bones of the ox" (cf. "On Fairy-stories"). Tolkien's draft letter to Mr. Rang seems almost to do both at once (*Letters* 379–380).

8. The Rawlinson and Bosworth Professor of Anglo-Saxon in Pembroke College, Oxford. Tolkien was the eighteenth professor to hold the chair, Godden the twenty-second.

9. The statement comes from Godden's review of *J.R.R. Tolkien, Scholar and Storyteller*, in which Tom Shippey's essay on "Creation from Philology in *The Lord of the Rings*" appears.

10. One of the earliest serious discussions of this nature was Tom Shippey's 1979 essay, "Creation from Philology in *The Lord of the Rings*," to which I have alluded several times already. From that foundation, Shippey has expanded on these ideas in many essays and in three full-length books on Tolkien.

11. Grimm refers to an apparition called a *fetch* (or *wraith*) in *Teutonic Mythology*. Scott uses the word in the Waverley Novels, e.g., *Quentin Durward* (which Andrew Lang later edited), as well as in his poetry (e.g., in *The Lay of the Last Minstrel*). Tennyson used the word in his poetry as well (e.g., "The Death of Œnone," "Maud; a Monodrama," and "In Memoriam A. H. H."). Lang used it in his translation of Homer's *Iliad*, and he made wraiths the subject of an entire chapter (V) of his *Book of Dreams and Ghosts* (1897). Morris used the word in his translation of the *Völsunga Saga*. MacDonald used it in his poetry (e.g., "The Homeless Ghost") and in his novels (e.g., *Castle Warlock* and *Mary Marston*). I could easily go on but will stop here so as not to test the reader's patience.

12. A translation into the Middle Scots dialect made by Gavin Douglas in 1513. Interestingly, Tolkien's friend C.S. Lewis greatly admired Douglas's translation, and Lewis used the word *wraith* in his own (incomplete) translation of the *Aeneid*, finally published (as *C.S. Lewis's Lost Aeneid*) in 2011.

13. From the 2nd ed., online (1989). See also Gilliver 223–4.

14. This is essentially the same wording of the primary sense given by Jamieson as well.

15. Shippey has discussed this idea several times. See "Orcs, Wraiths, Wights" 189–90, *Author* 121–2, *Road* 148–9, "History in Words" 32. Even so, the topic is hardly exhausted, and I feel I can add to the conversation.

16. The verb was originally strong, i.e., demonstrating ablaut, but has joined many others in becoming weak.

17. See also Blackwelder 275. The third instance occurs in the chapter "The Great River": "Behind them stood low crumbling cliffs, and chimneys of grey weathered stone dark with ivy; and beyond these again there rose high ridges crowned with wind-writhen firs. They were drawing near to the grey hill-country of the Emyn Muil, the southern march of Wilderland" (*FR* II, ix, 401).

18. Additional passages, including some that relate to Khamûl, have been published more recently in *Companion*.

19. Northern dialect is also the subject of his essay on Chaucer, previously discussed. In addition, Tolkien might have encountered northernisms while teaching in Yorkshire, at Leeds.

20. Of course, we have to be careful of reading too much into a single word, "bent"; after all, the same word is used to describe Gandalf and Treebeard, as it is Sauron and Gollum. Still, the usage here seems revealing.

21. Another root, **ker*, is supposed to have been an echoic root, giving rise to "ring" as a sound; see Watkins 40. Reconciling these two is a bit of a puzzler, but I will table that for the present.

22. Here I follow the spelling of Seamus Heaney (172). Heaney's Old English text is, in turn, based on the edition of C.L. Wrenn, Tolkien's successor to the Rawlinson and Bosworth Professorship at Pembroke College, Oxford. Note that Heaney renders the lines,

"the outlandish thing / *writhed* and convulsed and viciously / turned on the king" (173, emphasis added).

23. From Tolkien's translation of *Beowulf* (May 2014).

24. See Tolkien *Pictures* (plate 40) and Hammond and Scull *Artist & Illustrator* (52) for reproductions of this painting.

25. Joseph Bosworth was the Rawlinson Professor of Anglo-Saxon at Oxford from 1858–76. After he retired from the chair, his own name was added to it—the same chair which Tolkien would hold a half-century later (1925–45).

26. See also *Sauron* 243, where the form is *wraikwas*, which recalls the Gothic cognates I discussed above (e.g., Gothic *wraiqs*, *wraks*, etc.).

27. Notably, from Morris, 213. Morris defines *wryþe* variously as "turn, wriggle, toil, bind, thrust," but there is no suggestion of turning from the right to the wrong course. Likewise, Tolkien's definition differs from the one given in Stratmann 697.

28. For example, Morris (1854), Gollancz (1891), Mead (1908), Jewett (1908), and E.V. Gordon's posthumous edition, edited by his wife, with Tolkien's assistance (1953). Two representative examples: "That God from right would swerve away" (Jewett 41), and "That he would deal so wrong a way" (Mead 27).

29. This is a deliberate echo of Tolkien's metaphor in earlier versions of "On Fairy-stories" (149).

30. See Watkins 99. Also see Skeat, Zoëga, Grimm (688 *et seq.*), Stratmann, *et al.*, for many of these (and other) cognate forms.

31. In another diminution of the same sort, Saruman in "The Disaster of the Gladden Fields" is said to have fallen from would-be dragon to no more than a jackdaw (*UT* 277). And Old Man Willow's trailing roots are called "dragonets" (*FR* I, vi, 128).

32. Tolkien would later recall, "I desired dragons with a profound desire" (*TOF* 55).

33. The majority of these cognates were drawn from Grimm, 688.

34. See Rateliff's "Nomenclature in the Pryftan Fragment" 15–16.

35. The dictionary is in four unpaginated sections. Both words occur in part IV, defined as "a worme" and "Fyre," respectively.

36. Until recently, it had been believed that Tolkien owned his copy from 1907 on (*Chronology* 12); however, Carl Phelpstead has provided evidence against this date (9, 124n34). Regardless of the precise timing, Tolkien definitely knew this reference work.

37. I am not the first to make this observation. The idea goes back at least as far as 1978: "Tolkien tells us in the first paragraph that this is 'not a nasty, dirty, wet hole, filled with the ends of worms.' If we pause to consider what he writes, we may conclude that the alpha and omega of Bag End is not limited in its significance to the fact that Bilbo will make an end of that 'giant worm,' the dragon" (Mathews 8).

38. Recall that one of the riddles from *The Hobbit* is distinctly etymological in nature ("an eye in a blue face..."). This may be arguing backwards, but the point nevertheless buttresses Gollum's character. Shippey makes the same observation about Gollum's interest in roots as a kind of metaphor for philology in "History in Words" (29–30).

WORKS CITED

Beowulf, an Anglo-Saxon Poem, and The Fight at Finnsburg. Tr. James M. Garnett. 3rd ed. Boston: Ginn & Co., 1895.

Béowulf and The Fight at Finnsburh. Ed. James A. Harrison and Robert Sharp. 4th rev. ed. Boston: Ginn & Co., 1904.

Beowulf: A New Verse Translation. Tr. Seamus Heaney. New York: Norton, 2000.

Blackwelder, Richard E. *A Tolkien Thesaurus.* Garland Reference Library of The Humanities, Vol. 1326. New York: Garland Publishing, Inc., 1990.

Bosworth, Joseph. *A Dictionary of the Anglo-Saxon Language.* London: Longman, Rees, Orme, Brown, Green, and Longman, 1838.

_____. *An Anglo-Saxon Dictionary.* Ed. and enlarged T. Northcote Toller. Oxford: Clarendon, 1898.

Brockett, John Trotter. *A Glossary of North Country Words with Their Etymology and Affinity to Other Languages and Occasional Notices of Local Customs and Popular Superstitions.* 3rd ed. Newcastle Upon Tyne: Emerson Charnley, Bigg Market; and Simpkin, Marshall, & Co., 1846.

Cook, Albert Stanburrough. *A Literary Middle English Reader.* Boston: Ginn & Co., 1915.

Gilliver, Peter, Jeremy Marshall, and Edmund Weiner. *The Ring of Words: Tolkien and the Oxford English Dictionary.* Oxford: Oxford University Press, 2006.

Godden, Malcolm. Rev. of Mary Salu and Robert T. Farrell, eds., *J.R.R. Tolkien, Scholar and Storyteller: Essays in Memoriam. The Review of English Studies* N.S., 32.128 (November 1981): 488–93.

Gollancz, Israel. Ed. and tr. *Pearl: An English Poem of the 14th Century.* London: D. Nutt, 1891.

Grimm, Jacob. *Teutonic Mythology.* Vols. I–IV. Tr. from the 4th ed. James Steven Stallybrass. Mineola, NY: Dover, 1966.

Hammond, Wayne G., and Christina Scull. *J.R.R. Tolkien: Artist & Illustrator.* Boston: Houghton Mifflin, 1995.

Hooker, Mark T. *A Tolkienian Mathomium: A Collection of Articles on J.R.R. Tolkien and His Legendarium.* [N.P.]: Llyfrawr, 2006.

Jamieson, John. *An Etymological Dictionary of the Scottish Language.* Abridged from the quarto edition. Edinburgh: Abernathy & Walker, 1818.

Jeffrey, David Lyle. "Tolkien as Philologist." *Invention* 61–78.

Jewett, Sophie. *The Pearl: A Middle English Poem.* New York: Thomas Y. Cromwell & Co., 1908.

Lewis, C.S. *Studies in Words.* 2d ed. Cambridge: Cambridge University Press, 1967. Reprinted 2002.

_____. *C.S. Lewis's Lost Aeneid: Arms and the Exile.* Ed. A.T. Reyes. New Haven, London: Yale University Press, 2011.

Liddell, Henry George, and Robert Scott. *A Greek-English Lexicon.* New York: Harper, 1848.

Mathews, Richard. *Lightning from a Clear Sky: Tolkien, The Trilogy, and The Silmarillion.* The Milford Series: Popular Writers of Today, Volume 15. San Bernadino: Borgo Press, 1978.

Mead, Marian. *The Pearl: An English Vision-Poem of the Fourteenth Century Done Into Modern Verse.* Portland, ME: Thomas B. Mosher, 1908.

Moor, Edward. *Suffolk Words and Phrases.* London: Woodbridge, 1823.

Morris, Richard. *Early English Alliterative Poems in the West-Midland Dialect of the Fourteenth Century.* E.E.T.S. o.s. 1. London: Early English Text Society, 1854. 2d ed., 1869.

Morris-Jones, John. *An Elementary Welsh Grammar, Part I: Phonology and Accidence.* Oxford: Clarendon, 1921.

The Oxford English Dictionary. Oxford University Press, November 2010. June 2011.

Phelpstead, Carl. *Tolkien and Wales: Language, Literature, and Identity.* Cardiff: University of Wales Press, 2011.

Rateliff, John D. *The History of The Hobbit, Part One: Mr. Baggins.* Boston: Houghton Mifflin, 2007.

Salesbury, William. *A Dictionary in Englyshe and Welshe, Parts I–IV.* London: The Cymmrodorion Society, 1877.

Shippey, T.A. "Creation from Philology in *The Lord of the Rings.*" *J.R.R. Tolkien, Scholar and Storyteller: Essays in Memoriam.* Ed. Mary Salu and Robert T. Farrell. Ithaca: Cornell University Press, 1979. 286–316.

_____. "History in Words: Tolkien's Ruling Passion." *Scholarship* 25–39.

_____. "Light-elves, Dark-elves, and Others: Tolkien's Elvish Problem." *Tolkien Studies* 1 (2004): 1–15. Rpt. *Roots* 215–233.

_____. "Orcs, Wraiths, Wights: Tolkien's Images of Evil." *J.R.R. Tolkien and His Literary Resonances: Views of Middle-earth*. Ed. George Clark and Daniel Timmons. Westport, Connecticut: Greenwood Press, 2000. 183–98. Rpt. *Roots* 243–265.

Sisam, Kenneth. *Fourteenth Century Verse and Prose (with Glossary)*. Oxford: Clarendon, 1921. Rpt. with corrections, 1964.

Skeat, Walter W. *An Etymological Dictionary of the English Language*. 2d ed. Oxford: Clarendon, 1893.

Stratmann, Francis Henry. *A Middle English Dictionary*. New ed. by Henry Bradley. Oxford: Oxford University Press, 1891.

Tolkien, J.R.R. "Chaucer as a Philologist: *The Reeve's Tale*." *Transactions of the Philological Society*, London, 1934: [1]–70. Rpt. *Tolkien Studies* 5 (2008): 109–71.

_____. "The Gnomish Lexicon." Ed. Christopher Gilson, *et al. Parma Eldalamberon* 11 (1995): 17–75.

_____. *A Middle English Vocabulary*. Oxford: Clarendon, 1922.

_____. "Philology: General Works." *The Year's Work in English Studies* Vol. 4 (1923): [20]-37.

_____. *Pictures by J.R.R. Tolkien*. Ed. Christopher Tolkien. Boston: Houghton Mifflin, 1979.

_____. "The Qenya Lexicon." Ed. Christopher Gilson, *et al. Parma Eldalamberon* 12 (1998): 29–106.

_____. "Sigelwara Land." *Medium Ævum* 1.3 (December 1932): [183]-196; 3. 2 (June 1934): [95]-111.

_____. *Sir Gawain and the Green Knight, Pearl and Sir Orfeo*. London: George Allen & Unwin, 1975.

_____, and E.V. Gordon. *Sir Gawain and the Green Knight*. Oxford: Clarendon, 1925.

Turner, Allan. *Translating Tolkien: Philological Elements in* The Lord of the Rings. Frankfurt am Main: Peter Lang, 2005.

Watkins, Calvert. *The American Heritage Dictionary of Indo-European Roots*. 2d ed. Boston: Houghton Mifflin, 2000.

Wilson, Edmund. "Oo, Those Awful Orcs!" Rev. of J.R.R. Tolkien, *The Fellowship of the Ring. The Nation* CLXXXII (April 14, 1956): 312–314.

Zoëga, Geir T. *A Concise Dictionary of Old Icelandic*. Oxford: Clarendon, 1901. Rpt. Dover Books on Language. [Mineola, NY]: Dover, 2004.

"He chanted a song of wizardry": Words with Power in Middle-earth

B.S.W. BAROOTES

In Tolkien's Middle-earth, people do things with words.[1] Language sets the universe in motion, and it continues to be the primary means of creation in Middle-earth. Arda comes into existence through Eru Ilúvatar's primeval command. Yavanna's chant upon the green mound of Ezellohar produces Telperion and Laurelin, the Two Trees of Valinor. The death of the trees, too, is marked by the dirge of Yavanna. Even this sad song, sung in the deepest dark, is not without generative power, for it brings forth the last fruit and flower that become the Sun and the Moon. The making through song, however, is not limited to the Valar in the deeps of time. In *The Silmarillion*, the Elves' first action is the making of language—the exclamation "Ele!," which means "*behold!*" (*S* 358; cf. Flieger, *Light* 64), from which they take their name. In Aman and in the Hither Lands, the Elves' words work spells of building and of razing, of disguise and of release. On the Quest for the Silmaril, Finrod cloaks his companions in the image of Orcs through his elven craft, and uses his words to combat Sauron. Lúthien, anticipating Galadriel at Dol Guldur, sings down Sauron's tower and opens the dungeons of Tol-in-Gaurhoth. The Dwarves also demonstrate the connection between language and making. In Bag–End, the song of Thorin and company tells how "The dwarves of yore made mighty spells, / While hammers fell like ringing bells" (*H* I, 22). This is echoed in the *Lord of the Rings* in Gimli's song, in Moria, in Khazad-dûm when "forged was blade, and bound was hilt" and "delver mined" and "mason built" so "Beneath the mountains music woke: / The harpers harped, the min-

115

strels sang" (FR II, iv, 330). Of men, especially of men at the end of the Third Age, we have fewer reports of skill in speech and strength in song. Tolkien's mythology is one of decline and fall, a history of diminution or, to borrow the phrase Galadriel uses when speaking to Frodo, a "long defeat" (FR II, vii, 372). Although Tolkien emphasizes and celebrates the immense power of language and of story-telling, the ability to "do things with words" is not constant throughout the history of Middle-earth; it is not, as Mary Zimmer asserts (58), an ability accessible to anyone who can speak. In Middle-earth, heroic deeds, skill in art and craft, proximity to Valinor, and Light all lessen over time; so too does language.

This essay explores how Tolkien's Saga of Jewels and Rings traces the pattern of decline in the creative and sub-creative powers of language. Other scholars have analyzed and discussed the several sites of diminution and decay in Tolkien's world. W.A. Senior argues that "the sustained and grieved sense of loss, of which death is but one form, ... provides Tolkien with his most pervasive and unifying component of atmosphere and mood" (173). As Verlyn Flieger states, "The whole work is permeated by an air of deepening sorrow, a sense of loss, of estrangement" (Light 60). In Splintered Light, Flieger elucidates how the paired concepts of light and language lessen in clarity, intensity, and strength as the ages of Middle-earth pass.

Tom Shippey picks up this thread in his analysis of the Elbereth hymns that appear in The Lord of the Rings (Road 189; Author 202). Shippey uses the four iterations of the hymn to stress the pervading theme of loss and longing. Sung by the Noldorin elves, the song expresses the sorrow of displacement and of exile. It is not only the stories and songs of the legendarium that evoke a sense of separation. Elsewhere, Shippey addresses the question of genre in The Lord of the Rings, and to do so he employs Northrop Frye's hierarchy of literary modes (Author 221–5). Frye classifies five types of literature according to the nature of the protagonist and the world he inhabits (Anatomy 33). These are, in descending order, myth, romance, high mimesis, low mimesis, and irony. Although he suggests that The Lord of the Rings is a mosaic of modes, Shippey, I believe, agrees with Frye that the lower modes represent a "displacement" from myth (Anatomy 135–36; cf. Author 221–22): myth gives way to romance, which gives way to high mimesis, and so on. At the generic level as well, then, Tolkien's Saga demonstrates a pre-occupation with decay, loss, and displacement.

Following Shippey's lead, I employ a different Frygian source to clarify how Tolkien demonstrates the power of language and traces its decline. In The Great Code, Frye adapts the historical and linguistic models of the seventeenth- and eighteenth-century Italian linguist Giambattista Vico (5 ff). The application of this interpretive model to Tolkien's work allows us to see a clear pattern of progressive diminution of the creative and performative powers of language in his *legendarium*.[2]

In *The New Science*, Vico sets out a three-age model of human history: an Age of Gods, an aristocratic Age of Heroes, and, finally, an Age of the People (20 [par. 31]). Quite clearly, Vico's schema of history is one of diminution (cf. 115 [par. 372], for example). This model is not, however, strictly linear, nor is it teleological. At the end of the Age of the People, there is a *ricorso*, a return to the beginning of the cycle. This model offers useful correspondences to the history of Middle-earth: the Ages of Gods and Heroes are covered in *The Silmarillion* (including the "Ainulindalë" and the "Akallabêth"), and the condition of the world at the end of the Third Age, with its dearth of heroes and the absence of the Valar, is certainly what Vico would call a Vulgar Age. The return of the king—the restoration of the Númenórean kingdoms in Middle-earth which coincides with the defeat of Sauron and the forces of Darkness—functions as Tolkien's *ricorso*, or, to use his own term, the Recovery (*TOF* 67–8).[3]

A similar pattern appears in Vico's model of the history of language. This is also a tripartite model, and the phases of language, each characterized by different mode of verbal expression, correspond to the three historical ages Vico defines. He names his three phases of language the poetic, the noble or heroic, and the vulgar (see, for instance, 22 [par. 34]).[4] Frye, borrowing in part from Vico, initially renames these phases the hieroglyphic, the hieratic, and the descriptive (*Great Code* 5). Throughout his study, however, Frye consistently refers to the phases as the metaphoric, the metonymic, and (returning to Vico's term) the demotic (15 ff), and I shall use these labels throughout the present study.[5]

These three Viconian-Frygian phases represent a progressive displacement from primal unity, from an identity of subject and object. The idea of decline, then, is represented as a shift away from metaphor. The metaphoric phase is similar to what Frye calls, in the modal structure that Shippey employs, the mythic mode (cf. *Anatomy* 33).[6] This mode is "a world of total metaphor, in which everything is potentially identical with everything else" (*Anatomy* 136). The metaphoric phase takes its name from the formulation of metaphor: "this is that" (*Great Code* 7). Flieger locates an example of this identification in the primal utterance of the Elves, looking up at the newly rekindled stars at the very dawn of language in Middle-earth. This original expression is, for Flieger, emblematic of the unity of light and language in Middle-earth. Flieger points out that the doubled force of the perception and the subsequent response, the exclamation, is a separating agent, "dividing the see-ers from the seen" (*Light* 74), the subject from the object. Although Flieger does not acknowledge it, and although it does not in fact occur for many long years, we see here—at the advent of language—the first hint of displacement and the rise of the metonymic period.

The connection between word and thing, between signifier and referent, is the source of the power of language in the metaphoric phase. As Zimmer briefly notes, this power is demonstrated most clearly in "word magic" and "name magic" (50). She takes the terms from the first volume of Ernst Cassirer's *The Philosophy of Symbolic Forms*. Cassirer defines word magic as the ability to cause an event to occur through speech or narration (1.117)—what we often call an incantation and what Tolkien calls a spell (*TOF* 41). Name magic is a special kind of utterance whereby a speaker gains power and control over a person or thing by knowing and using its name (Cassirer 1.118). Frye makes an identical point when he writes that, in the metaphoric phase, to know and use the name of a person or thing "give[s] the knower some control over it" (*Great Code* 6).[7] The metaphoric phase, then, is a period of intense creative ability in language: to say is to do or to make, and to name is to make present or otherwise control. In this first phase, writes Frye, "the word [is] an element of creative power," and "language can be used with immediacy and vitality ... that later ages never consistently recapture" (*Great Code* 18, 20). This power appears in Middle-earth in the first period of the *legendarium*: in the Music of the Ainur, in the Shaping of Middle-earth, and in the works and deeds of the Elves in Valinor and Beleriand.

In the metonymic phase, this power lessens. Whereas in the metaphoric phase there is a direct connexion, indeed an identity, between subject and object—as Frye puts it, "this is that"—in the metonymic phase there is a separation of the two wherein the one is a substitute for the other: "this is put for that" (*Great Code* 7, 15). The separation between the sign and the referent results in a diminished form of language where to name is only to suggest or to allude, where words can only conjure memories and create fleeting illusions. As we shall see, this diminution is important for Tolkien's view of the waning power of words, for language in the metonymic phase self-reflexively calls attention to its diminished state. In the demotic phase of language, however, the power of words is reduced to almost nothing. In this language of the vulgar age, the distance between the signifier and the signified is further increased, and "the word has no power to be anything but a word" (*Great Code* 19). Speech and writing do no more than describe: they do not make or invoke. It is at this point, at the nadir of the Vico-Frye model, that we find the *ricorso* and the restoration of the power of language. In Tolkien's world, as I have mentioned above and will demonstrate below, this return is realized through Aragorn's Quenya oath at his coronation.

Tolkien's world begins in the metaphoric phase of language, in the Timeless Halls of Eru Ilúvatar (*S* 15). The Music of the Ainur forms the plan for the World, but Arda is only a vision (*S* 17)—an observable ("Behold your Music!") but unrealized and removable form—until Ilúvatar declares "*Eä!* Let these things Be!" (*S* 20). The Allfather's imperative utterance thus transforms the vision and makes "Eä, the World that Is" (*S* 20). Language is also the chief means whereby the Valar shape Middle-earth. In the period following the establishment of Valinor, Yavanna uses "a song of power" (*S* 38) to create the Two Trees. Sitting in Máhanaxar, the Ring of Doom, the Valar silently listen to her song:

> And as they watched, upon the mound [Ezellohar] there came forth two slender shoots; and silence was over all the world in that hour, nor was there any other sound save the chanting of Yavanna. Under her song the saplings grew and became fair and tall, and came to flower ... [*S* 38].

The Two Trees of the Valar, the greatest of the artifacts of Arda save the Silmarils, are wrought exclusively through the power of words, "the chanting of Yavanna." Accordingly, when the Trees are wounded and poisoned by Melkor and Ungoliant, it is the dirge of Yavanna, strengthened by the tears of Nienna (which were also a part of the making of the Trees), that, while unable to restore the Light, produces the last flower and fruit of which the Moon and Sun are made (*S* 98–9).

Metaphoric language is not used for creative purposes exclusively. Language is also a means of combat in the First Age of Middle-earth. In the story of the Quest for the Silmaril, as is told in *The Lay of Leithian* (*Lays* 154–309) and in "Of Beren and Lúthien" in *The Silmarillion*, there occurs a great singing contest between Sauron (called Thû in the poem) and the Noldorin king Finrod Felagund (originally called Inglor Felagund). Earlier in the journey, on the road from Nargothrond to Tol-in-Gaurhoth, Beren, Finrod, and their ten companions disguise themselves as Orcs: they adopt the clothing, gear, and weapons of their slain enemies, and "[b]y the arts of Felagund their own forms and faces were changed into the likeness of Orcs" (*S* 170). The "arts of Felagund" is perhaps a bit ambiguous, but the corresponding passage from *The Lay of Leithian* shows the Elvish king as a wielder of words with power:

> Then Felagund a spell did sing
> of changing and of shifting shape;
> their ears grew hideous, and agape
> their mouths did start, and like a fang
> each tooth became, as slow he sang [*Leithian* 2009–13].[8]

The elven king's song works physical changes on the company, and the progress of the transformation is tied to the progress of the spell: the effects of the song are simultaneous with Felagund's chanting.

The pairing of powerful poetic narration and images forms the bulk of the chant-battle between Finrod Felagund and Sauron-Thû. As Beren, Felagund, and their companions travel north on the road to Angband, they are waylaid at the Isle of Werewolves and are forced, in their orcish garb, to report to Thû. The encounter, in which "Felagund strove with Sauron in songs of power" (*S* 171), may be divided into two parts. The first part takes the form of an interrogation, what Tolkien, in a prose synopsis of the poem, calls "a contest of riddling questions and answers" (*Lays* 233). In a single-line stanza, Thû asks the band for news of the Elvish kingdoms of Beleriand and their own errands there: "Where have ye been? What have ye seen?" (*Leithian* 2100). As Christopher Tolkien notes in his commentary on Canto VII, the form of the poem changes here to reflect the shift to a different sort of linguistic engagement: "Lines 2100–6 are in a changed metre, especially suitable to a riddle contest, and their content (the reply to Thû's question ...) is riddling ('misleading accuracy')" (*Lays* 234). The disguised Felagund's reply truthfully states that the company has been in Elfinesse (Elvenesse) and has killed a band of thirty foes—of course, he is careful not to give any more detail than this. His ruse begins to falter hereafter: he knows too much of the elven lands and has "too little knowledge of Angband," as Tolkien notes in a comment scribbled in the margin of the manuscript (234). This weakening is marked by a return to the regular metre of the *Lay* where "the riddling element disappears" (C. Tolkien, 234).

The second part of the contest, also in a slightly varied metre—principally nonosyllabic rather than octosyllabic—should be seen as the battle proper; it consists of powerful chants traded back and forth by the combatants (*S* 171).[9] This passage shows the power ("magic and might") Tolkien locates in language and in story-telling. Sauron's initial attack conjures images of deceit and betrayal, and its variation of terms—revealing and uncovering, treachery and betrayal—suggests the sorcerer's several efforts to learn the identity of the company. Finrod Felagund's "song of staying" parries Sauron's attack. Indeed it is a direct response, for the shift from assailant to defender maintains and extends the rhyme scheme: the "betraying" qualities of Sauron's chant give way; there is a swaying which occurs in the liminal space between the two combatants; and the balance then tips in Felagund's favor with a move to steadfastness or "staying." The double-sense of the "song of staying" further emphasizes the elf-king's power. It is a song on the subject of staying: resistance, "secrets kept," freedom and escape, a song of transformative agility and the defensive symbolism of the tower. The song is also the very act of staying: his song is itself a manifestation of staying. To speak of a "release from bondage," of "snares eluded, broken traps, / The prison opening, the chain that snaps," makes these things happen. In the metaphoric phase of language, the act described is carried out through and realized by the story-telling. The chain snaps because it is said to do so.

In Felagund's chant there is also an element of movement, a flight out from under the shadow of death, from Sauron's terror—machinations and metal, fire and reek—to the natural world of birds, underground caverns, rivers, and the sea. This movement allows Felagund to distance himself and his cause from the oppressive weight of Sauron's presence and song of power and to focus the strength of natural creation in his words. Felagund's song invokes the beauty of Arda, the great Artifact, and combines its creative power with "Gnomish skill" (*Leithian* 2006), "all the magic and might ... / Of Elvenesse" (*S* 171). The singing of the birds, like the delving strength of flowing water that carved Nargothrond, is an image of sub-creation: birdsong within Elfsong within the Great Music that is the history of Eä.[10] What is more, the majesty of the sea (here evoked through the wave-like repetition of "on sand, / On sand of pearls") is closely identified with the "Ainulindalë" (*S* 19). The successive elements of the song also suggest a movement from fallen East to blissful West: from inland Beleriand, Tol Sirion near the spring of the great river, south to Nargothrond, further on to the shores of the mortal continent, and across the Sundering Sea ("Beyond the western world") to the immortal lands of Aman, the earthly paradise covered with gemstones rather than mundane pebbles.

This movement is something of an illusion—or, rather, it is only one side of the overall effect of the elvish spell. Indeed, there is both centrifugal and centripetal movement occurring simultaneously, and the latter is the more effective and important. Felagund's song gathers strength from the allusions it makes. It draws them to the location of the utterance: the birds and pearly sands are brought to the sorcerer's isle; the gloom is infiltrated by the light of day; and an air of immortality is breathed in spite of the suffocating weight of impending doom. The power of Felagund's language stems from its basis in the metaphorical phase. The metaphor causes its referent to be present. The language of this phase operates as literal invocation; the speaker's utterances release a quasi-physical power (*Great Code* 6) and manifest the named things in the moment and at the location of the singing.

Unfortunately for Felagund and Beren, this power is not limited to the forces of good. Sauron's resumed attack is the demonic equivalent of Finrod Felagund's invocation of connexion and solidarity. The brightness that Felagund introduces into the shadow of Sauron's isle is overpowered by renewed gloom and growing darkness. The Elvish cause is lost entirely when Morgoth's lieutenant recalls the disgrace of the Noldor at Alqualondë, the vile Kinslaying, and the hypocritical theft of the Telerin ships. To this defeating vision of the splintering of kindreds Sauron adds images of isolation and loneliness, suggesting barrenness, alienation, and solitude: "The wind wails, / The wolf howls. The ravens flee. / The ice mutters in the mouths of the Sea. / The captives sad in Angband mourn" (2199–2202). The empty sounds of these natural voices crying in the wilderness—the wind, the wolf, and the ice are all speakers—serve Sauron as metaphors for Finrod's song, sapping its strength. Sauron thus isolates the Elven king and causes him to fail. (It is worth noting, I think, that the muttering ice also recalls the Helcaraxë, the Grinding Ice. The ice is the space between the wastes of Araman and the far north of Middle-earth. Finrod's hard passage across the ice finalizes his flight from Valinor and his separation from his father Finarfin and his beloved, Amarië of the Vanyar.) Although Finrod Felagund conjures great beauty and bliss, Sauron has the mastery; his song is more potent. Whereas Felagund's spell bridges distances in space, Sauron's song of wizardry bridges space and time; the song of birds and waves on Elven sand are still (albeit distant) occurrences in the world at the time of the chanting, but Sauron takes a moment of history, the Kinslaying, and makes it fully present. After his song fails, Finrod and Beren are imprisoned, and the Elven king dies saving the outlaw mortal's life; Finrod Felagund becomes a memory, the subject of story and of song: "Thus died the king, / as elvish singers yet do sing" (*Leithian* 2636–7).[11]

While language is a means of creation and of action in the metaphoric phase, this power is greatly diminished in later ages. The metonymic phase is marked by a distinct distance between subject and object, between word and referent, between saying and doing. The best example of language in this phase is Galadriel's "Song of Eldamar": "I sang of leaves, of leaves of gold..." (*FR* II, viii, 388–9). Hers is not a song of making or of doing; it is a song of memory and of loss. It points to a moment in time—a period and a place—when and where she had the power of song and wielded words deftly; the song memorializes that making, but makes no new thing. The growing failures of language, of song, and of story-telling are manifested in the imagery, the diction, the grammar, and the structure of the poem.

Like her Quenya song "Namárië," Galadriel's "Song of Eldamar" is a lament; like the hymn to Elbereth, it is an exile's song. She cannot sing the leaves into budding anymore. The song yearns for a distant place and time characterized by an intense generative function of language. This intensity is immediately apparent and insisted upon through the structure of the song. Although much of the poem is in (rough) iambic heptameter, it opens with a forceful, declarative spondee: "I sang." Galadriel, or, rather, the Galadriel of a former time, is identified as a powerful singer. The vigor of the song of making is compounded in the following line where the same short phrase is repeated and maintains the same stress pattern. "Leaves" is repeated three times in the first line alone; these golden symbols of creative capacity are thick on the bough of the line. The song of wind brings forth the breeze—punctuated by a triplet of stressed syllables: "wind there came"—and joins it with the first product, the golden leaves.

In this later phase, however, language is slippery, and it behaves in unintended and problematic ways. Galadriel cannot wield this powerful tool as once she could. Repetition, formerly a mighty means of making, is now a fickle device. The repetition of Eldamar in the fifth and sixth lines serves as a painful reminder (for us, for the Fellowship, and for the singer herself) that this sort of singing did not and does not happen here in Lothlórien, in Middle-earth. The mention of Ilmarin in the fourth line serves this purpose as well. Furthermore, the choice of Eldamar, Elf-home, is telling. Although Ilmarin, Valimar, Valinor, or Tirion would all fit the line, "Eldamar" highlights Galadriel's status as an exile. Her home proper, the place she belongs, is not the site of her singing. Lothlórien, however beautiful and unstained, is a temporary dwelling. Like the other exiles who remember and sing of Elbereth as they wander in "this far land beneath the trees" (*FR* I, iii, 89), Galadriel is out of place in Middle-earth.[12]

The spatial separation is compounded with temporal distance through the use of "beyond" in "Beyond the Sun, beyond the Moon." This phrase suggests spatial separation: Tirion and Eldamar are physically sundered from Middle-earth not only by Belegaer but, as a result of the Akallabêth, by the curved air of the spherical world. The sun circles the globe and need not set beyond the Blessed Realm. "Beyond" also implies a temporal distance—or, more specifically, a spatial metaphor of temporality—something like a timeline. In this sense, we can locate Galadriel's original song of power in the long ages of stars and of the Two Trees. "Beyond" also means "before," when only stars shone on the Sea in the perpetual twilight of Ever-eve.

The gulf between the site of powerful song and this far land is also carefully negotiated through the precise use of tenses in the poem. The preterite of the opening lines underscores the finality of the original song of production: she sang, leaves grew, wind came to the call and shook the branches. Note how, in the seventh and eighth lines, the tensions of exile are highlighted through a shift from the present perfect to the present simple. As the Blessed Realm is fenced and veiled by mists of confusion, so too is knowledge of it obscured and imprecise. There long the golden leaves have grown: we know they grew and continued to grow upon the branching years. Are they growing even now? The song (and the singer) cannot be sure. She can be certain, however, that here and now fall the Elven-tears. It is a present simple point: tears fall; they fall now. The lyric now stresses both the immediacy of the sorrow and its recurrence: now, and now, and now. Life in *galadhremmin ennorath*, tree-tangled Middle-earth, is a perpetual present of loss and lamentation as the present continuous attests: "the leaves *are falling* in the stream." Nowhere is tense more evocative of the pain of exile and the faded (and fading) power of language in the metonymic phase than in the final couplet of the song where the tense suddenly shifts to the conditional: "But if of ships I now should sing, what ship would come to me, / What ship would bear me ever back across so wide a Sea?" (*FR* II, viii, 389). The uncertainty is daunting. Galadriel recognizes, indeed admits, that her power of song is diminished; she is reluctant even to begin.

The structure of the song further betrays the diminished capabilities of language in the latter days of Middle-earth and the singer's (perhaps unconscious) acknowledgement of her once-mighty capacities. The song is meant to be geometrically balanced. As I note above, the song is written in a rough iambic heptameter; it measures fourteen syllables by fourteen lines, what is often called a fourteener. Or, rather, it almost does. There is one important aberration. The eleventh line, the line that contains the phrase "too long," is just that—too long. There are fifteen syllables in this line. The extra syllable mars the symmetry of the poem.[13] The song that fails to produce a new thing, that can only remember and lament lost potency, is itself an imperfect creation.[14] The out-of-place syllable upsets the otherwise regular rhythm of the song; it is a wrinkle in the unchanging time of the poem which also foreshadows the temporal shift from stasis to flow that threatens Lothlórien (cf. *FR* II, vii, 381). There is a greater significance to his aberration, however. The out of place syllable is the stressed *I*: Galadriel herself does not fit—in Middle-earth or in her own song.

We thus witness a painful displacement of subject and object and an alienation of speaker from utterance. On the one hand, these manifest as a distrust of language and regret over lost capabilities. As I discuss above, the song ends in a moment of doubt, with the singer stranded in this far land. On the other hand, this late song becomes a sombre memorial to the earlier song of power it recounts. It is a metonymic utterance: Galadriel's lament is "put for" the song that produced the golden tree. There is some small creative power left in this song of memory. It calls the event into the mind of those who hear it, certainly, but this is only an illusion. Gimli and Legolas discuss the illusory nature of memory (and, by extension, metonymic language) as they leave Lothlórien behind. Gimli bemoans the parting, and Legolas seeks to comfort him: "the least reward that you shall have is that the memory of Lothlórien shall remain ever clear and unstained in your heart, and shall neither fade nor grow stale." Gimli, however, identifies the rub: "Maybe ... and I thank you for your words. True words doubtless; yet all such comfort is cold. Memory is not what the heart desires. That is only a mirror, be it clear as Kheled-zâram" (*FR* II, viii, 395). Even as it recalls the remembered thing, metonymic language calls to mind the insurmountable gap between the utterance and the referent, and thereby reinforces this separation. Indeed, metonymic language, the language of memory rather than making, calls attention to its own failings.

What little double-edged power remains in metonymic language completely disappears in the demotic phase. The Fading Days of the Third Age are the Age of the People, a world populated by men of lesser stature, by Hobbits, horsemen, and fat inn-keepers, and their language is accordingly diminished. Frye puts it plainly: "For descriptive [demotic] language, the word has no power to be anything but a word" (*Great Code* 19). This is certainly the case in Tolkien's world. Indeed, in several instances we see a disconnection between the word and its referent at the level of meaning and accessible truth. Whereas metonymic language still has some small connection to the past and ability to hail or invoke it, demotic language is, for all intents and purposes, entirely divorced from it. Even if there is some vestige of unity and understanding, it is invisible to the vulgar speakers: Théoden does not make the cognitive leap between a name for Fangorn Forest, "Entwood," and "the wood where Ents live" (*TT* III, viii, 155); the hobbits retain the expression "When the King comes back" long after they have forgotten that a King ever existed (*RK* Appendix A, 323). There is a total alienation of the word from the thing, and, consequently, of the speaker from the word.

This displacement results in a language absent of the power to make and to do. An early and poignant example of this phase of language is found at the end of the road to Rivendell, when Frodo confronts the Black Riders pursuing him. After he crosses the Ford of Bruinen, Frodo turns and commands the Riders to stand down:

> With a great effort Frodo sat upright and brandished his sword.
> "Go back!" he cried. "Go back to the Land of Mordor, and follow me no more!" His voice sounded thin and shrill in his own ears. The Riders halted, *but Frodo had not the power of Bombadil.* His enemies laughed at him with a harsh and chilling laughter [*FR* I, xii, 226; my emphasis].

The reference to Bombadil emphasizes the utter weakness of Frodo's use of language. Tom Bombadil is a figure of the mythic mode (*Author* 222), and his status as a wielder of metaphoric language is demonstrated several times during his brief encounter with the hobbits. He uses his song to release Merry from Old Man Willow and suggests that he is capable of a more violent undertaking (but chooses instead to put the rotten tree to sleep): "I know the tune for him…. I'll freeze his marrow cold, if he don't behave himself. I'll sing his roots off. I'll sing a wind up and blow leaf and branch away" (*FR* I, vi, 131). His words of "Carn Dûm in the Land of Angmar," spoken as he arms the hobbits with knives taken from the barrow, bridge time and space in the same manner as Felagund's song:

> The hobbits did not understand his words, but as he spoke they had a vision as it were of a great expanse of years behind them, like a vast shadowy plain over

which there strode shapes of Men, tall and grim with bright swords, and last
came one with a star on his brow. Then the vision faded, and they were back in
the sunlit world [*FR* I, viii, 157].

By contrast, Frodo's words are empty. The cold laughter of the Riders is
the only thing his ineffectual language elicits. They halt of their own volition
not because of any innate force in the utterance or the speaker. In fact, the
captain of the Ringwraith's response further reduces Frodo's position as a
speaker. The Black Rider raises his hand and halts speech altogether: "Frodo
was stricken dumb. He felt his tongue cleave to his mouth, and his heart labour-
ing" (*FR* I, xii, 227). This is only one example, of course, but it serves to demonstrate the degree to which language has sunk at the end of the Third Age.
Demotic language has displaced the remains of metonymic language and is a
far cry from the power of metaphoric language in the Elder Days. The condition of language at the end of the Third Age of Middle-earth is inextricably
linked to a great many factors: the absence of the Valar and the emigration of
the Elves, the near-absence of noble or heroic figures; the predominant presence of ordinary people, and the dilution and disappearance of ancient knowledge and lore. The ancient kingdoms have faded. It is a time of Bree-men and
Shire-folk. Words, accordingly, have lost their power to create; they now only
serve to describe, and, with the threat of Sauron's victory, the story they stand
to tell is grim.

All is not lost, of course. In the moment of eucatastrophe, "the sudden
joyous 'turn'" (*TOF* 75), the One Ring is destroyed in the Cracks of Doom.
This allows for the return of the king and the moment of *ricorso* in the history
of Middle-earth. Aragorn's ascension marks the restoration or Recovery
(Tolkien's term) of the many sites of diminution in Arda: light, geography,
and, most importantly, language. This last recovery is achieved in word and
in deed through the brief speech Aragorn makes at his coronation, a carefully
structured event. After introducing Aragorn, his titles, and his lineage to the
assembled people of Gondor, Faramir the last Steward brings out of the Rath
Dínen, the Tomb of Kings and Stewards, the crown of Eärnur the last king.
Holding the crown aloft, Aragorn speaks:

> *Et Eärello Endorenna utúlien. Sinome maruvan ar Hildinyar tenn' Ambar-
> metta!* ... Out of the Great Sea to Middle-earth I am come. In this place will I
> abide, and my heirs, unto the ending of the world [*RK* VI, v, 245–6].

The coronation speech is, on the surface, a simple declarative statement, but
these sentences carry the weight of the entire mythology. These words reveal
Aragorn in his full power, as though a covering were suddenly whisked away:
"Tall as the sea-kings of old, he stood above all that were near; ancient of days
he seemed and yet in the flower of manhood; and wisdom sat upon his brow,

and strength and healing were in his hands, and a light was about him" (246). Just as Strider gives way to Aragorn at the outset of the quest, so is the warrior transformed into the king, no longer Aragorn but Elessar; he is not a vision but an incarnation of the lost past. The words identify Aragorn as "the agent of ... renewal" (Ford 59). He earlier identifies himself as such when he first secretly enters Minas Tirith to aid Éowyn and Faramir in the Houses of Healing: "in the high tongue of old I am *Elessar*, the Elfstone, and *Envinyatar*, the Renewer" (*RK*, V, viii, 139). At his coronation, Aragorn's words in effect change his body so that he is seen clearly in mythical proportions. This cleansing or revealing is accompanied by a clear return of metaphor, even at the level of narration. His qualities and powers—wisdom, strength, and healing—take on quasi-physical existence.

This speech functions in each of the Viconian phases of language in ascending order, and, by arriving at the metaphoric phase, it traces the recovery. In terms of demotic language, the first sentence constitutes a reasonably accurate account of recent events, of how Aragorn arrived in his realm: he sailed up the river Anduin in the ships of the Corsairs of Umbar "borne upon a wind from the Sea to the kingdom of Gondor" (*RK* V, vi, 123). The speech also functions metonymically, for we learn that Aragorn's speech is not original but a repetition of "the words that Elendil spoke when he came up out of the Sea on the wings of the wind" (*RK* VI, v, 246). Aragorn is thus "put for" Elendil, and his utterance upon his arrival and establishment points to the foundation of the kingdoms of the West three millennia earlier. In the metaphoric phase of language, however, the coronation speech increases in power; it not only indicates but realizes the return. By uttering the words of Elendil, Aragorn makes the past present; the moment of his ascension is consequently compounded with the moment of foundation, of the creation of the kingdom. Aragorn does not simply imply Elendil; he *is* Elendil.

Much of the might of Aragorn's speech arises from its status as an oath (see Hostetter 340). As John R. Holmes argues, oaths are a powerful form of performative language in Middle-earth (251–53). The oath with the greatest implications is, of course, the infamous Oath of Fëanor (*S* 83). This oath, described as both a "torment" and a "burden" (*S* 246, 247), is an eternally binding contract—not even Manwë can undo it—and it drives much of the narrative and much of the tragedy of *The Silmarillion*. Most grievously, it leads to the three Kinslayings, including the massacre at Alqualondë that Sauron-Thû invokes in his battle with Finrod. Throughout Tolkien's mythology, oaths lead to trouble, pain, and sorrow: Finrod's sworn service to the kin of Barahir results in his death just as Fingolfin's earlier oath to follow Fëanor causes his exile from the Blessed Realm as well as his death; Beren's oath to Thingol repeatedly drives him out of the arms of Lúthien; the broken oath of the Dead

Men of Dunharrow holds them as specters for three millennia. Aragorn's oath at the coronation, by contrast, is productive. The same can be said of the oath he swears to Frodo at Bree: "I am Aragorn son of Arathorn; and if by life or death I can save you, I will" (*FR* I, x, 183). He makes good on this oath by escorting the Hobbits to Rivendell, joining them on the Quest as one of the Nine Walkers, and especially in marching the seven thousand weary soldiers of Gondor and its allies to the Black Gate in a show of force which, while ultimately hopeless, is designed to "give the Ring-bearer his only chance, frail though it be" (*RK* V, ix, 156). Aragorn's positive and successful oath corrects the negative oaths in the earlier parts of the *legendarium*—and accordingly corrects the decline of language.

Similarly, the coronation speech offers an inversion of a primeval instance of corruption, Melkor's act of naming Arda unto himself. As the Ainur enter the world, Melkor claims it: "This shall be my own kingdom; and I name it unto myself!" (*S* 21). The struggle to reclaim the world, to oust Morgoth and his servants, is the overarching theme of the whole Saga of Jewels and Rings. Aragorn symbolically achieves this through an inversion of Melkor's formula: rather than name Middle-earth unto himself as his kingdom, Aragorn commits himself to Middle-earth. By seemingly undoing the corruption of Arda, Aragorn symbolically restores or translates the world to the state at which it existed in the earliest days following Ilúvatar's command "*Eä!*" By giving his word, he renews—arguably recreates—the world.

There is, of course, an important caveat repeated in the preceding paragraph—"symbolically." After many long years of decline, Aragorn's speech cannot entirely escape the gravitational pull of the metonymic and demotic phases. Although his words refresh the world, they do not, in truth, reset it to its original state. Time, like the river in Galadriel's song in Lothlórien, flows away. The Fourth Age is not and cannot be the First Age: "the time comes of the Dominion of Men, and the Elder Kindred shall fade or depart" (*RK* VI, v, 249). In this respect, Aragorn's metaphoric utterance also functions metonymically, and thus identifies the double-bind of language. Like the songs of wizardry in the Elder Days, it bridges time and space. Like Galadriel's "Song of Eldamar," it recalls a golden age of powerful language only to see it fade into the past. While this last comparison undermines the power of Aragorn's speech on the one hand, on the other it points to an important feature of Tolkien's love for and understanding of language.

J.R.R. Tolkien was, first and foremost, a lover of language. He immersed himself in it professionally, investigating its intricacies and minutiæ. Language, for Tolkien, was also a private passion; it was the fundamental inspiration for his great works of fiction, *The Lord of the Rings* and *The Silmarillion*. He believed in the ability of a story, a spell, to cause images to appear and to stir emotions. A well-wrought chain of words can move a crowd to action or hold an audience enthralled. Yet Tolkien was acutely aware of an innate sadness built into language. Spoken or written, there is an inherent disconnect between words and their referents. In their everyday use (in the Primary World in which Tolkien wrote) and in the latter-day Middle-earth in his fiction, words do not have power; at best, they are "put for" the object they signify. In this state, language, although an agent of memory, preservation, and limited invocation, also serves as a painful reminder of the very separation it seeks to overcome. Throughout his mythology, Tolkien considers this paradox of language. He held a vision of an idealized form of language, now lost, wherein language could do more than conjure ethereal images; he saw a world where words have power to shape and affect real, physical objects. This world is Arda in its prime, in the Elder Days. Language ushers that world into existence, and, for a time, continues to be a significant force of creation and change. Songs bridge time and space and cause Light to grow from the earth; words can open or bar doors, create fire, and blot out the sun. Language in Tolkien's *legendarium*, however, is affected by loss and change, by displacement and splintering. Language is both the medium of preservation and the chief tool of enforcing the loss and separation it seeks to transcend. For all this pessimism, Tolkien maintained the hope that language could, in certain circumstances, transcend its own faded state. Tolkien's presentation of the functions of language in his mythology both acknowledges the diminution that accompanies the passing of days and offers a glimpse of Gil-Estel, the Star of High Hope.

NOTES

1. This essay, which grows out of my Master's thesis, was presented in an earlier form at the 44th International Congress on Medieval Studies, May 2009, as part of a session organised in honor of Professor Shippey. I wish to thank the organisers of and the participants in that session for their thoughtful comments, as well as my MA supervisor, Dr. Kevin Whetter of Acadia University, for his guidance and encouragement.

2. If the pairing of Tolkien and Frye appears at all suspect, the pairing of Tolkien and Vico perhaps seems nonsensical. In the former case, however, I am in quite good company. As Shippey notes (*Author* 221), Frye never explicitly mentions Tolkien in *Anatomy of Criticism*, although there are clear references to C.S. Lewis and Charles Williams (*Anatomy* 117). Frye's *Secular Scripture*, however, does make passing reference to *The Lord of the Rings*, and his notebooks contain numerous references to Tolkien's work which suggest Frye approved and thought highly of the text. I am in good company in the latter case as well. In his essay, "From Vico to Tolkien: The Affirmation of Myth against the Tyranny of Reason," Marek Oziewicz offers an insightful argument for why we should reflect on the parallels of Vico's and Tolkien's projects.

3. In *A Question of Time*, Flieger briefly mentions Vico, likening his notion of *ricorso* to the Nietzschean concept of Recurrence and Mircea Eliade's Eternal Return (25).

4. The chief Viconian source for the present discussion is found in the "Poetic Logic" section of the second book, "Poetic Wisdom," of *The New Science*.

5. These labels are, I believe, better suited to a discussion of Frye's development of the Viconian model given that his understanding of Vico's phases of language is informed by his reading of Roman Jakobson (*Great Code* 15). For Jakobson's parsing of the differences between the metaphor and the metonym, see "The Metaphoric and Metonymic Poles" in *Fundamentals of Language*, 90–96.

6. Frye himself acknowledges that "the sequence of literary modes in ... *Anatomy of Criticism*" is very close to Vico's model—indeed much closer than his adaptation of Vico's model is to the Italian thinker's original outline (*Great Code* 5). The overlap of the two sequences provides further insight into the Tolkien's mythology of loss and recovery. In Frye's hierarchy of modes, the ironic loops back into the mythic (*Anatomy* 62). In *The Lord of the Rings* this happens at the climax of the Quest of the Ring-bearer when the ironic figures, Sam and Gollum, enable the return to myth, and thus usher in the return of the king and the Recovery of Middle-earth.

7. Cassirer's "mythical view of language," in which a word "is itself a very real part of reality" (1.117), is strikingly similar to both Frye's metaphoric phase and his mythic mode of literature. In mythical language, writes Cassirer, "the world of things and the world of names form a single undifferentiated chain of causality and hence a single reality" (Cassirer, 1.118): this claim is echoed in Frye's characterization of the mythic mode as "a world of total metaphor, in which everything is potentially identical to everything else" (*Anatomy* 136).

8. Henceforth, I shall cite passages from *The Lay of Leithian* by line number. Citations from the prose text and commentary in *Lays* will be by page number.

9. I refer here to the more widely known version of this passage found in *The Silmarillion*. There are minor differences between this version and that found in *The Lay of Leithian* (2173–2205). For the most part, the differences are rather insignificant. It should be noted, however, that the final lines of the passage are different in each version. Where *The Silmarillion* reads "Thunder rumbles, the fires burn— / And Finrod fell before the throne" (*S* 171), *Leithian* adds a line and positions Felagund's defeat slightly differently: "Thunder rumbles, the fires burn, / a vast smoke gushes out, a roar— / and Felagund swoons upon the floor" (2203–05). The *Silmarillion* version emphasizes the struggle for mastery of the isle and the tower thereon: Minas Tirith on Tol Sirion was originally raised by Finrod Felagund (*S* 120, 205), but Sauron now sits on the throne. The earlier version, by contrast, focuses on the dazing of Felagund—he "swoons." It also introduces the unintelligible utterance of wrath, the roar, which, in a demonic inversion of the final chord of the Music of the Ainur, marks the end of the song of power. Moreover, true to Flieger's analysis of the paired tropes of light and language, the roar is combined with an obscuration of light by means of a "vast smoke."

10. Tolkien uses a similar image to emphasize the importance of sub-creation in "Leaf by Niggle." When Niggle arrives at his tree, the Tree, he immediately notices birds singing and building their nests therein (*TL* 89).

11. We hear an echo of these lines in the opening of Sam's song of Gil-galad, "Gil-galad was an Elven-king. / Of him the harpers sadly sing" (*FR* I, xi, 197), and I would argue that this echo is intentional, that Tolkien had the earlier passage in mind when he wrote Sam's song. Compare, as further evidence, Sam's observation in the Morgul Vale that he and Frodo are "in the same tale still" (*TT* IV, viii, 321) as "Hador, and Húrin, and Túrin, and Beren himself" (*FR* II, ii, 284).

12. On the significance of Lórien as an unstained space, see Shippey *Road* 217–19 and *Author* 196–99.

13. It is clear, I think, that this aberration is a conscious decision on Tolkien's part. An early draft of Galadriel's song is structurally sound, a perfect fourteen-by-fourteen measure. I include here lines from the draft that differ from the final version, with the changes identified in bold:

> And by the strand of **Tirion** there grew a golden Tree.
> Beneath the stars of **Evereve** in Eldamar it shone ...

But far away and far away beyond the Shadow-meres
Now long the golden leaves have grown upon the branching years.
And Lórien, O Lórien! the river flows away
And leaves are falling in the stream, and leaves are borne away;
O Lórien! Too long I dwell upon this Hither Shore
And in a fading crown I twine the golden elanor.
But if a ship I now should sing ... [*Treason* 284].

Admittedly, a couple of the changes are less important. Others, however, significantly alter the meaning of Galadriel's poem, and further identify it as a song that is acutely conscious of loss, separation, and the fading power of words. More importantly, the shift to the past perfect—"dwell" becomes "have dwelt"—is the source of the additional syllable that stains the face of the poem.

14. Tolkien draws inspiration for this model—the poem as (purposefully) imperfect artefact—from the fourteenth-century dream vision *Pearl,* where the carefully wrought form of the poem errs once in its rhyme scheme (an omitted line), in its concatenation, and in its stanzaic grouping. For a discussion of other associations between *Pearl* and Lothlórien, see Shippey *Road* 218–22 and *Author* 196–207; for the idea that *Pearl* is purposely imperfect, see David Carlson's *"Pearl*'s Imperfections."

Works Cited

Carlson, David. *"Pearl*'s Imperfections." *Studia Neophilologica* 63 (1991): 57–67.
Cassirer, Ernst. *The Philosophy of Symbolic Forms.* 3 vols. Tr. Ralph Manheim. New Haven: Yale University Press, 1953.
Flieger, Verlyn. *A Question of Time: J.R.R. Tolkien's Road to Faërie.* Kent, OH: Kent State University Press, 1997.
_____. *Splintered Light: Logos and Language in Tolkien's World.* 2d ed. Kent, OH: Kent State University Press, 2002.
Ford, Judy Ann. "The White City: *The Lord of the Rings* as an Early Medieval Myth of the Restoration of the Roman Empire." *Tolkien Studies* 2 (2005): 53–73.
Frye, Northrop. *Anatomy of Criticism: Four Essays.* Princeton: Princeton University Press, 1957.
_____. *The Great Code.* Orlando: Harcourt, 1982.
Holmes, John R. "Oaths and Oath Breaking: Analogues of Old English *Comitatus* in Tolkien's Myth." *Invention* 249–262.
Hostetter, Carl F. "Languages Invented by Tolkien." *Encyclopedia* 332–44.
Jakobson, Roman, and Morris Halle. *Fundamentals of Language.* The Hague: Mouton, 1956.
Oziewicz, Marek. "From Vico to Tolkien: The Affirmation of Myth against the Tyranny of Reason." *Tolkien's* The Lord of the Rings: *Sources of Inspirations: Views of Middle-earth.* Ed. Stratford Caldecott and Thomas Honegger. [Zollikofen]: Walking Tree, 2008. 113–36.
Senior, W.A. "Loss Eternal in J.R.R. Tolkien's Middle-earth." *J.R.R. Tolkien and His Literary Resonances.* Ed. George Clark and Daniel Timmons. Westport, CT: Greenwood, 2000. 173–82.
Vico, Giambattista. *The New Science.* Ed. and tr. Thomas Goddard Bergin and Max Harold Fisch. Ithaca: Cornell University Press, 1968.
Zimmer, Mary E. "Creating and Re-creating Worlds with Words: The Religion and Magic of Language in *The Lord of the Rings.*" *Invention* 49–60.

Inside Literature: Tolkien's Explorations of Medieval Genres

JOHN D. RATELIFF

C.S. Lewis once wrote of his old friend Tolkien that he had been "inside language" (Salu 12).[1] By this he meant that through the creation of his own invented languages ("a really possible tongue with consistent roots, sound laws, and inflexions, into which he poured all his imaginative and philological powers" [12]), Tolkien had gained insight into the way languages work, insights not achievable through external study, however painstaking, and had put this knowledge to good use, both in his scholarship and his fiction. In Lewis's words, "it was ... the source of that unparalleled richness and concreteness which ... distinguished him from all other philologists" (12).

I believe that we can expand on Lewis's insight, and that by looking beyond Tolkien's invented languages to his poetry and fiction—the "Lit" to his "Lang," so to speak—we can see a larger pattern emerge. As Richard West reported, "Professor Tolkien said himself that his medieval studies fertilized his imagination, that his typical response upon reading a medieval work was to desire not so much to make a philological or critical study of it as to write a modern work in the same tradition" (80).[2] Just as inventing his own languages gave Tolkien insights into language itself that most of his contemporaries lacked, so too his predilection not just for translating medieval works (*Beowulf*, *Sir Gawain*, *Pwyll Prince of Annwn*, *Sir Orfeo*)[3] but for writing new works in a variety of medieval genres (*The Fall of Arthur*, "Ides Ælfscýne," *The Lay of Sigurd*, "Imram") gave him insights into medieval literature not accessible to critics and authors who approached such works only from the outside, as museum specimens, fossils from an array of extinct genres. Over and over again, we find Tolkien writing new works in the mode and metre of *The Allit-*

erative Morte Arthure, in the language and style of Chaucer's *Canterbury Tales*, in the "Belle Dame sans Merci" perilous encounter mode of the Child Ballads. Taken individually, these new works seem mere curiosities: interesting in that they showed the vitality of their given genres—suddenly revealed to have only been in abeyance, sleeping but not dead—but not greatly significant to Tolkien's career as a creative writer, or to twentieth-century literature as a whole. But taken together, they show how Tolkien went beyond useful exercises or the creation of new works in medieval modes for their own sake: he used the insights thus gained to reproduce the appeal of medieval literature in his own modern works.

At the outset of our exploration, an obvious point to address is, if such a pattern underlies so much of Tolkien's work, why is its existence not a given of Tolkien studies? The reason, I believe, is threefold. First, many of the works that demonstrate the pattern are unfinished or unpublished or both, and hence have received relatively little attention to date (some are also written in languages other than modern English—i.e., the Old English of "Ides Ælfscýne" and the "Enigmata Saxonica," or the Middle English of "The Clerkes Compleinte" and "Doworst"—which naturally limits their audience). Second, many are works of poetry, not prose, and most interest in Tolkien has been in his prose work, not his poetry (even his alliterative poetry, at which he is admitted to excel). Third, most of these works are unconnected with Tolkien's *legendarium*, his Middle-earth cycle, which contains what are (rightly) considered his masterpieces; they more closely resemble the building blocks out of which those works were constructed, analogous to the "old stone" in his Allegory of the Tower (*MC* 7–8). We are too dazzled by the sun (*The Lord of the Rings*), the moon (*The Hobbit*), and the wandering planets (the ever-changing "Silmarillion" texts) to pay sufficient attention to the stars in all their constellations, however remarkable those reveal themselves to be once we turn our eyes to them.

First Category: Pastiche and Parody

So too with Tolkien's works in medieval modes: Once we turn our attention to them, we find they fall into a whole range or continuum, from pastiche and parody to wholly new works employing the metrical scheme or other distinctive attributes of a given genre or specific major medieval work. Sometimes the subject matter remains close to that of its progenitor, as in "The Lay of Aotrou and Itroun" or *The Fall of Arthur*; sometimes they are widely divergent, as in Ælfwine's "Annals." Of them all, none is closer to its original than "The Clerkes Compleinte,"[4] a clever pastiche of the "General Prologue" to *The Can-*

terbury Tales written in good Chaucerian Middle English. "The Clerkes Compleinte" shares not just the language and metre of Chaucer's Prologue but even some of the same lines,[5] while many others are direct reversals of Chaucer's originals. For example, "Whan that Aprill with his shoures soote / The droghte of March hath perced to the roote" becomes in Tolkien's poem "Whanne that Octobre mid his schoures derke / The erthe hath dreint, and wete windes cherke" (lines 1–2). Instead of Zephirus, the gentle West wind, we have Eurus, the sopping wet East wind (Chaucer line 5; Tolkien line 7); instead of gathering to travel to Canterbury in the south, "In al the North to Leedes done they wende ... the fairest toune of Yorkeschire" (lines 16–17). Similarly, "And smale foweles maken melodye / That slepen al the nyght with open eye" becomes "wrecche cattes youlen umbewhiles / That slepen nat but wandren on the tiles" (lines 9–10).

After thus closely paralleling Chaucer's text for the first twenty lines or so, Tolkien's diverges thereafter, so that rather than a description of how the pilgrims gather for their journey to Canterbury we get instead the mock-serious story of a hapless applicant to a university (Leeds) who fails miserably to gain admittance.

Closely associated with this both in the proximity of their medieval sources and their subject matter is the still-unpublished poem "Doworst,"[6] which takes its inspiration from *The Vision of Piers Plowman*. Tolkien's parody-poem is headed in Latin "Visio Petri Aratoris de Doworst" ("Vision of Peter [or Piers] Plowman about Do-Worst") to parallel the title of Langland's work, just as "Doworst" itself (no doubt deliberately) calls to mind the rubrics (or subtitles) given in many manuscripts to the latter sections of *Piers Plowman*: "Dowel" ("Do well," Passus VIII–XIV), "Dobet" ("Do better," Passus XV–XVIII), and "Dobest" ("Do best," Passus XIX–XX). In any case, unlike the first third of "The Clerkes Compleinte," in "Doworst" only one line (the first) closely mimics a specific line of the original, with Langland's "In a somer seson, whan softe was the sonne" becoming Tolkien's "In a summer season when sultry was ye sun"; thereafter follows a spirited scene, unfortunately soon cut short in our fragment, of dim-witted students ("lourdins [= stupid lazy louts] & lubbers ... wood in his wits was each wiȝt") coming to grief in their oral exams (or *vivas*).[7]

> The clamour of ye company was like ye cackle of hens
> till a bell rang brazenly—that abated their noise.
> They were summoned it seemed ...
> by four clerks very fell whom few could appease
> that should iudge them ungently ...

As we can see, the poem (or the fragment we have of it) is written in lively, almost colloquial, alliterative verse, with a strong tendency to use the same sound or letter on all three of the first of each line's four main beats. Tolkien's diction and spelling are also slightly more modernized here than in his Chaucerian piece, making his poem easily readable even to those unfamiliar with Middle English.

Two more parody poems gain their effect not from a don's-eye-view of university students[8] nor from spot-on mimicry of Middle English but from the adaptation of a very medieval tradition, the bestiary, into all-too-modern diction; the comedy here comes from that very juxtaposition. Published together under the omnibus title *Adventures in Unnatural History and Medieval Metres, being the Freaks of Fisiologus* (1927), these comprise "Fastitocalon," which long afterwards in heavily revised form[9] appeared in *The Adventures of Tom Bombadil* (1962), and "Iumbo, or Ye Kinde of Ye Oliphaunt," which, despite occasional assertions to the contrary, is not the same poem as the one titled "Oliphaunt" appearing in *The Adventures of Tom Bombadil* and *The Lord of the Rings*.[10] As the overarching name indicates, both "Fastitocalon" and "Iumbo" derive from the Bestiary tradition, specifically the popular Latin work ascribed to Physiologus ("The Naturalist"), an Anglicization of whose name (Fisiologus) Tolkien adopts for his pseudonym for both poems in their original Leeds publication.[11] In both Tolkien preserves the traditional two-part structure (*natura* and *significacio*) from the originals, with the first part describing the creature's supposed habits (e.g., Fastitocalon's floating on the surface and mimicking an island, or Iumbo's unfortunate addiction to mandragora), and the latter providing a tendentious moral.

Since both Old English and Middle English versions of the Whale poem survive—and it *is* definitely a whale, not a great turtle, in Tolkien's original 1927 text[12]—the question arises as to which was Tolkien's model. Tolkien himself stated that he took the actual title of his poem "Fastitocalon" from the Old English text (*Letters* 343),[13] but the full answer seems to be, typically with Tolkien, a little bit of both.[14] Metrically, however, Tolkien's poem resembles neither its progenitors nor indeed its companion piece, instead using a complex stanza (typically rhymed *aabccb.d.eed*, but occasionally *aabccb.d.eed.f.ggf*) ending in a variant of the bob-and-wheel typically associated with Middle English tail-rhyme romances. In fact, the poem which his seems to follow most closely in form is Chaucer's "Tale of Sir Topas," which seems to have been rather a favorite of Tolkien's (and which I have argued elsewhere [Rateliff 1982] was at least a partial inspiration for "Errantry").

By contrast, "Iumbo," as the second half of the overarching title suggests ("Adventure*s* [plural] in ... Medieval Metre*s* [plural]"), has an entirely different metrical system than its companion piece, and a much simpler stanza (although still more complex than its Middle English antecedent). Since the elephant-poem is absent from the Old English fragment, here we have only the Middle

English version to consider, and it quickly becomes evident that Tolkien adapted freely, trimming down the rather diffuse original into a more focused little tale.[15] Like "Fastitocalon," the language throughout is deliberately and thoroughly up-to-date; whereas the former made reference to margarine and picnics and jazz, here we find allusions to vacuum cleaners, pharmaceutics, and cocaine. Finally, as already noted, both poems end in a highly facetious, and egregiously inappropriate, moral, further mocking the incessant allegorizing of the original bestiary[16]:

> This mighty monster teaches us
>   That trespassing is dangerous,
>   And perils lurk in wait
>   For curious folk who peep in doors
>   Of other folks, or dance on floors
>   Too early or too late
>   with jazz;
> That too much grease is worse than none,
> To spare the margarine on bun
>   Content with what one has
>   on hand;
> That many noises loud and strong
> Are neither music nor a song
>   But only just a band.

Second Category: Adaptations in Medieval Metres

The four poems in the next category depart from the pastiche and parody we've discussed so far,[17] being much more serious and substantial works, in most cases running to hundreds or even thousands of lines. Each is clearly inspired by, and based upon, a specific medieval work and typically shares both form (metre) and content (subject matter) with its original. Yet none are simple re-tellings or translations of their models: these are highly original new works in long-extinct genres. Despite their medieval inspirations, all are written in modern English.

The first of these, "The Lay of Aotrou and Itroun" (written circa 1930; revised and published 1945), derives directly from the Breton Ballad "Aotrou Nann hag ar Gorrigan" ("Lord Nann and the Corrigan"), the most famous of Vicomte Hersart de la Villemarqué's *Barzaz-Breiz* (1839).[18] Yet while Tolkien follows the outlines of the original story, he vastly expands it: "The Lay of Aotrou and Itroun" is more than five times the length of the original (506 lines in Tolkien's version, versus about 85 in La Villemarqué's) and much more complex—indeed, Shippey notes that it's the longest poem Tolkien published in his lifetime (*Road* 280). Tolkien retains the metre of the original (four-beat couplets) but eliminates the occasional triplets that are such a distinctive feature of the old ballad and makes frequent use of alliteration (a feature altogether absent in La Villemarqué's original):

> ... winging bats
> their harbour sought, and owls and cats
> from hunting came with mournful cries,
> night-stalking near with needle-eyes—ll. 33–36 ["Aotrou" 254].

He also introduces line-breaks to create stanzas of variable length, but these serve a narrative, rather than metrical, function, marking pauses and shifts in the story. Perhaps most strikingly, he creates a variable refrain, a quatrain that appears at irregular intervals to punctuate the tale in increasingly ominous fashion. Most importantly, to an allusive and seemingly arbitrary tale of a perilous encounter Tolkien adds intentionality: his Lord Aotrou deliberately seeks out the fay, whereas the original's Lord Nann simply stumbles across her by mischance. The ballad vividly captures a single incident; Tolkien creates a plot to which that incident is the climax. In essence, Tolkien has transformed a Breton Ballad, the last remnant of old lore plucked from dying oral tradition a century before, into a full-fledged Breton lay,[19] like the actual surviving 13th century *Sir Orfeo* (which he both edited and translated)—which in turn coincidentally enough also survives both as a Breton lay (at 604 lines only slightly longer than "Aotrou") and in fragmentary ballad form (Child Ballad #19, "King Orfeo"). In the context of Tolkien's career, the chief impetus of which was to re-create the lost myths of England (or at least fashion a satisfactory fantasy analogue for them), the re-created Breton lay takes its place among what Shippey has called Tolkien's "asterisk texts" (*Road* 37, 311 ff): a reconstruction of a feigned "lost original" which may have never existed. Other examples include the poem "The Cat & The Fiddle: A Nursery Rhyme Undone and Its Scandalous Secret Unlocked" (1923)—better known as Frodo's song at Bree, reprinted in *The Adventures of Tom Bombadil* as poem #5, "The Man in the Moon Stayed Up Too Late"—which constructs a sixty-line framework (sixty-five in the *ATB* version) to explain the 5-line nursery rhyme "The Cow Jumped Over the Moon," now feigned to be the sole surviving stanza from the mythical original. And perhaps typifying this more than any other of Tolkien's works is "Sellic Spell" (published with his *Beowulf*, 2014), in which Tolkien re-creates the lost folktale believed to underlie *Beowulf* (cf. Klaeber xiii ff. and Anderson 142).

    If "The Lay of Aotrou and Itroun" demonstrates Tolkien's expansion of a medieval original upon his own highly distinctive lines (while still remaining true to its medieval sensibilities), then *The Fall of Arthur* [circa 1934], his (unfortunately unfinished) entry into the Matter of Britain, shows him combining two quite distinct sources into something distinctively Tolkienian. This retelling in alliterative verse of the story of Arthur's downfall and the ending of his realm is known to have been read with enthusiasm and approval by three of Tolkien's friends and fellow medievalists: E.V. Gordon, R.W. Chambers, and C.S. Lewis[20]—and rightly so, since even in its unfinished state it's an impressive and compelling work.

As noted by Christopher Tolkien in his commentary (*passim*, but see especially *Fall of Arthur* 79–84 & 116–122), Tolkien's poem is obviously closely modeled on *The Alliterative Morte Arthure*, sharing both its metre and, just as importantly, its distinctive treatment of Guinevere, in keeping with what is generally known as the "English" or "chronicle" tradition (stretching back through Laʒamon and Wace all the way to Geoffrey of Monmouth) regarding Arthur's queen: portraying her in a strikingly negative light for her betrayal of her husband[21]:

> lady ruthless,
> fair as fay-woman and fell-minded,
> in the world walking for the woe of men [*Fall of Arthur* III 54b–56].

The *Alliterative Morte* goes so far as to portray her as an active and willing participant (lines 3903–3918) in a bigamous (and possibly incestuous) marriage with Mordred when the treacherous prince, serving as Arthur's regent while the King is tied up on the continent warring against the Emperor Lucius, rebels against an absent Arthur. Furthermore, theirs is a longterm relationship, resulting in at least two children (note the use of the plural in 3550–3552, 3575–3576, 4320–4322).

Tolkien's affinity to the *Alliterative Morte* is not surprising, given its status as a key work in the 14th century West Midlands alliterative revival, which was part of Tolkien's special study as a medievalist (cf. his work on *Gawain* and *Pearl*).[22] But just as with his Eddic poems (see below), Tolkien didn't limit himself to one source and one tradition in *The Fall of Arthur*: instead, for his contribution to the Arthurian legend Tolkien has combined sources from two entirely distinct traditions.[23] In addition to the alliterative tradition focused on Arthur's wars, characterized by a negative portrayal of the queen and featuring Gawain as the king's greatest champion, he has incorporated major elements from *The Stanzaic Morte Arthur*, most notably in assigning a major role to Lancelot, who is merely a notable second-tier knight in the *Alliterative Morte* (cf. passing mention of his death among a dozen or so of Arthur's knights in lines 4262–4267).

In essence, Tolkien has converted a version of the story as found in *The Stanzaic Morte Arthur*, which concentrates largely on the tragic love story of

Lancelot and Guinevere, back into the alliterative mode and stern mood of *The Alliterative Morte Arthur* and successfully melded the two into a new and striking whole. This blending also incorporates elements of other works: Christopher Tolkien notes influence at various points from Geoffrey of Monmouth's Latin *Historia Regum Britainniae* (73ff), the Old French *Mort Artu* (199), Laȝamon's early Middle English *Brut* (146–148), Malory's *Morte d'Arthur* (84ff & *passim*). And, given Tolkien's thorough knowledge of medieval literature, other related sources (e.g., Wace's Anglo-Norman *Roman de Brut*) would no doubt repay scrutiny as well as possible sources for specific detail.

It is important to note, however, that though Tolkien is using the alliterative metre of the *Alliterative Morte* and has derived much of his characterization jointly from that work and the *Stanzaic Morte*, his is a new version of the Arthurian legend that incorporates elements from extant works but goes beyond them, adding wholly original elements (most strikingly Arthur's preemptive strike against the Saxon raiders' homelands and the knot of love and loyalty that binds Lancelot from coming to Arthur's aid)[24] and offering a strikingly original new version of the Arthur legend.

This combination of sources is even more evident in *The Lay of Sigurd* and *The Lay of Gudrún*, also dating from the 1930s (published in *Legend* [2009]). Here we are fortunate enough to have Tolkien's own comment on at least one of his motives in writing these poems, in his 1967 letter to W.H. Auden: "I hope to send you, if I can lay my hands on it ... a thing I did many years ago when trying to learn the art of writing alliterative poetry: an attempt to unify the lays about the Völsungs from the Elder Edda, written in the old eight-line fornyrðislag stanza" (*Letters* 379).

Here Tolkien is explicit that one of his reasons for writing this work was his desire to "learn the art," not just of writing alliterative poetry but specifically of mastering the *fornyrðislag* metre of the *Elder Edda*—the best evidence we have for my overall thesis of his desire to go "inside" medieval literature. But in addition, he confesses to an antiquarian aim ("to unify the lays about the *Völsungs* from the *Elder Edda*"). And, we must not overlook an artistic, although unspoken, one: a mere desire to master a tricky metre would not lead to the over four thousand lines of polished, powerful storytelling we have here.[25]

Tolkien's (considerable) achievement with these lays is matter enough for its own essay, or no doubt many essays, but for our purposes a quick look at how he constructed his *Lay* will be enough. His main source, obviously, was the *Elder Edda* itself, which he followed closely in story, tone, and format. For the huge gap in the *Edda's* version of the Sigurd story caused by missing pages from the surviving manuscript (the Codex Regius's so-called *Great*

Lacuna; cf. *Legend* 233), he had recourse to the *Völsunga Saga* (itself originally based on the now-missing material), rendering elements of the saga-story back into *Edda*-style poetry. But his work goes far beyond mere back-formation: he transforms the material in the process, working to resolve paradoxes and contradictions in the original (highly heterogeneous) legends. He also draws from at least one other source, the Middle High German epic *The Nibelungenlied*, from which he borrows a few touches here and there. Other elements are wholly original, including the frame for the entire tale, which creates a believable rationale explaining Odin's actions and provides a unifying narrative element for the whole—Tolkien had, after all, in his letter to Auden stated that his intention was to "unify" the Völsung material from the *Edda*. The end result is not so much a re-creation of the "lost" Sigurd story that once occupied those missing pages of the *Edda* manuscript as it is Tolkien's own contribution to that tradition: not a restoration of "The Long Lay of Sigurd" but, to give it Tolkien's own (sub)title, its proffered replacement by his own "The Longest Lay of Sigurd" (*Legend* 234).

Finally, with "Imram," we have what at first looks like another restoration, but soon turns out to be a new contribution to a familiar medieval legend: the Voyage of St. Brendan to the Earthly Paradise. Also known as "The Death of St. Brendan" (circa 1945; publ. 1955), at only 132 lines (140 in "The Notion Club Papers" version) this is the briefest of the works we're considering in this section. Unusually, instead of recasting a new version of the legend, Tolkien has crafted a coda to it, set in that brief final section of the original *Navigatio Sancti Brendani* (Barron and Burgess 64) where Brendan finally returns home to his own abbey, tells the monks there about the marvels he had encountered, and dies. In this sense "Imram" is very much the reverse of Tolkien's procedure in "The Lay of Aotrou and Itroun," where he expanded out the kernel of a sparse ballad account into a full story, recovering an old tale; here, he has pared away all but the bare essentials, focusing all Brendan's adventures down to three encounters.[26]

Paul Kocher long ago (1972), in the first and still most insightful critique of "Imram" (205), asserted that almost all the elements of Tolkien's poem could be found in the original *Navigatio*, but closer scrutiny shows that the "almost" is significant. Certainly the Tree of White Birds corresponds fairly well to the Paradise of Birds described in Sections IX and XI of *Navigatio* (34, 36), and the great Black Mountain spewing smoke and fire has close affinities to the Hell-Mountain of Section XXIV (56). But the third and final encounter, that with the Star, is wholly Tolkien's own, as is his description of Brendan leaving the round earth behind, sailing on the "unseen bridge" that is the Lost Road to reach "the last land," the "coasts that no man knows" that lie beyond (*Sauron* 298).[27] Any medieval reader familiar with the Brendan legend in all its many forms, from the 8th-century Latin original through Caxton's *Golden Legend*, would have been puzzled mightily both by the absence of any miracles in Tolkien's account and by the form these elements took in Tolkien's poem: that the Black Mountain—better known in Tolkien's *legendarium* under its later name, the Meneltarma— stands "on the foundered land / where the kings of kings lie low" (that is, Númenor), or that the beings who appear as white birds in the Tree are here "neither ... man nor angel ... but maybe ... a third / fair kindred ... [which] yet lingers / beyond the foundered land" ("Imram," lines 91–94 [298])—that is, the elves of Tol Eressëa.[28] And most of all the final stanzas, where Brendan turns evasive about the lands beyond, bend away from the traditional accounts into Tolkien's distinctive cosmology of Eärendil (the Star) and the Straight (or Lost) Road.

Here, then, we have reached a transitional point in Tolkien's exploration of medieval genres, where the medieval model and his own *legendarium* begin to seamlessly merge. For this poem is both an *imrám* in its own right, like *The Voyage of Bran* (*Imram Brain*), *and* a part of Tolkien's *legendarium*. Here he uses the Brendan legend as an artifact from the past to bolster *his own imram*, "The Story of Ælfwine" (*Lost Tales II*, *Lost Road*). Bridging the gap between the historical worlds of mid-twentieth century Britain ("Notion Club Papers," *Lost Road*), early tenth-century England, and sixth-century Ireland, on the one hand, and the realm of legend and myth, on the other,[29] "Ælfwine" in turn ties into and resonates with a still older *imrám* ("older" both in terms of Tolkien's career and the internal chronology of the *legendarium*): The Voyage of Eärendil. Thus in "Imram" the old legend is transmuted to serve Tolkien's own ends and thoroughly co-opted into his new mythology.

Third Category: New Wine in Old Bottles

Given the length of this paper already, here we'll just briefly mention some typical examples of the final category, what I call Tolkien placing new wine in old bottles, such as "Enigmata Saxonica Nuper Inventa Duo" (1923). The title itself is a pleasingly ingenious Tolkienian pun, meaning literally "Two Newly Discovered Saxon Riddles," but with a secondary meaning that could be translated as "Two *Newly Written* Saxon Riddles." Here he recasts two nursery rhymes into the form of *Exeter Book* riddles, creating a merged form that clearly belongs to both traditions at once. Both are not only in alliterative verse but actually written in Old English; indeed, the second of the two, "Hild Hunecan," is both rhymed *and* alliterative. Also of note in this context is Tolkien's poem "The Nameless Land" (written 1924; published 1927), written in the difficult *Pearl* stanza and, like *Pearl*, describing a glimpse of a fair otherworld into which entry is forbidden to mortals.[30] And one could hardly ask for a better example of a medieval form wholly co-opted by Tolkien for use in his new mythology than Ælfwine's "Annals," where the form (chronicle), language (Old English), and format of *The Anglo-Saxon Chronicle* are used to tell events in Tolkien's invented history; not only does Tolkien write these in good literary Old English, but he casts his entries into the same format, starting each year's entry with *Her* ("Here"):

[AN CCCCLU.] Her Hengest 7 Horsa fuhton wiþ Wyrt georne þam cyninge ... 7 his broþur Horsan man ofslog. 7 æfter þam Hengest feng ^{to} rice, 7 Æsc his sunu.
—*The Anglo-Saxon Chronicle* [A, the Parker Ms], Earle and Plummer I:12

The Year 455: Here Hengest and Horsa fought with Vortigern the King ... and his brother Horsa was slain, and after that Hengest took the kingship and Ash his son.
—*The Anglo-Saxon Chronicle,* Ingram 26

MMD. Hér þurh searucræftas aþóhton and beworhton þá Nold-ielfe gimmas missenlice, 7 Féanor Noldena hláford worhte þá Silmarillas, þæt wǽron Eor-clanstánas.
    Year of the Valar 2500: Here through cunning craft the Noldor elves devised and created [a-thought and be-worked] many gems, & Fëanor the Noldor lord wrought the Silmarils, that were Holy/precious Stones.
—Ælfwine's "Annals of Valinor" (*Shaping* 282)

But the finest example of Tolkien's absorption of an old genre to create a new thing comes in the remarkable poem "Ides Ælfscýne," one of the *Songs for the Philologists* (?circa 1924–1925; 1936). This takes the form of a Child ballad and encapsulates in its purest form a theme that greatly attracted Tolkien and which he used over and over again in his works: the Perilous Encounter between a mortal man and a fay-woman.[31] Had such a ballad really existed when Francis Child was compiling his five-volume set, he probably would have set it alongside either "Clerk Colvill" (ballad #42), which itself shares strong affinities with "The Lay of Aotrou and Itroun," or the even better-known "Thomas Rymer" (ballad #37). Thanks to Shippey's inclusion of "Ides Ælf-scýne" in *Road* (356 [text] and 357 [prose translation]), this is probably the best-known of Tolkien's poems in Old English, but it is badly in need of a high-quality verse translation if it is ever to receive the acclaim it deserves.

Final: Subsumed into a New Context

Finally, we have Tolkien putting what he'd learned from his close study of medieval genres to work. This took many forms, from writing alliterative verse for the Rohirrim that strictly follows the (reconstructed) rules any Mercian poet would have been expected to adhere to a dozen centuries before (something which Tolkien had been practicing for two decades and more by that point in his career), to appending Anglo-Saxon-style chronicles to the "Silmarillion" (as "The Annals of Valinor" and "The Annals of Beleriand") and even, in modified form, to *The Lord of the Rings* as well (under the rubric "Tale [or Tally] of Years"). Sometimes the influence shows in small ways, like passing grace notes that link his world back to our medieval past—as when he deliberately echoes lines from "The Wanderer" in a song of Rohan, or revives an old saying from the time of *Sir Gawain and the Green Knight* as a hobbit proverb ("third time pays for all"). Sometimes the influence is massive, as with *Beowulf* (which Tolkien translated not once but twice, into both alliterative verse and prose)—so massive, in fact, that Tolkien himself, who rarely acknowledged his borrowings, singles out *Beowulf* alongside *The Silmarillion* as his two main sources for *The Hobbit* (*Letters* 31); Bonniejean Christensen devoted a whole dissertation to exploring *Beowulf*'s impact on *The Hobbit*, the most extensive of many subsequent studies exploring the same topic. The influence may be remote, wholly subsumed into its new context—the legends of the Tuatha dé Danaan, in works such as the *Cath Maige Tuired* (*The [Second] Battle of Mag Tuired*), were clearly Tolkien's primary source for the elves of the First Age, whereas the elusive otherworld of *The Mabinogi* seems to have provided the main model for the older and wiser elves of the Third Age. And just as Tolkien often mixed sources within a single tradition to great effect in works like *The Lay of Sigurd* and, I suspect, *The Fall of Arthur*, in his *legendarium* he could mix works from different traditions, as when the Finnish tale of Kullervo from *The Kalevala* gets blended with the Völsung legend to create The Tale of Túrin, one of the three "Great Tales" that formed the core of *The Silmarillion*.[32]

Conclusion

In the end, Tolkien's body of work is crowded with too many works (of which we have by no means surveyed all) written in medieval genres for it to have been accidental or coincidental. Tolkien's returning to medieval genres time and time again was not exactly *methodical*—a phrase that I would never apply to Tolkien—so much as *persistent*; it gave him an immersion that may be unparalleled in its depth and breadth. But if the bones lie nearer to the surface in the works I've focused on, which for the most part lie outside his *legendarium*, these merely point the way to the similar, and massive, influence from such works that lies more deeply hidden in the *legendarium*: Tolkien's work is so suffused with medieval borrowings that today it serves as most readers' portal into medieval literature, making the real thing more familiar and accessible to modern readers. To return to the Allegory of the Tower: by learning the craft of creating new stones in the shape and style of the damaged or lost original blocks, Tolkien enabled himself to build his own Tower, offering an accessible and appealing view out onto a long-neglected sea.

NOTES

1. This and the following quotations in this paragraph are taken from the September 3, 1973, *Times* obituary of Tolkien. Although unsigned, this piece has long been believed to have been written by Lewis (cf. Carpenter 133). That ascription was challenged in the early 1990s by Kathryn Lindskoog as part of her general assault on Lewis's posthumous publications (cf. Tim Powers, "J.R.R. Tolkien Obituary Not By Lewis After All," *The Lewis Legacy* 57:1, and *Sleuthing C.S. Lewis* 117–118), but its authenticity was confirmed by Lewis scholar Stephen Schofield, who discovered that the *Times'* records showed "the obituary of J.R.R. Tolkien was written by C.S. Lewis, who retained copyright in the text" (Ralph Nodder, Syndication Manager, Times Newspapers Ltd., qtd. *The Canadian C.S. Lewis Journal* 83 [Summer 1993]: 9). In addition, Lewis is known to have written such an obituary: I am indebted to Walter Hooper, who received this information from Edith Tolkien, who had been told it by Lewis himself; my thanks also to Douglas Anderson, for letting me know that Priscilla Tolkien also confirms this anecdote. Internal evidence supports the ascription as well: the obituary was clearly written by someone who knew Tolkien well, including details of biography and his early writings on the *legendarium* not at that time public, and particularly well-informed about Tolkien's behind-the-scenes work at Oxford, even including a list of late-period fellow Inklings. Perhaps most telling, the obituary's author at one point seems to paraphrase one of Lewis's letters, describing the relationship between *The Hobbit* and *The Silmarillion* in almost exactly the same language that Lewis had used in a 1958 letter (unpublished at the time the obituary appeared, since it is not included in the 1966 edition of *Letters of C.S. Lewis*) to Thomas Howard:

"*The Hobbit* is merely *a fragment of his myth, detached, and adapted for children*" [CSL to Thomas Howard, October 14, 1958, *Collected Letters* Vol. III, 981; emphasis mine].

"*The Hobbit* (1937) was *in origin a fragment from this cycle* ['the private mythology'] *adapted for juvenile tastes*" [*Times* obituary (Salu 14); emphasis mine].

2. West here is paraphrasing "[a] remark made to an audience at Oxford who had come to hear Tolkien lecture on philology and instead heard him recite a poem of his own composition" (92–3n10); his source for this comment was Eugene Vinaver, who had been present at the event in question. Unfortunately we cannot identify the occasion, nor the poem or presumptive topic of the lecture.

3. Tolkien's translations of *Sir Orfeo* and *Sir Gawain and the Green Knight* were published in 1975. His two translations of *Beowulf* (an earlier incomplete one in alliterative verse dating from the Leeds period [1920–25] and a later complete translation in prose probably dating from the early thirties) were published in 2014. His incomplete translation of the First Branch of the *Mabinogi* unfortunately remains unpublished.

4. This sixty-line poem was published (pseudonymously) at Leeds in 1922 and rediscovered by Anders Stenström in 1984, who published it in *Arda* IV (1988). This re-publication was accompanied by an insightful commentary by T.A. Shippey (who praises the excellence of its Middle English diction [3–7]), as well as a translation into modern English. Its provenance was subsequently confirmed by Christopher Tolkien, who provided a calligraphic manuscript copy that was reproduced in *Arda* VI (1990).

Tolkien of course knew Chaucer well, having worked for years on an abortive student's edition of Chaucer ("the *Clarendon Chaucer*") in collaboration with George Gordon (cf. *Guide* 153–6) as well as writing an extensive piece on Chaucer's use of dialect. He twice performed a Canterbury tale, from memory, in the original Middle English, at the Summer Diversions in Oxford organized by the poet laureate, John Masefield, in collaboration with Tolkien's friend, fellow Inkling, and fellow Chaucer scholar Nevill Coghill: "The Nun's Priest's Tale" in 1938 and "The Reeve's Tale" in 1939, preparing his own edition of the latter for the occasion. This edition has since been reprinted in *Tolkien Studies* 5 (2008): 173–183; the same issue includes a reprint of Tolkien's lengthy 1934 essay (delivered as a lecture in 1931), "Chaucer as Philologist: *The Reeve's Tale*" (109–170).

5. Lines 11 ("So priketh hem nature in her corages"), 15 ("And specially from every schires ende"), and 19a ("Bifel that in that sesoun") are exact matches both as to placement within the poem and wording within the lines.

6. Most of what little is known about "Doworst" comes from Douglas A. Anderson's article on Tolkien's friendship with R.W. Chambers (*Tolkien Studies* 3 [2006]: 137–147; see particularly 139, 144n6). Tolkien gave Chambers a calligraphic manuscript copy of the poem on December 21st 1933, which Chambers thought highly enough of to have bound; this manuscript subsequently passed (1942) to Chamber's colleague Winifred Husbands, who in turn (1957) left it to Professor Arthur Brown; its whereabouts since Brown's death in 1979 are unknown. However, we have the first twenty lines from the manuscript's first page reproduced in facsimile in the Australian fanzine *A Elbereth Gilthoniel* 2 (June/July 1978): 3. I am grateful to Matt Blessing of the Marquette Archives and to Gary Hunnewell for helping me to locate a copy of the latter.

Tolkien's familiarity with Langland is less well-documented than is the case for Chaucer, but in addition to "Doworst" it should be noted that two excerpts from *Piers Plowman* (totaling 436 lines) were included in Sisam's *Fourteenth Century Verse and Prose* (76–93), to which Tolkien provided a glossary so detailed that it was sometimes printed as an independent work—*A Middle English Vocabulary* (1922).

7. A similar work gathering together student's blunders for the amusement of their teachers is *Some Thoughts on Examinations, by An Examiner.* This little booklet is cited to anonymous in its University College, London form; I am indebted to Douglas Anderson for the information that the author was probably Walter Raleigh (1861–1922), who had been Professor of English Literature at Oxford University when Tolkien was an undergraduate there and during his *Oxford English Dictionary* days. The pamphlet was the first publication from the Elizabethan hand-press used by A.H. Smith of University College, London to teach printing to his students; their next release for the following semester's class being the renowned *Songs for the Philologists* (1936). Tolkien was well aware of *Some Thoughts*, since he quotes from it in a 1941 letter to R.W. Chapman (*Letters* 57), the relevant passage he alludes to reading as follows in the original:

The brilliant man who did not know and the learned man who did not think met in the Second Class and disliked each other. The poet sat in the Third and laughed.

8. An additional piece that might be associated with this group is Tolkien's poem "Knocking at the Door," as indicated by its original subtitle: "Lines Induced by Sensations when Waiting for an Answer at the Door of an Exalted Academic Person." These academic overtones were removed from the later version of the poem published as "The Mewlips" in *The Adventures of Tom Bombadil* (*ATB* #9).

9. "heavily revised form": the *ATB* version is reduced from seven stanzas to three and from seventy-eight lines to just forty-four. Of these, only two lines (the fourteenth and sixteenth of the *ATB* text, corresponding to the fifty-third and fifty-fifth in the older text) remain unchanged between the two versions, with fragments of perhaps another dozen lines surviving into the later version as well. Despite the loss of its first half and major recasting of the remnant, the *ATB* text is recognizably a descendent of the Leeds version, even retaining

the complex bob-and-wheel form of a tail-rhyme romance. And, of course, in the final poem Fastitocalon himself (or Himself, since Tolkien always refers to him in Upper Case in both versions) is unambiguously a great turtle, not a whale as in the original.

10. Despite their shared topic, "Iumbo" is a wholly different poem from the later better-known "Oliphaunt" of *The Lord of the Rings* (*TT* IV, iii, 254–5, c. April 1944) and *The Adventures of Tom Bombadil*: the two Oliphaunt poems have not a single line in common and are written in completely different metres and rhyme schemes.

The original "Iumbo" has nine stanzas and a total of eighty-three four-beat lines; "Oliphaunt" has twenty-two two-beat lines in a single stanza. Whereas the stanzas in "Iumbo" rhyme *abab.b.cbcc* and make playful use of heavy but erratic alliteration, "Oliphaunt" has short simple lines rhyming *aabbccdd*&c (which, it might be noted, is the rhyme scheme of the Middle English original). Finally, "Iumbo" uses a deliberately elaborate polysyllabic vocabulary (pendulous, unmasticated, repartee, Brobdingnagian), while "Oliphaunt" eschews words of more than two syllables (the sole exception being *oliphaunt* itself) and shows a decided preference for words of a single syllable; its first eight lines are made up entirely of monosyllabic words, and only ten bi-syllabic exceptions dot the remaining lines (or, to put it another way, eighty-four of the poem's ninety-six words are monosyllabic).

11. Both Old English and Middle English versions of this bestiary survive: the Old English in a fragment of 179 alliterative lines covering three creatures (The Panther, The Whale, and The Partridge) preserved in the Exeter Book and the Middle English in a single manuscript of just over six hundred lines rhyming in simple couplets describing thirteen creatures, including both the Whale and the Elephant. The popular Latin version from which both ultimately derive (itself translated in turn from a Greek original) traditionally includes forty-nine creatures, according to Cook (*The Old English Physiologus* [1921] iii); however, the translation by Curley (*Physiologus: A Medieval Book of Nature Lore* [1979]) includes fifty-one chapters, of which "On The Elephant" is Chapter XX (29–32) and "On the Whale, that is, the Aspidoceleon" Chapter XXXI (45–46).

12. Cf. its "vast and blubbery back" (line 38) and the mentions in stanza one of being rendered down for (whale)-oil, the fate of most of the world's whales over the nineteenth and early twentieth century. The change from whale to turtle may suggest the influence of a theory advanced by A. S. Cook that the creature was originally thought of as a sort of serpent (hence the name, "asp-turtle"), and only became a whale in later bestiary tradition (Cook, *The Old English Elene* lxxiii–lxxxv; cited by Curley 83).

13. "not ... my own invention entirely but a reduced and rewritten form ... of an item in old 'bestiaries' ... I took [the name] from a fragment of an Anglo-Saxon bestiary that has survived." (*Letters* 343).

14. For example, this particular bestiary poem falls into two parts, one about the creature's luring prey into his jaws with a tantalizing smell (muddled allusions to ambergris, perhaps?) and the other about his sometimes being mistaken for an island when floating on the surface. The Old English text, following the Latin original (cf. Curley 45–46), first describes the treacherous mock-island and then the fish-lure. By contrast, like the Middle English version, Tolkien's 1927 text puts the allurement of its fellow fish first (although changing it so that his Fastitocalon sings rather than attracts underwater prey by scent, a nice adaptation of whalesong to sinister purpose), and its mimicking an island second—perhaps simply because this makes for a more dramatic sequence. In his 1962 revision he eliminates the first half entirely, to the poem's great improvement.

15. For example, he ignores the original's rather salacious concern with elephant conception—not surprising, perhaps, for Tolkien, who is so shy on the topic that he actually censored "The Reeve's Tale" in the version he delivered in 1939. He also drops its explicitly allegorical conclusion in favor of a more rambunctious account of an elephant drugged up on mandragora going on a rampage like a cocaine fiend, with the inevitable (and literal) crash to follow. He does, however, preserve the two-part structure (*natura* and *significacio*) from

his original, as he had in "Fastitocalon" (where, indeed, the moral survives, although in much reduced and agreeably pithy form, all the way into the 1962 version).

16. Before leaving the bestiary poems, we might note that almost twenty years later, "Iumbo"'s replacement, "Oliphaunt," completely rejected the bestiary format and instead took the form of an entirely different Old English genre: the riddle, adopting the first-person tone of actual surviving riddles from the *Exeter Book* (that it answers its own question is not a disqualification, since this is also a feature of some genuine surviving riddles). Also, both "Oliphaunt" and the revised "Fastitocalon" have been incorporated into Middle-earth, acclimatized through the addition of a few significant details.

Finally, Tolkien is known to have written two more bestiary poems: "Reginhardus, the Fox" and "Monoceros, the Unicorn" (cognate with Chapters XVIII and XXXVI of the Latin *Physiologus*), both of which remain unpublished; cf. *J.R.R. Tolkien: A Descriptive Bibliography*, entry C20, 346, and *Guide*, 296. I am grateful to Merlin de Tardo for drawing these to my attention.

17. Similar in inspiration and tone is "The Battle of Eastern Fields," Tolkien's first known published poem (1911), which I omit here only because it is based upon Thomas Babington Macaulay's *Lays of Ancient Rome* (1842) rather than a true medieval source. Nevertheless this pastiche-parody of Macaulay's attempts to re-create the lost lays of pre–Imperial Rome (in itself a very Tolkienian enterprise and possible model for his own work along similar lines a century later), published when Tolkien was not yet twenty, shows affinities with his pastiche/parodies of real medieval works, showing how far back this impulse lay in his career.

18. This source was first noted by Tolkien scholar Rhona Beare some thirty years ago. "Lord Nann" was reasonably well-known in English, probably because it was included by Keightley in *The Fairy Mythology* (1850), 433–436, to represent Breton lore; it also appears in Tom Taylor's *Ballads and Songs of Brittany* (1865), 8–14. The story was also retold by Lewis Spence in *Legends & Romances of Brittany* (1917), 57–59, complete with illustration of Nann encountering a very classical-looking Korrigan. Tolkien, who owned a copy of the 1846 edition of *Barzaz-Breiz* in the original Breton, would have been aware of the controversy over whether La Villemarqué's texts represented authentic medieval tradition or were modern pastiches concocted by La Villemarqué himself.

19. That Tolkien had recast the ballad into a Breton *lai* was first noted in passing by Shippey in the original 1982 edition of *The Road to Middle-earth* (182). This idea was picked up by Jessica Yates in her pioneering essay "The Source of 'The Lay of Aotrou and Itroun,'" where she notes that Tolkien's piece is in the metre of a Breton lay (69)—something which might also account for his eliminating the ballad's triplets in favor of octosyllabic couplets. Yates (like Shippey) also stresses that Tolkien adds a good number of explicitly Christian elements to the poem, rather unusually for him, given his usual extreme reticence in his work about matters of faith. [See in this volume Larsen, "Alone."—Eds.]

20. We know of Gordon's reaction through Carpenter's biography (Carpenter 168); Chamber's praise is quoted both by Carpenter (ibid.) and in Christopher Tolkien's recent edition of *The Fall of Arthur* (10); Lewis's is revealed by his statement in his essay "The Alliterative Meter." In the opening paragraph of this piece, Lewis states his hope that "Professor Tolkien will soon, I hope, be ready to publish an alliterative poem" (119). Thanks to Dimitra Fimi, I can now confirm that Lewis's statement goes back to the original publication of his essay in the undergraduate magazine *Lysistrata* [1935], except that there the wording was slightly different: "Professor Tolkien will soon, I hope, be ready to publish an *important* alliterative poem" (Lewis, "Metrical Suggestion" 13; emphasis mine).

Asked by Walter Hooper to identify the poem in question, Tolkien replied that it was *The Fall of Arthur*:

Professor Tolkien tells me that Lewis was probably referring to his poem, "The Fall of Arthur," which has never been completed or published. Though Professor Tolkien's alliterative poem, "The Homecoming of Beorhtnoth Beorhthelm's Son," was in existence when Lewis wrote this essay, Professor Tolkien does not recall showing it to him before it was revised and published in *Essays and Studies*, vol. VI, new series (1953), pp. 1–18 [Lewis, *Selected Literary Essays* 15].

Even if we were to assume Tolkien was mistaken about which specific poem Lewis is referring to here, his statement to Hooper is still good proof that he did show *The Fall of Arthur* to Lewis at some point, just as Lewis's stated desire to soon see it in print indicates his admiration for Tolkien's poem.

21. The only other fairly well-known Arthurian tale to portray Guinevere in such a negative light is the relatively minor tail-rhyme romance *Sir Launfal*, written by Thomas Chestre, circa 1420.

22. JRRT to HM Co., June 30th 1955: "Anglo-Saxon and *Western Middle English and alliterative verse have been ... my main professional sphere* ... I write alliterative verse with pleasure, though I have published little beyond the fragments in *The Lord of the Rings*, except 'The Homecoming of Beorhtnoth' ... I still hope to finish a long poem on *The Fall of Arthur* in the same measure." (*Letters* 218–219; emphasis mine).

23. In this he was following the example of Sir Thomas Malory, who had similarly drawn in his *Le Morte d'Arthur* on the same two primary sources; cf. Christopher Tolkien's commentary (84–85, 94, 111).

24. Even more original, had he completed it, would be the final section of the work focusing on Arthur's departure to Avalon and Lancelot's attempts to find out his ultimate fate therein; as it is, this striking emphasis exists only in elusive outlines and notes.

25. "over four thousand lines": 339 stanzas (2712 lines) + 166 stanzas (1328 lines) = 4040 lines total.

26. Amusingly enough, one of the more striking encounters Tolkien omits is the monks' landing on the whale-island Fastitocalon, here called "Jasconius" (Section X, 35). A great whale had, of course, played a small but significant role in another of Tolkien's works many years before, in *Roverandom* (1925–27), where the ancient whale Uin carries the title character within sight of Fairyland (Eldamar) (73–74).

27. Kocher considers the Star analogous to the heavenly light that illuminates the Earthly Paradise (211), but this is problematic, not least because we are told in the *Navigatio* (Sections I and XXVIII, 26 and 63) this light is Christ himself, whereas Brendan's light in "Imram" is not a part of the undying lands but a sort of sentinel at the edge of the world ("at the parting of the ways / a light on the edge of the Outer Night/ beyond the Door of Days" [*Sauron* 298]) marking the division between mortal lands and what lies beyond, positioned where the Lost Road leaves the round earth behind—in fact, Eärendil himself.

28. In the original *Navigatio*, they identify themselves as angels assigned to serve Lucifer who "fell" because of loyalty to a bad master. Given the old tradition (or rather, *one of* the old traditions) of the elves' origins as lukewarm angels, it is perhaps significant that their description in the *Navigatio* could equally well be a description of one of Lewis's *eldils*, or one of the disembodied Eldar of Tolkien's later mythological writings.

29. Note that in the discussion that follows the poem's presentation to the Notion Club (*Sauron* 261, 264–5), its members specifically comment on how the Tree and Volcano derive from the original *Navigatio* but point out the changes made to them and also that some elements of the poem seem wholly new, such as "your Volcano is not a hell-smithy, but apparently a last peak of some Atlantis," the white birds being neither human nor angels but "a third *fair* race," and especially "that bit about the 'round world' and the 'old road' ... where did you get that from?" One character specifically cites both "the *Navigatio Sancti Brendani*"—i.e., the original Latin version of the legend—and "that early Anglo-French thing, Benedeit's *Vita*." This latter, the earliest adaptation of the Brendan legend into another language, appears in Barron and Burgess's book as "The Anglo-Norman Version" [circa 1120], tr. Glyn S. Burgess, 65–102. They do not make any mention of Brendan's third and most elusive memory, the Star.

30. Perhaps significantly, just as the bestiary whale celebrated in "Fastitocalon" appears in the Brendan legend, so too is Brendan himself mentioned in "The Nameless Land" poem as one of the nameless narrator's precursors:

> Such loveliness to look upon
> Nor Bran nor Brendan ever won ...
> Than Tír na nÓg more fair and free,
> Than Paradise more faint and far ...
> —ll. 44–5, 49–50 [Lost Road 99].

31. The most significant example of this motif is in Beren's meeting with Lúthien, the core event in *The Silmarillion* (and, arguably, of the entire *legendarium*) and of such importance to Tolkien personally that he had a reference to it carved on his tombstone. Other examples include "The Lay of Aotrou and Itroun," two more from *Songs for the Philologists*, "Ofer Wídne Gársecg" ("The Mermaid" 14–15) and "Ólafur Liljurós" (*SP* 5), perhaps "Shadow Bride" (*ATB* #13), the story of Mithrellas and Imrazôr the Númenórean (*UT* 248, 316), the story of Tuor and Idril, and the story of Aragorn and Arwen, among others.

32. The other two being the story of Beren and Lúthien (see above) and the story of Tuor and the Fall of Gondolin.

WORKS CONSULTED

All references to unpublished Tolkien material refer to the Tolkien Manuscripts in the Bodleian Library's Department of Western Manuscripts, Modern Papers, Tolkien Papers.

The Alliterative Morte Arthure. Benson 113–238.
Anderson, Douglas A. "R.W. Chambers and *The Hobbit.*" *Tolkien Studies* 3 (2006): 137–147.
The Anglo-Saxon Chronicle. Tr. Rev. James Ingram. Everyman's Library 624. London: Dent, 1912; 1938 printing.
[*The Anglo-Saxon Chronicle.*] *Two of the Saxon Chronicles Parallel, with Supplementary Extracts from the Others.* Ed. John Earle, rev. Charles Plummer. Oxford: Clarendon Press, 1892.
Benson, Larry D., ed. *King Arthur's Death.* Indianapolis and New York: Bobbs-Merrill, 1974.
Beowulf and *The Fight at Finnsburg.* Ed. Fr. Klaeber. 3rd ed. Boston: Heath, 1950.
Cath Maige Tuired. Tr. Elizabeth A. Gray. Dublin: Irish Texts Society, 1983.
Chaucer, Geoffrey. *The Canterbury Tales. The Complete Poetry and Prose of Geoffrey Chaucer.* Ed. John H. Fisher. 2d ed. Fort Worth: Harcourt Brace, 1989. See "The General Prologue" (9–24); "The Reeve's Tale" (69–76); and "The Tale of Sir Topas" (247–251).
Chestre, Thomas. *Sir Launfal.* Ed. A.J. Bliss. London: Nelson, 1960.
Child, F.J. *English and Scottish Popular Ballads.* Ed. Helen Child Sargent and George Lyman Kittredge. Boston and New York: Houghton Mifflin, 1904.
[*Elder Edda*] *Poems of the Elder Edda.* Tr. Patricia Terry. Rev. ed. Philadelphia: University of Pennsylvania Press, 1990.
Hammond, Wayne G., with the assistance of Douglas A. Anderson. *J.R.R. Tolkien: A Descriptive Bibliography.* Winchester: St. Paul's Bibliographies and New Castle, DE: Oak Knoll Books, 1993.
The Kalevala, or, Poems of the Kaleva District. Compiled Elias Lönnrot. Tr. Francis Peabody Magoun, Jr. Cambridge, MA: Harvard University Press, 1963. For the Tale of Kullervo, see Runos 31–36.
Keightley, Thomas. *The Fairy Mythology.* London: H.G. Bohn, 1850.
Kocher, Paul. *Master of Middle-earth: The Fiction of J.R.R. Tolkien.* Boston: Houghton Mifflin, 1972.
Langland, William. *The Vision of Piers Plowman.* Ed. A.V.C. Schmidt. London: Dent, 1978.

Lewis, C.S. "The Alliterative Metre." *Rehabilitations and other Essays*. London: Oxford University Press, 1939. 117–132.

_____. "The Alliterative Metre." *Selected Literary Essays*, ed. Walter Hooper. Cambridge: Cambridge University Press, 1969. 15–26.

_____. *The Collected Letters of C.S. Lewis*. Ed. Walter Hooper. Vol. III: 1950–1963. San Francisco: HarperSanFrancisco, 2007.

_____. "A Metrical Suggestion." *Lysistrata* II (May 1935): 13–24.

_____. [Obituary for J. R.R. Tolkien.] *The Times* 3 September 1973: 58. Rpt. Salu and Farrell 11–15.

Lindskoog, Kathryn. *Sleuthing C.S. Lewis: More Light in the Shadowlands*. Macon, GA: Mercer University Press, 2001.

The Mabinogi and other Medieval Welsh Tales. Tr. Patrick K. Ford. Berkeley and Los Angeles: University of California Press, 1977.

The Middle English Physiologus. Ed. Hanneke Wirtjes. Early English Text Society, no. 299. Oxford: Oxford University Press, 1991.

Navigatio Sancti Brendani. Tr. John J. O'Meara. *The Voyage of St Brendan: Representative Versions of the Legend in English Translation*. Ed. W.R.J. Barron and Glyn S. Burgess. Exeter: University of Exeter Press, 2002; paperback edition, 2005. 13–64.

The Nibelungenlied. Tr. A.T. Hatto. Penguin Classics. London: Penguin Books, 1965.

The Old English Physiologus. Ed. and tr. Albert Stanburrough Cook, verse tr. by James Hall Pitman. Yale Studies in English LXIII. New Haven: Yale University Press; London: Oxford University Press, 1921.

Physiologus: A Medieval Book of Nature Lore. Tr. Michael J. Curley. Chicago: University of Chicago Press, 1979; trade paperback edition, 2009.

Powers, Tim. "J.R.R. Tolkien Obituary Not By Lewis After All." Ed. Kathryn Lindskoog. *The Lewis Legacy* 57 (Summer 1993):1.

Rateliff, John D. "J. R. R. Tolkien: 'Sir Topas' Revisited." *Notes and Queries* 227 (N.S. 29. 4) (August 1982): 348.

Salu, Mary, and Robert T. Farrell, eds. *J.R.R. Tolkien: Scholar and Storyteller*. Ithaca: Cornell University Press, 1979.

Schofield, Stephen, ed. *The Canadian C.S. Lewis Journal* 83 (Summer 1993): 9.

Sisam, Kenneth, ed. *Fourteenth Century Verse and Prose*. Oxford: Clarendon Press, 1921. After 1923 includes Tolkien's *A Middle English Vocabulary* as a glossary/appendix.

Some Thoughts on Examining, by an Examiner. London: University College London, 1936.

Spence, Lewis. *Legends & Romances of Brittany*. London: George G. Harrap, 1907.

The Stanzaic Morte Arthur. Benson 1–111.

Taylor, Tom. *Ballads and Songs of Brittany*. London and Cambridge: MacMillan, 1865.

Tolkien, J.R.R. "Adventures in Unnatural History and Medieval Metres, being The Freaks of Fisiologus": (i) "Fastitocalon," (ii) "Iumbo, or Ye Kinde of Ye Oliphaunt." *The Stapeldon Magazine* VII. 40 (June 1927): 123–127.

_____. Ælfwine's "Annals." *Shaping* 281–293 ("The Earliest Annals of Valinor") and 337–341 ("The Earliest Annals of Beleriand").

_____. "Ælfwine of England / The Story of Ælfwine." *Lost Tales II* 312–334 and *Lost Road* 77–87.

_____, tr. *Beowulf*. Unpublished translations in alliterative verse (Bodleian A29/1.41–56 and A29/1.9b) and Modern English prose (Bodleian A29/2). Boston: Houghton Mifflin Harcourt, 2014.

_____. "The Cat and the Fiddle: A Nursery-Rhyme Undone and Its Scandalous Secret Unlocked." *Yorkshire Poetry* II.19 (October/November 1923): 1–3.

_____. "Chaucer as Philologist: *The Reeve's Tale*." *Transactions of the Philological Society* (1934): 1–70. Rpt. *Tolkien Studies* 5 (2008): 109–171.

_____. "The Clerkes Compleinte." *The Gryphon*, n.s. 4.3 (December 1922): 95. Rpt. *Arda*

IV (1988, for 1984): 1–2. A slightly later calligraphic version appears in facsimile in *Arda* VI (1990, for 1986): 2–3; a transcription of the latter is reprinted in *Tolkien Studies* 6 (2009): 49–50.

_____."Doworst." *A Elbereth Gilthoniel: The Newsletter of The Fellowship of Middle Earth* 2 (June/July 1978): [3].

_____."Enigmata Saxonica Nuper Inventa Duo." *A Northern Venture: Verses by Members of the Leeds University English School Association.* Leeds: The Swan Press, 1923. 20. Rpt. in Anderson 124–125.

_____. *The Fall of Arthur.* Ed. Christopher Tolkien. Boston and New York: Houghton Mifflin Harcourt, 2013.

_____. *Finn and Hengest: The Fragment and the Episode.* Ed. Alan Bliss. Boston: Houghton Mifflin, 1983.

_____."Ides Ælfscýne." *Songs for the Philologists.* 10–11. Rpt. *Road* 356–358.

_____."Imram." *Time and Tide* December 3rd, 1955: 1561. Rpt. "The Notion Club Papers," *Sauron* 261–264, 296–299.

_____."Knocking at the Door: Lines Induced by Sensations when Waiting for an Answer at the Door of an Exalted Academic Person." *The Oxford Magazine* 55.13 (February 18, 1937): 403.

_____. "The Lay of Aotrou and Itroun." *The Welsh Review* IV.4 (December 1945): 254–266.

_____. "The Nameless Land." *Realities: An Anthology of Verse.* Ed. G.S. Tancred. Leeds: The Swan Press, 1927. 24–25. Rpt. *Lost Road* 98–100.

_____. "The Notion Club Papers." *Sauron* 145–327.

_____. "Ofer Wídne Gársecg" ("The Mermaid"). *Songs for the Philologists* 14–15. Rpt. *Road* 359–361.

_____. "Ólafur Liljurós" *Songs for the Philologists* 5.

_____, tr. *Pwyll, Prince of Annwn.* [Unfinished and unpublished translation of the First Branch of the Mabinogi]. Bodleian A.18/1.135–153.

_____, ed. Geoffrey Chaucer. "The Reeve's Tale" (1939). *Tolkien Studies* 5 (2008): 173–183.

_____. *Roverandom.* Ed. Christina Scull & Wayne G. Hammond. Boston: Houghton Mifflin, 1998.

_____, tr. *Sir Gawain and the Green Knight/ Pearl/ Sir Orfeo.* Ed. Christopher Tolkien. London: Allen & Unwin, 1975.

_____, and E.V. Gordon, *et al. Songs for the Philologists.* London: Privately Printed in the Dept. of English, University College, London, 1936.

_____, and Kenneth Sisam. *A Middle English Vocabulary.* Oxford: Clarendon Press (1922).

La Villemarqué, Théodore, Vicomte Hersart de. *Barzaz-Breiz: Chants Populaires de la Bretagne.* (1839, 1845, 1867). Ed. Yann-Fañch Kemener. Paris: Editions du Layeur, 2003.

Völsunga Saga: The Story of the Völsungs and Niblungs, with Certain Songs from the Elder Edda. Tr. Eiríkr Magnússon and William Morris. Ed. H. Halliday Sparling. The Scott Library, Vol. xxxi. London: Walter Scott, n.d.

The Voyage of Bran (Imram Brain). Tr. Kuno Meyer (1895). Medieval Irish Series Cambridge, ON: In Parentheses Publications, 2000.

"The Wanderer." *Seven Old English Poems.* Ed. John C. Pope. 2d ed. New York and London: W. W. Norton, 1981. 28–32.

West, Richard C. "The Interlace Structure of *The Lord of the Rings.*" In *A Tolkien Compass.* Ed. Jared Lobdell. La Salle, Illinois: Open Court Press, 1975. 77–94.

Yates, Jessica. "The Source of 'The Lay of Aotrou and Itroun.'" In *Leaves from the Tree: Tolkien's Shorter Fiction.* London: The Tolkien Society, 1991. 63–71.

"Poor Sméagol": Gollum as Exile in *The Lord of the* Rings[1]

YVETTE KISOR

To say that Tolkien's Middle-earth is peopled with exiles is to state the obvious. Aragorn, exile-king from a long line of exile-kings; the Noldorin Elves, long exiled from Valinor; even Frodo, who acknowledges his journey with the Ring is no quest: "But this would mean exile, a flight from danger into danger, drawing it after me" (*FR* I, ii, 72).[2] Perhaps the only more obvious thing to observe is that Tolkien was strongly influenced by his knowledge and love of Old English literature.[3] Poems like *Beowulf* and "The Wanderer" provide numerous elements that help shape Tolkien's world, and Tolkien's concept of exile bears their imprint. In fact, if one considers the Anglo-Saxon notion of exile it is not Aragorn or the Noldor, or even Frodo, who best captures it— it is Gollum.

Tolkien did not specifically refer to Gollum as an exile, at least not in his written work. The concept of exile permeates his *legendarium*, however, and can be seen in the stories of almost every race in Middle-earth, most notably the histories of the Noldorin Elves and the Númenóreans. In *The Lord of the Rings* proper there are only a few references to these histories; as with so much of Tolkien's construction of Middle-earth, the information is buried in the appendices or found in the posthumous *The Silmarillion*. Gildor refers to himself and his people as "Exiles" who are "tarrying here a while, ere we return over the Great Sea" (*FR* I, iii, 89), and a second reference to the "Elves in these lands of exile" comes in the "Farewell to Lórien" chapter (*FR* II, viii, 394), but these comments are opaque to novice readers. The explanation for these allusions is relegated to the Appendices, where references to the Elves as Exiles as well as a much truncated account of their history can be found.[4] Similarly, the exile of the Númenóreans is referred to only obliquely in *The Lord of the Rings* where we are told that "the power and craft of Númenor waned in exile" (*RK* V, iv, 96) but not what that means, and while references to Númenor are more frequent, a fuller explanation must wait for Appendix A.[5] There too one will find Aragorn's history fleshed out, where he is referred to "as a king that is in exile" (*RK* App. A, 341), a story that underlies the description of him approaching Gondor with the Fellowship as "a king returning from exile to his own land" (*FR* II, ix, 409). So too with the Dwarves, where an account of the exile of Durin's folk found in Appendix A fleshes out the barest of references in the Prologue.[6] Even the temporary internal displacement of Rohan's women and children due to war is referred to as exile (*RK* V, ii, 56; V, iii, 76).

It is in the accounts of the Elves and the Númenóreans, though, that exile finds its fullest expression. As he describes their histories in various letters, especially the long letter to Milton Waldman (*Letters* 143–61), Tolkien identifies the principal subject of the "Silmarillion" as "the fall of the most gifted kindred of the Elves, their exile from Valinor (a kind of Paradise, the home of the Gods)" and "the history of the War of the Exiled Elves against the Enemy" (148).[7] He repeatedly refers to the rebellious Noldorin as Exiles with a capital "E,"[8] suggesting how crucial the reality of exile is to their identity.[9] He does this less frequently with the Númenóreans but it does occur, though generally in reference to the kingdoms of Arnor and Gondor rather than the Númenóreans themselves; thus Tolkien's reference to "Númenor in Exile on the coasts of Middle-earth" (*Letters* 206) and "the Exiled kingdoms in Arnor and Gondor" (*Letters* 347) while the Númenóreans are simply "exiles" (lower-case; see *Letters* 156–7, 194). Exile is fundamental to Tolkien's concept of both Elves and Men and appears to be grounded in his own Christian sense of mankind as fallen and estranged from God/bliss/Paradise. In a letter to his son Christopher he details his sense of the loss of Eden as a part of the human condition, noting the many "sad exiled generations from the Fall" but asserting that "certainly there was an Eden on this very unhappy earth. We all long for it, and we are constantly glimpsing it: our whole nature at its best and least corrupted, its gentlest and most humane, is still soaked with the sense of 'exile'" (*Letters* 110).[10]

But what of Gollum? Tolkien never specifically calls him an exile, much less an Exile, and as the concept manifests in Gollum's character and situation it appears less biblical than Anglo-Saxon. In his influential article on the language of exile in Old English poetry, Stanley Greenfield discusses four aspects of the exile state that find expression in poetic formulae: the status of the exile, the exile's state of mind, movement within or into exile, and the expression of deprivation. Each of these can be applied to Gollum in illuminating ways, and a consideration reveals how for Gollum his Ring, his Precious, takes the place of king or homeland in the *comitatus* relationship. Further, Gollum's repetitive manner of speech works as a kind of analogue to poetic formulae, and his use of language can be examined further to reveal the nature of his state of exile. In particular, his use of pronouns reveals a separation not only of self from home but self from self, and as his use of pronouns changes through the course of his journey, one can chart the course of Gollum's changing relationship with the world—and the degree to which he determines that relationship through his use of referential language.

In some Old English poetry, particularly elegies like "The Wanderer" or "The Wife's Lament," the speaker laments his or her exile-state without always being very specific about how that exile arose. In other poems, however, it is clearer. Figures such as Grendel in *Beowulf* and Adam and Cain in *Genesis* are exiled by God because of crimes they have committed or are associated with. Cain murdered his brother Abel and Grendel is associated with that crime ("him scyppen forscrifen hæfde / in Cāines cynne" [106–7; him the Shaper had condemned with Cain's kin]),[11] and as for Adam—well, we all know about the forbidden fruit and the resulting exile from Paradise.[12] This is reflected within Anglo-Saxon law where exile appears as a state reached either as a result of crime committed or having lost one's lord. Gollum fits into this scheme in fairly obvious ways—like Cain he has committed murder, and if Déagol is not quite a brother he is Sméagol's friend and close companion, further linked to him through the rhyming names, and Sméagol has been exiled from his kin-group due to his crimes that follow upon the murder of Déagol and the theft of the Ring: "he became very unpopular and was shunned (when visible) by all his relations. They kicked him, and he bit their feet. He took to thieving, and going about muttering to himself, and gurgling in his throat. So they called him *Gollum*, and cursed him, and told him to go far away; and his grandmother, desiring peace, expelled him from the family and turned him out of her hole" (*FR* I, ii, 63).[13] This idea of exile as punishment for crime, particularly murder of a close kin, is echoed as well in the exile of the Noldor from Valinor after the kin-slaying at Alqualondë (*S* 87–90).

Whatever the cause of exile, Old English poetry uses conventional language to describe the exile-state, and we find the same recurrence of key phrases in descriptions of Gollum's exile-state, both those by observers and by Gollum himself. The tone is set in Gandalf's account of Gollum's origins in "The Shadow of the Past." As well as giving the account of Gollum's expulsion from the family home and kin-group quoted above, Gandalf tells Frodo that "[h]e was altogether wretched" (*FR* I, ii, 64) and "he is very old and very wretched" (69) and calls Gollum a "miserable creature" (68) and a "[w]retched fool" (68). These key words and phrases, as well as others used by Gollum himself, recur throughout the text and take on a kind of choric quality analogous to the formulaic language of Old English poetry.

In his classic study of poetic formulae expressing the theme of exile, Stanley Greenfield notes the conventional language that describes and creates images of exile. The most common phrase used to describe the status of exile is *wineléas wrecca* ("friendless exile"); the other is *earm án-haga* ("miserable lone-dweller") (201–2). Analogous phrases are used by and about Gollum with regularity. The modern word *wretch* develops directly from the Old English *wrecca*, which the OED defines as "One driven out of or away from his native country; a banished person; an exile" and indeed we find the phrase "poor wretch" recurring in descriptions of Gollum, particularly by Frodo and Sam (three times: Frodo once [*TT* IV, i, 221] and Sam twice [*TT* IV, ii, 230, 232]). All of these occur in the opening chapters of Book IV; the phrase "the little wretch" is used here as well (241). A second phrase used repeatedly in reference to Gollum and loosely analogous to *earm án-haga* is "miserable creature"; this also occurs three times, twice used by Gandalf and once by the narrator (*FR* I, ii, 68; *TT* IV, vi, 298; *RK* V, iv, 89).[14] Variations on these phrases include "wretched creature" (*TT* IV, i, 220), "that piece of misery" (*TT* IV, vi, 298) and "miserable enemy" (*TT* IV, i, 221).

Along with terms like *wineléas wrecca* referring to the status of the exile, Greenfield isolates adjectives that reference the exile's state of mind, in particular *héan* (low, mean, abject, poor, humbled, humble), *earm* (poor, miserable, helpless, pitiful, wretched), *geómor* (sad, sorrowful, mournful, murmuring, miserable, wretched), and *-cearig* (careful, sorrowful, pensive, wary, chary, anxious, grieving, dire), and related compounds (203). These are used either by the narrative voice describing the exile, generally modifying the third person pronoun, or by the exile in his or her own voice, modifying the first person pronoun. Analogous adjectives continually used to describe Gollum's state are "poor" and "wretched"—the first favored by Gollum himself (sixteen times, twelve by Gollum) and the second by those describing Gollum (ten times, only once by Gollum); "miserable" and "lost" also recur, though less frequently ("miserable" is used four times, never by Gollum, and "lost" is used three times, always by Gollum). When used by others or by the narrator to describe Gollum these adjectives follow the pattern seen in Old English verse and modify the third person pronoun, but since Gollum rarely uses the first person pronoun to refer to himself, self-referential uses are more complicated. I will return to Gollum's pronoun use shortly, but in terms of his self-descriptive use of recurring adjectives, these generally modify either the third person singular or the first person plural pronouns, as Gollum generally refers to himself in the third person or as a collective self. Thus at times Gollum references the loneliness and misery of his state by lamenting "we're so lonely" (*TT* IV, i, 221) and "wretched we are" (222) while at others he refers to himself as "[p]oor, poor Sméagol" and says "he's lost now" (223). The most frequently used language to describe Gollum's exile-state is the phrase "poor Sméagol"—Gollum uses it ten times, sometimes with additional adjectives "[p]oor thin Sméagol!" (*TT* IV, ii, 229), "poor little Sméagol" (*TT* IV, iii, 249), "poor hungry Sméagol" (*TT* IV, iv, 262), etc. This phrase belongs exclusively to Gollum; the only time any other voice uses it he is imitating Gollum: "I suppose the whole time it's been *The Precious for poor Sméagol*" (*TT* IV, viii, 323) says Sam.

Along with phrases denoting the status and state of mind of the exile, Greenfield considers phrases referencing movement connected with exile, specifically movement away from home, movement within exile including the endurance of hardships, and seeking, usually a new home or lord (203–6). The second of these ideas, movement that occurs in the exile-state, is captured in a few phrases; for example Gandalf's account of Gollum's history with the Ring describes him after his expulsion: "He wandered in loneliness, weeping a little for the hardness of the world" (*FR* I, ii, 63) and these are later references to "his wanderings" (*TT* IV, ii, 241) and "his lonely wandering" (228). However, the ideas of movement away from or towards a home or lord are not captured in quite the same way. Gollum never laments the loss of his home or his search for a new one, nor does he speak longingly of a lost lord, nor indeed of any kind of personal relationship. The loss that Gollum laments, the loved object that he seeks, is not lord or home but the Ring. In this way Gollum's situation is more complicated than that usually depicted in Old English elegiac poetry since he experiences, in essence, two exiles—one from his home and one from the Ring, his Precious. "Poor, poor Sméagol, he went away long ago. They took his Precious, and he's lost now" (*TT* IV, i, 223). Gollum, at least, associates his present troubles not with his first exile, from his home, an event precipitated by the Ring, but with his second exile, his loss of the Ring, and the driving force of his existence is his attempt to get the Ring back.

This unique situation is reflected as well when it comes to the final category identified by Greenfield, expressions of deprivation. In Old English poetry this follows a very specific pattern: the past participle of a verb of deprivation preceded by the genitive or instrumental of the thing removed. It is typified by phrases like *wine-mágum bedroren* ("deprived of companions") or *wuldre benámed* ("deprived of glories") or *hróðra bedǽled* ("deprived of comforts"). The items removed "range from the physical ones of gold and land to abstract concepts of comforts and joys" (Greenfield 202). For Gollum, however, there is no range—the focus of his loss is singular; it is the Ring. Further, there is no specific analogue to this poetic formula in Tolkien's account. Perhaps there is no need—Gollum is so completely associated with the Ring, his sense of identity so bound up with it, that any formula of deprivation is superfluous. There is an analogue, however, to an iconic image from the Old English poetic corpus, and it has become iconic in Tolkien as well. In "The Wanderer,"

Old English elegy of exile *par excellence*, there is a moment when the Wanderer becomes lost in reminiscence, confusing memory with his present exile-state: "þynceþ him on mōde þæt hē his mann-dryhten / clyppe and cysse and on cnēo lecge / handa and hēafod" ("The Wanderer" 41–43; it seems to him in [his] mind that he embraces and kisses his lord, and lays hands and head on his knee ...).[15] That motion of embrace, and laying his hands on his lord's knee, is echoed in the oft-noted moment when Gollum returns and finds Frodo and Sam asleep on the stairs of Cirith Ungol: "and slowly putting out a trembling hand, very cautiously he touched Frodo's knee—but almost the touch was a caress. For a fleeting moment, could one of the sleepers have seen him, they would have thought that they beheld an old weary hobbit, shrunken by the years that had carried him far beyond his time, beyond friends and kin, and the fields and streams of youth, an old starved pitiable thing" (*TT* IV, viii, 324). This moment has been seen as the moment when Gollum almost recaptures his old pre–Ring self, a moment of possible redemption,[16] and rightly so, but it is also an expression of Gollum's exile and a moment when the nature of that exile moves close to what exile meant for the Anglo-Saxons—not exile from a Ring of Power, but from one's lord and from one's home.[17]

This image captures visually a moment when Gollum moves close to his Sméagol-self; this movement between Gollum and Sméagol, or Slinker and Stinker as Sam puts it, is a function of his exile-state and recurs throughout the text not only visually but in Gollum's use of referential language. Before proceeding further in considering Gollum as an exile and the conventional language repeatedly used by and about him, some comment is necessary regarding the character's unusual manner of speaking, his dual nature, and even his name. Throughout this essay I have generally referred to the character as Gollum, though I have included references to him as Sméagol. Since I am focusing on exile in my consideration of the character, it makes sense to acknowledge the new name he is given and comes to embody when he is banished from his home. Many scholars, however, particularly those interested in his dual nature, refer to him by some combination of his two names, even though he is never given such an appellation in the text of *The Lord of the Rings*. Thus as early as 1961 Auden refers to him as "Sméagol-Gollum" (48) and the entry for the character in Tyler's *The Complete Tolkien Companion* is found under "Sméagol-Gollum" (589–92).[18] Even Tolkien refers to him at least once as "Sméagol-Gollum" (*Letters* 296). Jane Chance consistently uses "Gollum-Sméagol" (*Tolkien's Art* 147, 154; *Mythology* 82–3, 86) while other critics prefer the slash mark to the hyphen; Marjorie Burns has "Gollum/Sméagol" (163) as do Charles Keim (305) and Michael Stanton (64), whereas Roger Schlobin (73) and Dinah Hazell (48) prefer "Sméagol/Gollum." Shippey alternates between "Sméagol/Gollum" ("Another Road to Middle-earth" 242) and "Gollum/

Sméagol" (243) while Maggie Fernandes refers to the character as both "Gollum-Sméagol" (267) and "Sméagol/Gollum" (269).

The duality of the character captured by this hybrid name is frequently commented on, but this doubleness is not always fully explained or explored and is understood in various ways.[19] Charles Nelson, for example, talks about the character's "dual personality" (51) as an aspect of his function as a false guide (as opposed to good guide figures such as Gandalf). Jane Chance sees the character as a "divided self" (*Tolkien's Art* 147, 154) illustrating "the fragmenting and divisive consequences of his fall into vice" (148); she discusses service as a way for Gollum to regain his sense of self (*Mythology* 24, 82–3). Brent Nelson too characterizes Gollum as a divided self (468, 478, 481) figuring his plight as one of alienation (468) manifest as an inner struggle between "Sméagol, the voice of pre-fallen conscience, against Gollum and his Cain-like desire" (478). Charles Moseley discusses the character in terms of the "motif of the divided self" (58) seeing in Gollum "the potential to have been other" (58)—i.e., "his earlier identity as Sméagol" (54). Similarly, Perkins and Hill describe Gollum as "a split character" but define the division through the Ring, identifying a split between Gollum, who would kill for the ring, and Sméagol, "bound by the power of the ring not to harm the hobbits" (60–1). Stanton too defines the two sides of the character in terms of the Ring: "Gollum, in other words, is that side of the character pretty much totally identified with or consumed by the Ring [whereas] Sméagol has a tiny bit of personality that remains free of the Ring's influence" (63). Others take a more essentialist view of the dual nature of the character. According to Walter Scheps, "Gollum's two selves ... counterpoint the struggle between good and evil" (51), while Fernandes specifically opposes this view, asserting that the contest is "not good and evil fighting each other" but rather "two individuals within one body, *id* and *ego* debating," and she diagnoses "a split personality" or "schizophrenia" (267, emphasis in original).

She is not the only critic to psychologize Gollum's condition. While Hazell simply refers to the character's "divided nature" (47) without further explanation, Catharine Stimpson sees Gollum not only as "a divided self" (32), but as a "study in psychic damage" (39). Rogers and Rogers talk of Gollum's "dual nature" and "split personality" (70) while Ruth Noel sees his "divided personality" as a "symptom of his madness" (64). Other critics, however, are less willing to take on the role of psychiatrist, and define Gollum's psychosis in terms of popular understandings of mental dissociation rather than the DSM.[20] Thus Flieger, though she calls the character "psychotic, driven mad," defines his madness in terms of "what the popular psychoanalytic terminology of the mid-twentieth century called a split or multiple personality, a schizophrenic" ("Wild Men" 103).[21] Stanton is another example of this tendency to frame a discussion of the character's duality in terms of the popular under-standing of Tolkien's time, seeing Gollum as "a classic case of split or dual per-sonality, as conceived by the popular or literary imagination, not the clinical report" noting that the "idea of doubling, the doppelgänger, split or dissociated personality, fascinated the age Tolkien grew up in, and indeed the whole nine-teenth century" (63). Like Stanton, Sue Zlosnik in her study of "Gothic Echoes" in *The Lord of the Rings* sees Gollum as an inheritor of the doppel-gänger tradition (56) in which the buried Sméagol identity engages in "a battle for consciousness with the monstrous and corrupted figure he has become under the influence of the Ring" (55–6). She observes "The Ring's power to disintegrate the subject and transform it into something abject" (56), and in a similar vein Gergely Nagy explores Gollum as a "lost" subject, seeing the character as undergoing "conflicting subject constitution processes," both the reconstitution of his lost identity as Sméagol (through relationship with Frodo) and the deconstitution of his subjectivity (through Sauron and the Ring) (65, 68–9).

Along with the duality of his character, Gollum's unusual manner of speaking has been a locus of critical interest. As Shippey observes, "it was [Tolkien's] idea, and a brilliant one, to mark Gollum out by his strange use of pronouns" noting that the character's "consistent verbal oddity gives a distinc-tive sense of personality, or lack of personality, which is entirely original" (*Author* 30). Daniel Hughes too notes that Gollum's speech "is the most mem-orable and immediately detachable part of the earlier book [*The Hobbit*]" (77). Gollum's odd speech patterns have been part of the character from his creation, and, as Rateliff has shown, Tolkien emphasized them through revision (Rateliff 167).[22] Many have seen Gollum's unusual speech as aligning him with the infantile or the bestial. Brian Rosebury, for example, associates his language with the "argot of the nursery" (81) and Chance describes how for "the Gollum side of Sméagol ... his speech fragments into ... baby-talk" ("Subversive Fan-tasist" 157), commenting elsewhere on "the simple baby talk of Gollum" (*Mythology* 59); Flieger likewise observes that "Gollum talks baby-talk" ("Wild Men" 104). Similarly, Fernandes finds that Gollum "has a childish, broken lan-guage" (268) and Rogers and Underwood note his speech is "childlike" (129) while Moseley finds that his language has "degenerated into sounds that are barely above mere animal noise" (45).

For most, though, both the strangest and the most important aspect of Gollum's speech is his nonstandard use of pronouns. As one critic remarked, "Gollum talks to himself" in a "self-referencing voice" (Rogers and Underwood 128) or, more explicitly, Gollum "speaks as two persons" (Rogers and Rogers 111). The "I" voice is usually identified as the more whole and originary Sméagol voice, whereas the "we" voice exhibits Gollum's total identification with the Ring[23]; his use of "precious," both lower and upper case, to refer to both the Ring and himself denotes this.[24] This split between "I" and "we" is much clearer in *The Lord of the Rings*, and much more important. In *The Hobbit*, as Shippey has observed, after his opening "I guess it's a choice feast" (*H* V, 83), Gollum never uses "I" again (*Author* 30). It is only in the later *The Lord of the Rings*, when he is separated from the Ring and comes under the influence of Frodo, that the Sméagol character becomes apparent verbally. In this later iteration, Gollum's strange use of self-referencing pronouns becomes much more than simply an odd quirk of the character. As Rosebury has pointed out, Gollum "speaks of himself in the third person or in the plural except at moments of intermittent rationality" (46) and this "unstable sense of grammatical person [suggests] mental dissociation" (81).

This unusual self-referential pronoun use is linked to grammatical wholeness; Chance has noted that as the character's "sense of self ('I') has begun to return ... Gollum now speaks in complete sentences" (*Mythology* 88) and she constructs this in part as a return to civilization and normalcy "reflected in his use of whole and complete sentences with subject, verb, and object" ("Fantasist" 157). Thus the Gollum side of the character "speak[s] ungrammatically" whereas "Sméagol tends to speak in complete sentences, using the first-person pronoun" (157).[25] Nagy discusses this mental disintegration in terms of subject constitution, noting that as the Sméagol-subject begins to be reconstructed, largely through contact with Frodo, "Gollum is now again able to produce meaningful language" (63).

Gollum's unusual use of pronouns includes not only his use of self-referential language but extends to unconventional ways of referring to others, and in both guises can be connected to the conventional language of the exile-state. As has already been noted, Gollum generally refers to himself as either "he" or "we" rather than "I." This strange usage is remarkable and commented on even by other characters within the text—Frodo muses that Gollum's self-referential use of "I" instead of "we" is a sign "that some remnants of old truth and sincerity were for the moment on top" (*TT* IV, iii, 251). Gollum's tendency to refer to himself collectively occurs alongside his use of the third person singular when he should use the first person pronoun.[26] When he uses the third person pronoun, referring to himself as if he were a separate being, he constructs Sméagol as a third person separate from himself, refusing through his use of pronouns to acknowledge Sméagol as himself: "Poor, poor Sméagol, he went away long ago. They took his Precious, and he's lost now" (*TT* IV, i, 223). But perhaps even more remarkable is Gollum's use of referential language when he mentions and addresses others. When he refers to others he frequently uses the nongendered third person pronoun rather than the gendered one: "it" when "he" or "she" would be more appropriate.[27] Further, in conversation he uses the third person when he should use the second person, addressing his speech partner as "he" instead of "you"[28]—suggesting a gesture of exclusion, a refusal to enter into direct relationship with another being. This pattern too can be traced to reveal Gollum's changing sense of his relationship with those around him.

Initially when Frodo and Sam meet Gollum in Book Four of *The Two Towers* he is using the third person singular pronoun to refer to himself when he should use the first person. When he does use the third person singular pronoun to refer to someone other than himself (or the Sméagol part of himself), he does so in an unconventional way. In their initial meeting he addresses Frodo as "he" (third person) when he should use "you" (second person) since they are in direct conversation. In response to Frodo's assertion that he will not remove the elven rope "unless there is any promise *you* can make that *I* can trust" Gollum replies: "*We* will swear to do what *he* wants, yes, yess" (*TT* IV, i, 224; emphasis mine). Where Frodo uses the first person singular (I) to refer to himself—a sign of his psychological wholeness—Gollum uses the first person plural (we)—a sign of his psychological division. And where Frodo refers to Gollum using the second person (you), expressing a willingness to enter into a direct relationship with him, Gollum uses the third person (he) to refer to Frodo—suggesting a gesture of exclusion, a refusal to enter into direct relationship where Frodo is willing to do so. Yet Gollum does make the promise, and once he does his speech patterns change.

As the narrator notes, Gollum's patterns of pronoun use are different after his promise: "From that moment a change, which lasted for some time, came over him. He spoke with less hissing and whining, and he spoke to his companions direct, not to his precious self" (*TT* IV, i, 225). And indeed that is what we see in the very next example of Gollum's speech: "Very lucky *you* came this way. Very lucky *you* found Sméagol, yes" (*TT* IV, i, 225; emphasis mine). Gollum not only uses the second person pronoun, suggesting a willingness to be in a direct relationship with another being, he even begins to use the third person masculine pronoun conventionally, figuring "Baggins," whom he had declared an "it" at their last meeting, as "he" when he thinks back to their long-ago encounter in the riddle-game: "*He* guessed it long ago, *Baggins* guessed it" (*TT* IV, ii, 227–8; emphasis mine). But this period of relative psychological wholeness, indicated through his patterns of pronoun use, does not last long. Soon "Sam thought he sensed a change in Gollum again ... and he went back more and more to his old manner of speaking" (227–8). And indeed from that point Gollum lapses again into the speech patterns evident in their initial encounter, and when he does use the third person masculine pronoun (he) it is almost always when the second person pronoun (you) is called for.[29] The two speech patterns, one featuring more conventional pronoun use and the other more fragmented usage, are most remarkable in the conversation Sam overhears between the Sméagol and Gollum parts of his personality, where they are brought into sharp contrast.[30] When Gollum refers to Frodo as "the hobbit," suggesting distance and the lack of a relationship, Sméagol responds by calling Frodo "master" and referencing his relationship to him as one of obedient servant. When Gollum takes that title and removes it from Frodo, suggesting that "we [could be] master," Sméagol gives Frodo a new appellation, calling him "nice hobbit" and referring to him, for the first time in appropriate usage, as "he." Gollum counters by accepting the "he" but insisting that "he's a Baggins" and refusing to accept Sméagol's attempts to designate Frodo as a unique and separate Baggins, different from that other Baggins (240–1).[31]

Perhaps most telling of all is Gollum's gloating speech when he attacks Sam in the chapter "Shelob's Lair." As he grabs Sam from behind, he refers to Sam, in spite of the fact that he is addressing him directly, as "*him* ... the nassty hobbit" and "*this one*" only to conclude with a victorious "he's got *you, you* nassty filthy little sneak!" (*TT* IV, ix, 335; emphasis mine).[32] Only at the moment of attack can he address Sam directly and acknowledge a direct relationship with him. It is only when he seeks to take a life that he can acknowledge a relationship with another being.

Gollum's use of pronouns separates him from the rest of the world, and while much of the repetitive language used by and about Gollum suggests the repetitive poetic formulae used to describe the exile-state in Old English poetry, his unusual use of referential language suggests a state of mind perhaps less associated with the Anglo-Saxon concept of exile than with the modernist notion of alienation. His lack of felt connection with any being or place is reflected in Gollum's unconventional pronoun use just as his obsession with the Ring has infiltrated other aspects of his referential language—his Precious is sometimes the Ring and sometimes himself,[33] and it is often nearly impossible to determine which Gollum intends as the conflation between the two is all but complete. As is so often the case, Tolkien proves himself to be a writer with deep roots in the medieval tradition at the same time he is revealed as belonging squarely in the twentieth century.

NOTES

1. An early version of this essay was presented at the Forty-second International Medieval Congress at Western Michigan University in Kalamazoo, Michigan in May 2007, as part of Session 121, "War and Exile in Tolkien," under the title "Gollum as Exile"; that paper presentation was supported by a grant from the Ramapo College Foundation.

2. Though at other times Frodo refers to exile much more casually, commenting at Rivendell that "I have had a month of exile and adventure, and I find that has been as much

as I want" (*FR* II, i, 233). Leslie Donovan's entry on "Exile" in *Encyclopedia* details several of these examples; she does not, however, consider Gollum as an exile.

3. This is widely acknowledged; perhaps the best treatments of Tolkien's use of medieval sources are *Road* and *Author*. Shippey has long observed Tolkien's use of medieval works including elegies such as "The Wanderer" and "The Ruin," and above all the poem *Beowulf*; see for example his Appendix A "Tolkien's Sources: The True Tradition" in *Road* (343–52).

4. See, for example, *RK*, App. A, 314; App. B, 363; App. E, 395, 401; and App. F 406, 416.

5. See the accounts in *RK*, Appendix A, esp. 313–19 (also App. A, 328 , 330; and App. D, 386); the kingdoms of Arnor and Gondor are referred to repeatedly as "the realms in exile" (App. A, 317, 318; App. B, 365).

6. The reference is to "Thorin Oakenshield, descendant of kings, and his twelve companions in exile" (*FR* Prologue, 20); the larger story is found in Part III of Appendix A (*RK* 352–62), not to mention *The Hobbit*.

7. Paul Kocher stresses the "rebellion and self-exile" of the Elves (156).

8. See *Letters* 149–151; also 176–7, 386, 425. However, this usage is not consistent; see also 204 and 281.

9. This practice has been widely adopted; *The Complete Tolkien Companion* defines Exiles (capitalized) as "The High-elves of Middle-earth, the NOLDOR" (Tyler 220).

10. This connection has been observed at least in passing by several critics, most notably Verlyn Flieger (*A Question of Time* 145, 217; "Do the Atlantis Story ..." 52). Lee and Solopova, too, see a connection between the Elves' exile from Valinor and the human state of exile from Eden (252); see also Miranda Wilcox, esp. 138–9. Perhaps more directly relevant to the sense of exile Tolkien expresses in this letter is the "Salve Regina," the final prayer of the Rosary:

> Salve, Regina, Mater misericordiæ,
> vita, dulcedo, et spes nostra, salve.
> Ad te clamamus exsules filii Hevæ,
> ad te suspiramus, gementes et flentes
> in hac lacrimarum valle ...

The third line, which translates as "we exiled children of Eve cry out to you," is of a piece with the ideas Tolkien expresses in this letter. I am grateful to John Houghton for bringing this connection to my attention.

11. The text of *Beowulf* is that of Fulk et al., *Klaeber's Beowulf*; the translation is my own.

12. Genesis 2:15–3:24; an expanded and somewhat different version is found in the Old English "Genesis B."

13. A few scholars have noted the parallel with Cain and applied either the term "exile" or "outcast" to Gollum. John Garth calls him "an outcast haunting the dank, treacherous borderlands of civilization," noting that the murder of Déagol "brands Gollum with the mark of Cain" (49) and Brent Nelson, who connects Gollum to both Cain and *Beowulf*'s Grendel, observes that "after his figurative fratricide, Gollum begins a watery exile" (475), for he is sent "into exile" by his "community" (478). Verlyn Flieger calls Gollum "murderer, outcast, maddened by reminders of joys he cannot share," identifying him as "the twisted, broken, outcast hobbit" who partakes of "both the *Beowulf* kinds of monster in one figure" ("Frodo and Aragorn" 141). Elsewhere she identifies him as "an outlaw, shunned by his relatives, expelled from his family, and driven into the wild" ("Tolkien's Wild Men" 103), and Robert Eaglestone asserts that Gollum is "both exiled and self-exiled from society" (77). See also Bonniejean Christenson, "Tolkien's Creative Technique" (6).

14. The primary narrator and author of *The Lord of the Rings*, if we accept Tolkien's conceit, is Frodo.

15. I am using the text of the poem found in John C. Pope's *Eight Old English Poems*; the translation is my own.

16. This moment is remarked on by almost every scholar who discusses Gollum even briefly; Tolkien comments on it in several times in *Letters* (110, 221, 234, 252, 255, 330).

17. In his discussion of Gollum and Othello as manifestations of the "Other," Robert Gehl associates both characters' struggles with identity (including Gollum's duality) with their lack of connection to both their original homes and their present surroundings (259); though he does not use the word or discuss the concept of exile per se, the situation he describes could be expressed by that term.

18. Charles Keim opens his essay "Of Two Minds: Gollum and Othello" by noting the difficulty such handbooks have in locating the character: under "Gollum" or "Sméagol" (294).

19. The most in-depth discussion of the duality of Gollum is Keim's. He describes not simply a split, but a division of self that lacks a central consciousness to mediate between the two identities.

20. DSM: the *Diagnostic and Statistical Manual of Mental Disorders*, the standard classification by the American Psychiatric Association, in which Dissociative Personality Disorder ("split personality") is different from Schizophrenia [Eds.].

21. In contradiction to this, Keim asserts that "Gollum is not schizophrenic" because the two sides of his personality are aware of one another (295).

22. Christensen makes a similar point regarding the "revisions of Gollum's diction," emphasizing the changes necessitated by the reconceiving of the character in *The Lord of the Rings* ("Gollum's Character Transformation" 17).

23. Rogers and Rogers describe "one hissing, cringing 'we' and one 'I,' more coherent and with more backbone" (111) and Stanton notes that "Sméagol has pale eyes and speaks of himself as 'I'; Gollum has green eyes and speaks of himself as 'we'" (63).

24. As Rateliff notes, "it is quite clear that 'my precious' originally applied only to Gollum himself and not the ring: Gollum 'always spoke to himself not to you,' usually in first person plural, yet he refers to the ring as 'it'" (167). This point is made as well by Douglas Anderson in his *The Annotated Hobbit*; as he observes "Gollum uses the phrase 'my precious' to refer only to himself" but in the revised 1951 edition "the phrase might be taken to refer to the ring" (120n8). Christensen claims that in the original 1937 version "Gollum refers to himself and to Bilbo as 'precious.' In the revised edition the word of endearment is extended to the ring" ("Gollum's Character Transformation" 11). This development is made clear in an early draft of *The Two Towers* in which Frodo responds with surprise when Gollum offers to swear "on the precious": "he had thought that *precious* was Gollum's self that he talked to" (*War* 97–8, emphasis in original). Whether "precious" refers to himself or to the Ring is indicated to some extent through the use of capitalization, but ambiguity is still possible, particularly in the revised 1951 version of *The Hobbit*. Any confusion present can, of course, be attributed to the misunderstandings of the purported authors of *The Hobbit* and *The Lord of the Rings*, Bilbo and Frodo. For the development of capitalization in the passage quoted above, see *War* 99n15.

25. Fernandes has noted this as well, observing not only that Sméagol "uses I, when referring to himself, as if aware of his identity" but that his side of the split character is marked through "more correct use of language when compared to the other debating personality" (268).

26. There is an interesting oddity in Gandalf's account of Gollum's origins in "The Shadow of the Past." Since this story concerns Sméagol before he encountered the Ring, we would expect him to exhibit a unified sense of self and normal pronoun use. Yet as he looks over Déagol's shoulder at the Ring in his hand, Sméagol says "Give us that, Déagol, my love" (*FR* I, ii, 62). This use of the plural pronoun could be explained as a mistake on the part of Gandalf, who is telling this story to Frodo and imagining Sméagol's speech, perhaps because he is so accustomed to Gollum's use of the plural pronoun, or even as due to the proximity of the Ring itself. However, an easier explanation might be found in the British colloquial use of the plural "us" when the singular "me" would be expected, particularly with the verb

"give." See the OED entry under "us, pron. b., and adj." definition 7; see also John Algeo's *British or American English?*, 107 and Michael Swan's *Practical English Usage*, 429.

27. This is obscured somewhat in the opening chapter of *The Two Towers* ("The Taming of Sméagol") because Gollum is consistently referring to and addressing Frodo and Sam as a group: "they," "them," "nice little hobbitses," etc. (*TT* IV, i, 221), and in English the third person plural makes no distinction of gender. It is much clearer in the "Riddles in the Dark" chapter of *The Hobbit* where almost Gollum's entire conversation with Bilbo is characterized by his use of "it," most memorably "What has *it* got in *its* pocketses?" (*H* V, 93 and ff.; emphasis mine) and "Thief, thief, thief! Baggins! We hates *it*, we hates *it*, we hates *it* for ever!" (*H* V, 98; emphasis mine); he also calls Bilbo "the Baggins" here (*H* V, 94). See *Author* 30, Rateliff 167.

28. See, for example, *TT* IV, i, 224; ii, 242; iii, 246, 255 *et passim*.

29. See Note 28.

30. In Peter Jackson's film version, the differing speech patterns are obscured in favor of a more visual delineation of the two personalities. As Fernandes notes, "Gollum and Sméagol speak nearly always in the same register in the film" but "the actor's performance deliberately shows totally different characters" (268). Rosebury notes that Jackson uses "alternating half-profile shots representing the two sides of his riven mind" (216) and Shippey finds the "more emphatic" staging by Jackson to be "entirely in line with Tolkien's intention" ("Another Road to Middle-earth" 243).

31. It is perhaps worth noting that in his most Gollum-like moments, as he tricks Gollum into following him from the pool of Henneth Annûn, Frodo lapses into Gollum's speech-patterns, referring to himself in the third person as "Master" (*TT* IV, vi, 296).

32. Tolkien worked to establish this through revision; in earlier versions Gollum alternates between second and third person in reference to Sam in this speech; see *War* 196.

33. See Note 24.

WORKS CITED

Algeo, John. *British or American English? A Handbook of Word and Grammar Patterns*. Cambridge: Cambridge University Press, 2006.

Auden, W.H. "The Quest Hero." *Texas Quarterly* 4.4 (1961): 81–93. Zimbardo and Isaacs 31–51.

Burns, Marjorie. *Perilous Realms: Celtic and Norse in Tolkien's Middle-earth*. Toronto: University of Toronto Press, 2005.

Chance, Jane. *The Lord of the Rings: The Mythology of Power*. 1992. Rev. ed. Lexington: University Press of Kentucky, 2001.

_____. "Subversive Fantasist: Tolkien on Class Difference." *Scholarship* 153–68.

_____. *Tolkien's Art: A Mythology for England*. 1979. Rev. ed. Lexington: University Press of Kentucky, 2001.

Christensen, Bonniejean. "Gollum's Character Transformation in *The Hobbit*." Lobdell 9–28.

_____. "Tolkien's Creative Technique: *Beowulf* and *The Hobbit*." *Mythlore* 15.3 (#57) (1989): 4–10.

Clark, George, and Daniel Timmons, eds. *J.R.R. Tolkien and His Literary Resonances: Views of Middle-earth*. Contributions to the Study of Science Fiction and Fantasy 89. Westport, CT: Greenwood Press, 2000.

Croft, Janet Brennan, ed. *Tolkien and Shakespeare: Essays on Shared Themes and Language*. Critical Explorations in Science Fiction and Fantasy 2. Jefferson, NC: McFarland, 2007.

Donovan, Leslie A. "Exile." *Encyclopedia* 178.

Eaglestone, Robert. "Invisibility." Eaglestone, *Reading* 73–84.

_____, ed. *Reading* The Lord of the Rings: *New Writings on Tolkien's Classic*. London and New York: Continuum, 2005.

Fernandes, Maggie. "Logos, the Silver Path to *The Lord of the Rings*: The Word in Novel and Film Writing." *The Ring Goes Ever On: Proceedings of the Tolkien 2005 Conference: 50 Years of* The Lord of the Rings. Ed. Sarah Wells. Coventry, England: The Tolkien Society, 2008. 2, 260–70.

Flieger, Verlyn. "Do the Atlantis story and abandon Eriol-Saga." *Tolkien Studies* 1 (2004): 43–68.

_____. "Frodo and Aragorn: The Concept of the Hero." Isaacs and Zimbardo 40–62. Rpt. Zimbardo and Isaacs 122–45.

_____. *A Question of Time: J.R.R. Tolkien's Road to Faërie*. Kent, OH: The Kent State University Press, 1997.

_____. "Tolkien's Wild Men: From Medieval to Modern." *Medievalist* 95–105.

Fulk, R.D., Robert E. Bjork, and John D. Niles, eds. *Klaeber's Beowulf and The Fight at Finnsburgh*. Fourth Edition. Toronto: University of Toronto Press, 2008.

Garth, John. "Frodo and the Great War." *Scholarship* 41–56.

Gehl, Robert. "Something is Stirring in the East: Racial Identity, Confronting the 'Other,' and Miscegenation in *Othello* and *The Lord of the Rings*." Croft 251–66.

Greenfield, Stanley. "The Formulaic Expression of the Theme of 'Exile' in Anglo-Saxon Poetry." *Speculum* 30.2 (April 1955): 200–6.

Hazell, Dinah. *The Plants of Middle-earth: Botany and Sub-creation*. Kent, OH: The Kent State University Press, 2006.

Hughes, Daniel. "Pieties and Giant Forms in 'The Lord of the Rings.'" Isaacs and Zimbardo 72–86.

Isaacs, Neil D., and Rose A. Zimbardo, eds. *Tolkien: New Critical Perspectives*. Lexington: University Press of Kentucky, 1981.

Keim, Charles. "Of Two Minds: Gollum and Othello." Croft 294–312.

Kocher, Paul. "Middle-earth: An Imaginary World?" *Master of Middle-earth: The Fiction of J.R.R. Tolkien*. Boston: Houghton Mifflin, 1972. Rpt. Zimbardo and Isaacs 146–62.

Lee, Stuart D., and Elizabeth Solopova. *The Keys of Middle-earth: Discovering Medieval Literature through the Fiction of J.R.R. Tolkien*. New York: Palgrave, 2005.

Lobdell, Jared, ed. *A Tolkien Compass*. La Salle, IL: Open Court, 1975.

The Lord of the Rings: The Two Towers. Dir. Peter Jackson. New Line Home Entertainment, 2004. Special Extended DVD Edition.

Moseley, Charles. *J.R.R. Tolkien*. Writers and Their Work. Plymouth, England: Northcote House, 1997.

Nagy, Gergely. "The 'Lost' Subject of Middle-earth: The Constitution of the Subject in the Figure of Gollum in *The Lord of the Rings*." *Tolkien Studies* 3 (2006): 57–79.

Nelson, Brent. "Cain-Leviathan Typology in Gollum and Grendel." *Extrapolation* 49.3 (Winter 2008): 466–85.

Nelson, Charles W. "From Gollum to Gandalf: The Guide Figures in J.R.R. Tolkien's *The Lord of the Rings*." *Journal of the Fantastic in the Arts* 13.1 (2002): 47–61.

Noel, Ruth S. *The Mythology of Middle-earth*. Boston: Houghton Mifflin, 1977.

The Oxford English Dictionary. Oxford University Press, November 2010. June 2011.

Perkins, Agnes, and Helen Hill. "The Corruption of Power." Lobdell 57–68.

Pope, John C. *Eight Old English Poems*. 3rd ed. Ed. R.D. Fulk. New York and London: Norton, 2001.

Rateliff, John D. *The History of the Hobbit—Part One: Mr. Baggins*. Boston and New York: Houghton Mifflin, 2007.

Rogers, Deborah Webster, and Ivor A. Rogers. *J.R.R. Tolkien*. Twayne's English Author Series 304. Boston: Twayne, 1980.

Rogers, William N. II, and Michael R. Underwood. "Gagool and Gollum: Exemplars of Degeneration in *King Solomon's Mines* and *The Hobbit*." Clark and Timmons 121–31.

Rosebury, Brian. *Tolkien: A Cultural Phenomenon*. New York: Palgrave: 2003.

"Salve Regina." Michael Martin. Thesaurus Precarum Latinarum, April 1998. July 28, 2012. http://www.preces-latinae.org/thesaurus/BVM/SalveRegina.html.

Scheps, Walter. "The Fairy-tale Morality of *The Lord of the Rings*." Lobdell 43–56.

Schlobin, Roger C. "The Monsters Are Talismans and Transgressions: Tolkien and *Sir Gawain and the Green Knight*." Clark and Timmons 71–81.

Shippey, Tom. "Another Road to Middle-earth: Jackson's Movie Trilogy." Zimbardo and Isaacs. 233–54.

Stanton, Michael N. *Hobbits, Elves, and Wizards: Exploring the Wonders and Worlds of J.R.R. Tolkien's* The Lord of the Rings. New York: Palgrave, 2001.

Stimpson, Catharine R. *J.R.R. Tolkien*. Columbia Essays on Modern Writers 41. New York and London: Columbia University Press, 1969.

Swan, Michael. *Practical English Usage*. Third edition. Oxford: Oxford University Press, 2005.

Tyler, J.E.A. *The Complete Tolkien Companion*. 1976. Rev. ed. New York: St. Martin's Press, 2004.

Wilcox, Miranda. "Exilic Imagining in *The Seafarer* and *The Lord of the Rings*." *Medievalist* 133–54.

Zimbardo, Rose A., and Neil D. Isaacs, eds. *Understanding* The Lord of the Rings: *The Best of Tolkien Criticism*. Boston and New York: Houghton Mifflin, 2004.

Zlosnik, Sue. "Gothic Echoes." Eaglestone, *Reading* 47–58. Rpt. *J.R.R. Tolkien's The Lord of the Rings*: New Edition. Ed. Harold Bloom. Bloom's Modern Critical Interpretations. New York: Infobase, 2008. 117–28.

The Presence of the Past in *The Lord of the Rings*

JOHN B. MARINO

> But all the while I sit and think
> of times there were before,
> I listen for returning feet
> and voices at the door.
> [*FR* II, iii, 292]

Only I hear the stones lament them: *deep they delved us, fair they wrought us, high they builded us; but they are gone.* They are gone. They sought the Havens long ago.
[*FR* II, iii, 297, emphasis in original]

1. Introduction: The Past and the Present

The past has had a mystique for quite some time, most notably in the Romantic era's medievalism, and most particularly in the Gothic imagination. Old ruins and old relics of a medieval past have evoked for the reader the idea and emotion that the dark past can be very alive in the present. The past continues to haunt the present, like a shadow that lingers on the periphery of the setting of the text. J.R.R. Tolkien, most notably in *The Lord of the Rings*, develops this aspect of his setting in that the adventuring characters are continually encountering ancient places and objects, even people, that bring the faded, or fading, world of *The Silmarillion* into the present in the Third Age of Middle-earth; throughout *The Lord of the Rings*, there are many things "of old," of Elder Days. The past is not only past; it is ever present.

Tolkien makes this present past an object of sentimentality in the sense that he consistently invokes a nostalgia throughout the narrative. As the characters affectively respond to relics of the past, the reader is to also respond accordingly. There is evidence of a general sentimentality throughout *The Lord of the Rings*, such as the stream, even in Mordor, found by Frodo and Sam:

> Out of a gully on the left ... water came dripping down: the last remains, maybe, of some sweet rain gathered from sunlit seas, but ill-fated to fall at last upon the walls of the Black Land and wander fruitless down into the dust ... to be lost among the dead stones [*RK* VI, ii, 197–98].

This sentimentality is most often applied to surviving relics of a fading past in particular.

For example, the central object of the quest, the One Ring, the Ring of Power, is itself a relic of the past. When Frodo approaches Mount Doom, the Ring becomes a greater burden: "As it drew near the great furnaces where, *in the deeps of time*, it had been shaped and forged, the Ring's power grew, and it became more fell, untameable save by some mighty will" (*RK* VI, i, 177; my emphasis). Sauron's Second-Age activities are not neatly contained in the past, over and done in that he was destroyed and banished to the outer darkness. Rather, he lingers in Middle-earth in the Third Age, re-formed to once again bring havoc. The existence of the Ring itself enables Sauron to again attempt his tyranny. He and the Ring are both past and present beings.

2. People: The Continuity of the Past and the Present

Sauron, originally a Maia, is of the remote past and the present, the former being the events of the First Age (and earlier) and the latter referring to the Third Age at the time of *The Lord of the Rings*. His nature seems to be virtually sempiternal in that he is never said to have died, but to retreat into other realms, perhaps the spiritual realm of darkness, and to re-form again after an indeterminate time of exile. Indeed time has very different meaning in a state of great existence, so perhaps the past and present are all one. How different is time to a being of vast age?

Gandalf, like Sauron, is a Maia and so from the past as well, even though "Of the Rings of Power" (*S* 299–300) relates his arrival in Middle-earth as one of the Istari. He is sent to counter Sauron, so he is bound to Sauron in time and task. His purpose is tied to Sauron's machinations. In this way, the past is not neatly contained within the time period of former events: persons, places, and things bridge a chronological distance. In other words, the "past" persists. Appropriately, Gandalf keeps two relics of the persistent past: the ring Narya and the sword Glamdring, the latter of which is "the work of Elvish smiths in the Elder Days" (*FR* II, iv, 324). Also, he appears old, but he does not age. He is matched, tested, against another great spirit of the remote past, the Balrog, a First-Age servant of Melkor who persists in imprisonment into the Third Age. It is "[a]n evil of the Ancient World" (*FR* II, vii, 371). As Gandalf attests, "There are older and fouler things than Orcs in the deep places of the world" (*FR* II, iv, 323).

And, like Gandalf—himself a Ring bearer—another group of personages from the past, the Ring-bearing Nazgûl bridge a gap (if there is a gap) between an earlier age and the present. Gandalf speaks of the "King of Angmar long ago, Sorcerer, Ringwraith, Lord of the Nazgûl, a spear of terror in the hand of Sauron, shadow of despair" (*RK* V, iv, 92). The Nine Rings allow them to persist, not necessarily granting a long life, but giving a continuous existence, a perpetual presence in the here and now. To Tolkien, the past is not something over and done, dead like some languages, but living and breathing in the present. This is what he saw in words, whether on Welsh coal trucks or in *Beowulf* (Carpenter 33–34, 42).

Glorfindel is another being of an earlier age, and in this he is emblematic of the elves as a whole in that his relevance, except for momentously encountering the wraiths at the ford, is diminishing; the elves are fading, they are has-beens. Perhaps this is where Tolkien does write discontinuity between past and present; the elves are of the past and are gradually fading into the past, not to have a future in Middle-earth. A few examples are the leaders of the elves: Elrond, Galadriel, and Celeborn. When these three speak together with Gandalf, on the way north after Sauron's defeat, they can be mistaken for "memorials of forgotten things now lost in unpeopled lands" (*RK* VI, vi, 263). These characters hearken back to an earlier age of Middle-earth, but their longevity bridges the gap between past and present. Elrond's lineage goes deep into the past of both men and elves, and these ancestors still live in him. He says, "But my memory reaches back even to the Elder Days. Eärendil was my sire, who was born in Gondolin before its fall; and my mother was Elwing, daughter of Dior, son of Lúthien of Doriath. I have seen three ages in the West of the world ..." (*FR* II, ii, 256). And Celeborn and Galadriel are even older; at the end of his prologue to *The Fellowship of the Ring*, Tolkien states that when Celeborn departed Middle-earth "... with him went the last living memory of the Elder Days in Middle-earth" (*FR* Prologue, 25). On departing Lórien, Frodo observes of Galadriel: "Already she seemed to him, as by men of later days Elves still at times are seen: present and yet remote, a living vision of that which has already been left far behind by the flowing streams of Time" (*FR* II, viii, 389). They both *were* (when the world was younger) and *are* (at the end of the Third Age).

Yet, the past does persist, even ambiguously so in the persons of Tom Bombadil and Treebeard, for which is older? They are both said to be the oldest being in Middle-earth, and so Tolkien preserves the mystery of their origins. Tom is said to be "older than the old ... oldest and fatherless" (*FR* II, ii, 278), and he has been in Middle-earth since "before the seas were bent" (*FR* I, vii, 142). Treebeard refers to his knowledge of what was "a long, long time ago" (*TT* III, iv, 67), and we can imagine that for him a long time is a very long time indeed. His experience goes back to the very youth of the world (78). He is said to be "the oldest of the Ents, the oldest living thing that still walks beneath the Sun upon this Middle-earth" (*TT* III, v, 102), "the oldest of all living things" (*TT* III, viii, 164), and "Eldest" (*RK* VI, vi, 259). The Ents as a whole are connected to the days of legend (*TT* III, viii, 155), and they are "a power that walked the earth, ere elf sang or hammer rang" (149). There is an emotionalism behind Treebeard's vast age, and both hobbits and the reader are to gaze in the Ent's eyes with sentimentality. Pippin says:

> "One felt as if there was an enormous well behind them, filled up with ages of memory ... but their surface was sparkling with the present ... [I]t felt as if something ... between deep earth and sky had suddenly waked up, and was considering you with the same slow care that it had given to its own inside affairs for endless years" [*TT* III, iv, 66–67].

Whoever is oldest, Bombadil or Treebeard, we may be content to place their origins in the remotest past, and they continually present the reader with a mystery, representing a past even before the reckoning of time. And Tolkien does not allow the distant past to remain in the past. Perhaps Bombadil embodies the continuity of the past in the present and the nostalgic view of history when he finds the brooch on the barrow mounds after rescuing the hobbits from the wight and carrying the treasure out to leave it on the grass. He picks up a brooch, gazes at it, and wistfully recalls the lady who wore it long ago. He waxes sentimental:

> He chose for himself ... a brooch set with blue stones .... He looked long at it, as if stirred by some memory ... saying at last:
> "... Fair was she who long ago wore this on her shoulder. Goldberry shall wear it now, and we will not forget her!" [*FR* I, viii, 156–57].

Tolkien is here not content merely to have a history in the background of his text, but he presents a nostalgic view of history. As Bombadil emotionally reacts to a relic of the past, we the readers are supposed to emotionally react to objects and places, brooches and ruins, that recall an almost forgotten time had it not been for these reminders of people and places long ago. There are stories behind the relics and ruins. This is evident when Merry, on the Barrow-downs, dreams of the men of Carn Dûm (*FR* I, viii, 154). He experiences the past, an attack by these men, as if it happened to him; this is an incident in which the past briefly comes alive again in the present. The past cannot stay put in the past and intrudes on the present, forcing itself on Merry's mind while he dreams.

Even Aragorn embodies the continuity of the past and the present in that he descends from a long line of the old kings stretching back into a shadowy past, "the last remnant in the North of the great people, the Men of the West" (*FR* II, i, 233). His role as one who builds continuity between past and present, a link in a long and old line of kings, resembles that of the horse Shadowfax, of which it is said: "In him one of the mighty steeds of old has returned" (*TT* III, vi, 126–27). And throughout *The Lord of the Rings*, we witness not the coming of the king but the *return* of the king, a restoration of a dynasty that has persisted throughout the many years, albeit in the shadows. As we are told, "Renewed shall be blade that was broken, / The crownless *again* shall be king" (*FR* I, x, 182; my emphasis). In the same poem he is associated with age, the past: "The old that is strong does not wither, / Deep roots are not reached by the frost." His sword, another relic, reflects Aragorn's representation of both past and present, establishing a continuity by its existence before even the men of Rohan established their land (*TT* III, ii, 40). He ascends to kingship centered in the realm of Gondor, which is itself a relic of the distant past, a people descended from the Númenóreans, a history of whom is related in *The Silmarillion* as the background of *The Lord of the Rings*. Although this line is fading over the years (fading being another consistent aspect of Tolkien's story), it yet persists. It is fad*ing* and not fad*ed*. There is interaction between this idea of fading and Tolkien's presentation of history. When we are conscious of something or someone fading, there is a suggestion of what something once was and what something now is. The past is recalled in comparison to the present and therefore impinges on the present. Aragorn belongs to a fading line that nevertheless persists.

3. Places: Ruins and Fading Glory

Quite often in *The Lord of the Rings* it is a place that excites nostalgia and leads a character into contemplative viewing of that place, meditating on a diminished people, civilization, and culture. This continues the theme of *fading*, diminishing; races of men can also be fading, such as the men of Númenor, an old and diminished line of kings that nevertheless can be revived by the like of Aragorn, yet significantly not quite at their former glory. They do persist, however. The ruins of their monuments and fortresses, notably towers, are the objects of nostalgia as adventurers, the Fellowship, travel across the landscape that was once a mighty realm. Connected to events of the past, there is great age in Isengard (*TT* III, viii, 159; III, ix, 174), in the Dead Marshes (*TT* IV, ii, 235, 240), in the road through Ithilien (*TT* IV, iv, 257, 259), Minas Tirith (*RK* V, iv, 96; VI, iv, 235; VI, v, 246), Minas Morgul (*RK* V, x, 160), and in Cirith Ungol (*TT* IV, iii, 252; *RK* VI, i, 176), where nearby an aged and hungry spider is connected to the darker aspects of *The Silmarillion* (*TT* IV, ix, 332). There is also the black stone of Erech, which is associated with a long past oath taken by the long since dead (*RK* V, ii, 55; V, ix, 152). There are other remains of other races, such as the realm of Moria. But Tolkien assigns some noteworthy ruins to Men. Aside from the tombs of the Barrow-downs, another remnant, there are the ruins of Amon Sûl, Weathertop. And Orthanc is also a remnant of past glory, although not in ruins, of course. One mysterious race of Men, the Woses or Wild Men, are ancient and associated with the aged Púkel statues on the road to Dunharrow (*RK* V, iii, 68; V, v, 105–6). Merry reacts emotionally to these statues and "gazed at them with wonder and a feeling almost of pity, as they loomed up mournfully in the dusk" (*RK* V, iii, 67). This place elicits sentimentality and wonder:

> Such was the dark Dunharrow, the work of long-forgotten men. Their name was lost and no song or legend remembered it. For what purpose they had made this place, as a town or secret temple or a tomb of kings, none in Rohan could say. Here they laboured in the Dark Years, before ever a ship came to the western shores, or Gondor of the Dúnedain was built; and now they had vanished, and only the old Púkel-men were left, still sitting at the turnings of the road [*RK* V, iii, 68].

The very mystery of this place hearkens to a deep past for the sentimental contemplation of character and reader.

Gondor, specifically Minas Tirith, is the surviving glory of Men, "recalling somewhat of the might of Númenor, ere it fell" (*FR* II, ii, 257). But this singular statement of glory that *is* recalls the greater glory of what *was*. One can gaze on Minas Tirith with appreciation of its present strength only to wax nostalgic at the past strength of the race of Men who built it and dominated much of Middle-earth, excepting Elven lands. Men once had a realm that stretched across the entire region of Middle-earth from the western shores (not far from the Barrow-downs) to what is now Minas Morgul, and from the area near the realm of the Witch-king of Angmar in the north to as far south as Umbar. We as readers may emotionally react when we encounter a reminder of what was, the past a shadowy background to give more significance to the narrative in the present, the fading glory. As we encounter what is, we cannot escape what was. After all, to have something fad*ing* assumes what it is faded *from*.

Places like Gondor have one foot in the past and the other in the present. One example, connected to Aragorn, is the Argonath. Here the past persists in the present as a memorial, a very present testimonial to the line of kings. Appropriately, the Fellowship reacts to this reminder of the past emotionally (sentimentally in Aragorn's case), and we are supposed to react this way as well:

> [G]reat pillars rose like towers ... Giants they seemed to him, vast grey figures silent but threatening ... the craft and power of old had wrought upon them, and still they preserved through the suns and rains of forgotten years the mighty like-nesses in which they had been hewn ... two great kings of stone: still with blurred eyes and crannied brows they frowned upon the North ... Great power and majesty they still wore, the silent wardens of a long-vanished kingdom. Awe and fear fell upon Frodo ... as the boats whirled by, frail and fleeting as little leaves, under the enduring shadow of the sentinels of Númenor [*FR* II, ix, 409].

The presence of the past in the present is such that "the craft and power of old had wrought upon them" excites "Awe and fear," an emotional response to the relics of the past. The Argonath awaken Aragorn's pride, his sense of self-hood bound to his very present identity with the past:

> Frodo turned and saw Strider, and yet not Strider; for the weatherworn Ranger was no longer there. In the stern sat Aragorn son of Arathorn ... a light was in his eyes: a king returning from exile to his own land [409].

He then further cements the continuous line from past to present, a "return-ing," when he connects himself to "Isildur and Anárion, my sires of old" and identifies himself as "Elessar, the Elfstone son of Arathorn of the House of Valandil Isildur's son, heir of Elendil" (409). Lineage is important in *The Lord of the Rings* as a connection between past and present, whether it be the blood of Westernesse or Númenor (*RK* V, i, 31; V, iv, 84; V, viii, 144; Appendix A, 343), the noble Eagles (*RK* VI, iv, 226) or the White Tree (*RK* VI, v, 250). Aragorn establishes his connection with the past by referring to his "sires of old." He is directly connected to "the power and majesty" of the kings of the Argonath (*TT* III, ii, 36). At one point Aragorn "looked as if some king out of the mists of the sea had stepped upon the shores of lesser men" (*TT* III, v, 104). He seems that he has "come on the wings of song out of the forgotten days" (*TT* III, vi, 115). In Aragorn the past lives.

Aragorn and companions also touch the past at Weathertop, where they see the ruins of Amon Sûl. This incident demonstrates Tolkien's nostalgia, an emotional response to reminders of the past. There are essentially three stages to this emotional recognition of the past. First, the ruins are described: "Along the crest of the ridge the hobbits could see what looked to be the remains of green-grown walls and dikes, and in the clefts there still stood the ruins of old works of stone" (*FR* I, xi, 197). Here the past is embodied by a physical object, or remains, in the present. Second, a sense of wonder is invoked by the ruins and environs; Merry says, "I wonder who made this path, and what for" (197). Ruins appeal to the viewer's sense of curiosity in that one wonders about the history, the past, behind the present artifact. Third, there is an affective and contemplative response to what remains. Aragorn explains:

> ... long before, in the first days of the North Kingdom, they built a great watchtower on Weathertop. Amon Sûl they called it. It was burned and broken, and nothing remains of it now but a tumbled ring, like a rough crown on the old hill's head. Yet once it was tall and fair. It is told that Elendil stood there watching for the coming of Gil-galad out of the West, in the days of the Last Alliance [197].

Sam then breaks out in song with "The Fall of Gil-galad" (*FR* I, xi, 197–8), a melancholy air which is characteristic of the songs of Middle-earth, or as Aragorn later says about another song, "It is a fair tale, though it is sad, as are all the tales of Middle-earth, and yet it may lift up your hearts" (*FR* I, xi, 203). Melancholy is the stuff of Tolkien's nostalgia.

This melancholy is constructed when Tolkien uses the past, lingering in the present in the form of relics and ruins, to orient the reader's emotions just as his characters have affective responses. For example, Aragorn says of the Road, "It is a strange road, and folk are glad to reach their journey's end" (*FR* I, xi, 200). The Road is not just a road. It is a special road, indicated by the definite article and a capital *R*, *The* Road, and it has roots in the distant past. A trip on The Road can be an emotional experience as one is all too glad to arrive at a destination. The Road takes on mythic significance, particularly in light of Bilbo's poem about The Road in both a general and particular sense (*FR* I, i, 44). Aragorn later relates the story of Beren and Lúthien (*FR* I, xi, 203–6), a melancholy tale indeed (especially coming from one whose romance is similar); and as this ends we are told that "As Strider was speaking they watched his strange eager face, dimly lit in the red glow of the wood-fire. His eyes shone, and his voice was rich and deep" (*FR* I, xi, 206). The atmosphere and character of the tale-teller is charged with emotion. Such reactions to stories, as well as to relics and ruins, are common in *The Lord of the Rings*, especially when the "Silmarillion" material is used as a backdrop and provides the emotionally charged history. When the adventurers draw near to Rivendell:

> The hobbits were glad to leave the cheerless lands and the perilous Road behind them; but this new country seemed threatening and unfriendly. As they went forward the hills about them steadily rose. Here and there upon heights and ridges they caught glimpses of ancient walls of stone, and the ruins of towers: they had an ominous look [*FR* I, xii, 213].

Not only do they attribute an emotional atmosphere to these ruins, finding them "ominous," but here the past is not merely past, but all too present: as Aragorn states, "a shadow still lies on the land" (214).

There are also remnants of a sinister past, continued by a sinister present, such as the dreaded realm of Mordor, the capital of which is a direct continuation, an endurance, of the past: "The Dark Tower was broken, but its foundations were not removed; for they were made with the power of the Ring, and while it remains they will endure" (*FR* II, ii, 257). Even the mere naming of that place excites an emotional reaction: "That name the hobbits only knew in legends of the dark past, like a shadow in the background of their memories; but it was ominous and disquieting" (*FR* I, ii, 53). The name evokes a mystery, an obscurity, that is fearsome in the very remoteness of its object. It is interesting that for Boromir Lothlórien invokes the same reaction (*FR* II, vi, 352–53). The *Old* Forest similarly evokes wonder and fear; one hobbit says, "That's a dark bad place, if half the tales be true" (*FR* I, i, 30).

> It was not called the Old Forest without reason, for it was indeed ancient, a survivor of vast forgotten woods; and in it there lived yet, ageing no quicker than the hills, the fathers of the fathers of trees, remembering times when they were lords [*FR* I, vii, 141].

Mordor is likewise connected to the continuation of the past in the present, as Gandalf explains to Frodo:

> [Sauron] has indeed arisen again ... and returned to his ancient fastness in the Dark Tower of Mordor. That name even you hobbits have heard of, *like a shadow on the borders of old stories*. Always after a defeat and a respite, the Shadow takes another shape and grows again [*FR* I, ii, 60; my emphasis].

The realm of Mordor, like Sauron himself, endures both in legend and actuality. It is the shadow of the past that excites a fearsome wonder in the audience of the tales: "... to them Mordor had been from childhood a name of evil, and yet unreal, a legend that had no part in their simple life; and now they walked like men in a hideous dream made true" (*RK* V, x, 162). Similarly, as Gandalf shows worry at the mention of Cirith Ungol, we are to fear for Frodo and Sam, who by that way are to enter Mordor (*RK* V, iv, 85, 88).

Another ominous place that recalls the distant past is the mysterious Barrow-downs, which is connected to the past of great Men. Tom Bombadil communicates a deep respect and immense sorrow when he tells the four hobbits about the history of this place: "Tom said that it had once been the boundary of a kingdom, but a very long time ago. He seemed to remember something sad about it, and would not say much" (*FR* I, viii, 158). Here there is a clear emotional response to the past.

It is not only the haunts of Men that excite a reverence and fear of the past, but the old places of the Dwarves as well, specifically the dreaded Mines of Moria—as well as the Elven realm of Eregion/Hollin before the western door in the shadow of the Misty Mountains, the latter ruins speaking to the heart of Legolas (*FR* II, iii, 297). The impassioned Dwarf Glóin exclaims at the council of Elrond:

> Moria! Moria! Wonder of the Northern world! Too deep we delved there, and woke the nameless fear. Long have its vast mansions lain empty since the children of Durin fled. But now we spoke of it again with longing, and yet with dread; for no dwarf has dared to pass the doors of Khazad-dûm for many lives of kings, save Thrór only, and he perished [*FR* II, ii, 253–54].

Here a mere name, embalmed with a long, remote history, can still draw on the wonder of Dwarves and consequently the wonder of Tolkien's reader. When in Moria, its mystique is powerful enough to invoke a song from Gimli, who recalls the past splendor of this now dark realm, referring to the Elder Days, mostly a Golden Age: "The world was fair in Durin's Day" (*FR* II, iv, 330). This is very different from the way Moria is now, a place of darkness and shadowed memories; he says, "I have looked on Moria, and it is very great, but it has become dark and dreadful" (332). The very name evokes an emotional response, as "It is a name of ill omen," and "The name of Moria is black" (309). The naming of Moria stirs the imagination of the hearer: "The wildest imaginings that dark rumour had ever suggested to the hobbits fell altogether short of the actual dread and wonder of Moria" (329). Although the experience of Moria itself is far worse than the rumors, there has built up a verbal tradition of the ancient horror. Yet not all is dark, as the glorious past and the ominous present exist side-by-side, even complimenting each other, as when Gimli beholds the enduring starry Crown of Durin in the water outside the west entrance of Moria, in the water of Kheled-zâram, which connects the past with a promise for the future (348).

Then the Fellowship enters the realm of Lothlórien, the epitome of the remote Elven past that continues in the present. Legolas connects this land with where his people "wandered in ages long ago" (*FR* II, vi, 352). From the very beginning of the Lothlórien portion of the narrative, a portion important enough to merit three chapters, the Fellowship connects a stream to the story of Nimrodel in a way that brings to life the remote and sorrowful past (353–5). Gimli had shown sentimentality towards Kheled-zâram, and similarly Legolas extols Nimrodel of "many songs long ago" (353). Tolkien orients the reader's emotional reaction at the very beginning of this emotional portion of the narrative that brings to life the past in the present. There is a contrast of remote Lothlórien with the time of the Shadow, the "latter days" (355–56). Perhaps the most significant paragraph describes Frodo's first experience of this place:

> As soon as he set foot upon the far bank of Silverlode a strange feeling had come upon him, and it deepened as he walked on ... it seemed to him that he had

stepped over a bridge of time into a corner of the Elder Days, and was now walking in a world that was no more. In Rivendell there was memory of ancient things; in Lórien the ancient things still lived on in the waking world ... on the land of Lórien no shadow lay [364].

For Frodo, "It seemed to him that he had stepped through a high window that looked on a vanished world," where what he sees is "ancient as if they had endured for ever" (365); and he "felt that he was in a timeless land that did not fade or change or fall into forgetfulness" (365–6). Rivendell is similarly timeless, as Bilbo comments, "I can't count days in Rivendell" (*FR* II, iii, 286).

This place is beautiful, but it is fading. The coming of the One Ring tolls the bell of disaster: whether the Ring survives or is destroyed, the power of Galadriel's Ring will diminish. Time cannot be held back much longer. Legolas affirms this, explaining the Elves' strange experience of time, more specifically the experience of the Lothlórien folk; Frodo says that time seems unmoving there and that they seemed to be in a past time. Treebeard testifies that "They are falling rather behind the world in there" (*TT* III, iv, 70). In Lothlórien there is an "ageless time" (*TT* III, v, 106). Legolas says:

> Nay, time does not tarry ever ... but change and growth is not in all things and places alike. For the Elves the world moves, and it moves both very swift and very slow. Swift, because they themselves change little, and all else fleets by: it is a grief to them. Slow, because they do not count the running years, not for themselves. The passing seasons are but ripples ever repeated in the long long stream. Yet beneath the Sun all things must wear to an end at last [*FR* II, ix, 404–5].

All will fade.

Yet, the past does persist. An obvious example is the appropriately named Old Forest; in the comparison made between the forest of Fangorn and the Old Forest, the common link is that of great age (*TT* III, ii, 45)—in fact, they were long ago part of the same wood that stretched across Middle-earth (*TT* III, iv, 72). Treebeard, supposedly the oldest of the old, says of Fangorn Forest that in some places "the trees are older than I am" (71). Treebeard brings a sentimental response to this distant past as he remembers Tasarinan in the Spring, Ossiriand in the Summer, Autumn in Neldoreth, Winter in Dorthonion:

> And now all those lands lie under the wave,
> And I walk in ... my own land, in the country of Fangorn,
> Where the roots are long,
> And the years lie thicker than the leaves
> In Tauremornalómë [72].

The mysterious names serve to build the romantic response to the past. Treebeard does more than recall the distant past. He waxes sentimental, and Tolkien's readers are to respond in kind.

4. Objects: The Past in Hand

Objects, artifacts and relics, also connect the past and the present, like the Phial of Galadriel that bears the light of a Silmaril (*TT* IV, ix, 329) or the Palantíri that served the searching eyes of Númenor (*TT* III, xi, 199–200, 202–3). There are also the swords of Merry and Pippin (*FR* I, viii, 157; *RK* V, i, 28; V, vi, 119–20), the horn given Merry by Éowyn (*RK* VI, vi, 256), and Boromir's horn of Gondor (*RK* V, i, 27). The past survives in swords and rings, especially swords borne by members of the Fellowship and the Rings of Power. Aragorn's sword is a family heirloom that is an indicator of his right to be king. Boromir states, "Yet we are hard pressed, and the Sword of Elendil would be a help beyond our hope—if such a thing could indeed return out of the shadows of the past" (*FR* II, ii, 260). This broken sword changes its name when it is reforged (*FR* II, iii, 290), but it still essentially represents the past— a sword and a line of kings—that is alive in the present, however faint its glimmer of hope. The swords Glamdring and Sting are also artifacts of the distant past, still sharp and deadly in the present, for they are "the work of Elvish smiths in the Elder Days" (*FR* II, iv, 324). Before entrance into Théoden's hall, Aragorn and Gandalf must yield their swords, which are connected to the remote past when they were forged (*TT* III, vi, 115). Frodo's Sting is likewise connected to the land of Beleriand (*TT* IV, ix, 331), which we know from the "Silmarillion" material; the naming of the land builds the mystique of the sword forged long ago. These swords are emblematic of the past's ability to live and breathe in the present, emblematic as the Mathom-house in the Shire.

Languages are old. The Palantíri are old. And much else in *The Lord of the Rings* has great age. But at the center of the narrative are the Rings from a previous age that yet bear much influence on the present age. In fact the One Ring establishes continuity between the past and the present, as Elrond explains:

> Sauron was diminished, but not destroyed. His Ring was lost but not unmade. The Dark Tower was broken, but its foundations were not removed; for they were made with the power of the Ring, and while it remains they will endure [*FR* II, ii, 257].

As Galadriel testifies, "The evil that was devised long ago works on in many ways" (*FR* II, vii, 381).

5. Conclusion: The Past's Persistence

Legends of the past, predominantly the stories that will be collected in *The Silmarillion*, ever shadow the present, such as the story of Beren and

Lúthien (*FR* I, xi, 204–6; *RK* VI, vi, 252). The vast history behind *The Lord of the Rings*, evident in the Appendices, creates a verisimilitude, but Tolkien adds to history a sentimentality, a pervading nostalgia, such as in the explanation of the Quendi:

> They were a race high and beautiful, the older Children of the world, and among them the Eldar were as kings, who now are gone: the People of the Great Journey.... They were valiant, but the history of those that returned to Middle-earth in exile was grievous; and though it was in far-off days crossed by the fate of the Fathers, their fate is not that of Men. Their dominion passed long ago, and they dwell now beyond the circles of the world, and do not return [*RK* Appendix F, 415–16].

This comparison of past and present asks for an effective response to what no longer is.

When discussing *The Lord of the Rings* it may be incorrect to establish neat boundary lines between the past and the present when the past is quite present throughout the narrative. People, places, and things are old, indeed ancient, and establish continuity from one age to another. The remote past is seldom only remote, but continuously overshadows and haunts the present, and we are to respond to the past sentimentally as when Aragorn relates "the sadness of Mortal Men" and asks *Ubi sunt*?: "Where now the horse and the rider? Where is the horn that was blowing?" answering his own question:

> They have passed like rain on the mountain, like a wind in the meadow;
> The days have gone down in the West behind the hills into shadow.
> Who shall gather the smoke of the dead wood burning,
> Or behold the flowing years from the Sea returning? [*TT* III, vi, 112].

Night-wolves, Half-trolls and the Dead Who Won't Stay Down[1]

Marjorie Burns

1. Wolves

Halfway through his essay "On Fairy-stories," in a section titled "Children," J.R.R. Tolkien takes issue with Andrew Lang by referring to his own boyhood preferences in books.[2] He begins with fairy-stories, saying only that those that succeeded with him were those that "awakened *desire*." He then tells us the *Alice* books "merely amused" him and *Treasure Island* left him "cool." Better were tales of Red Indians, and better yet was "the land of Merlin and Arthur." But best of all, he concludes, was "the nameless North of Sigurd of the Völsungs, and the prince of all dragons" (*TOF* 55).

This last, the Sigurd story from *Völsunga saga*,[3] is a remarkably telling preference for a boy who would someday become the author of *The Lord of the Rings*. No other tale, not even *Beowulf* (itself really a saga), is so densely packed with scenes and characters and tidbits that Tolkien would later take for his own. This is true even of the first version of *Völsunga saga* Tolkien read as a boy, a greatly shortened, heavily amended version that appears as the final chapter in Andrew Lang's *Red Fairy Book*.

Much hangs on that early encounter. If William Morris (working with Eiríkr Magnússon) had not made his 1870 translation of *Völsunga saga* (the first translation into English), and if Andrew Lang had not trimmed it down and placed it in his 1890 *Fairy Book*, would we still have *The Lord of the Rings*? I don't think we would, though we might have something else by a man named

J.R.R. Tolkien. But fortunately for us Tolkien discovered "The Story of Sigurd" during those formative years of middle childhood; and once he read it, it stuck. It stuck the way true childhood passions do, and it shaped what he became, leaving its mark not only on the literature for which he is famous but inspiring Tolkien to attempt a poetic rewriting of the Volsung story himself.[4]

The list of what Tolkien encountered in Lang's greatly shortened and softened retelling is impressive in itself: a gold-loving dwarf, a cursed and destructive ring, a supernatural horse, an advice-giving bearded old man, a shieldmaiden, an evil counselor, talking birds, an inherited broken sword (soon to be reforged), and a treasure-guarding dragon. Once Tolkien became acquainted with the unamended saga in his early teens, he found the following as well: oathbreakers, readers of the future, magically healing leaves, secretive runes, dreams that warn or reveal, catchy aphorisms, and—most important for this opening section—detailed, impressive accounts of humans in wolfish form.[5]

Early in *Völsunga saga*, King Siggeir and his army attack the Volsungs. They kill King Volsung and capture his ten sons, placing them in stocks. Here they sit throughout the day; then (quoting from Morris and Magnússon)[6]:

> [A]t midnight, as they sat in the stocks, there came on them a she-wolf from out the wood; old she was, and both great and evil of aspect; and the first thing she did was to bite one of those brethren till he died, and then she ate him up withal, and went on her way [298].

Each night she comes again, this wolf rumored to be King Siggeir's mother using "troll's lore and witchcraft" to change her outer guise. Each night she eats one of the brothers until only Sigmund, the eldest, remains. But now Sigmund's sister (the wife of King Siggeir) works up a plan. She arranges to have Sigmund's face covered with honey as a distraction for the wolf.

> [S]o the next night came the she-wolf according to her wont, and would slay him and eat him even as his brothers; but now she sniffs the breeze from him ... and licks his face all over with her tongue, and then thrusts her tongue into the mouth of him. No fear he had thereof, but caught the she-wolf's tongue betwixt his teeth, and so hard she started back thereat, and pulled herself away so mightily, setting her feet against the stocks, that all was riven asunder; but he ever held so fast that the tongue came away by the roots, and thereof she had her bane [299].

This is not a passage a reader would likely forget, and it certainly impressed Tolkien—so much so that he borrows closely from the saga passage in his story "Of Beren and Lúthien." Here King Finrod Felagund, Beren, and ten unnamed companions have been cast into Sauron's "deep pit, dark and silent" (*S* 171). Just as in *Völsunga saga*, the wolf that comes to them in their captivity and eats them, one by one, is no ordinary wolf.[7] Like Sigmund, Beren alone survives, and again like Sigmund, Beren is saved through help that comes from a woman.

Two chapters and some years later, Sigmund and his son, Sinfjotli (now living an outlaw's life in the woods) come upon two men, "spell-bound skin-changers," lying fast asleep. Wolf-skins are hanging above the men, and these Sigmund and Sinfjotli place upon themselves and, through the magic of the skins, turn themselves into wolves. Once they have done so, they must remain in this guise for nine days at a stretch. Only on the tenth day can the skins be removed, and so they continue—howling like wolves but thinking and under-standing like men—until Sigmund, in a moment of anger, turns on Sinfjotli and bites him in the throat.

Even in his wolfish state, he regrets what he has done, and curses the wolf skins, wishing them "to the trolls." But Sinfjotli survives (through an applica-tion of magical leaves); and when the nine days are once more up, the two of them burn the skins, praying "no more hurt might come to anyone" from those skins. And yet, the saga tells us, "in that uncouth guise they wrought many famous deeds" (302–303).

The wolf that devours nine brothers and the werewolves that Sigmund and Sinfjotli become are the most dramatic examples of wolves in *Völsunga saga*, but they are not the only ones. In one incident, wolf flesh is used in hostile magic; in another, a wolf hair signals the presence of a traitor; and still else-where a murderer is "given forth to be a wolf" (291). This last may seem an odd expression, but those familiar with saga language will understand that the murderer has been outlawed and must leave society. In the eyes of others, he has become a wolf or a vargr, and *vargr*—an Old Norse word meaning both outlaw and wolf—is where Tolkien got his wargs.[8]

All of this wolfishness (as werewolves or as a means of creating magic or as an expression applied to human violence) is standard Old Norse fare, as are wolves that appear in dreams (a clear indication of evil) and wolves used as mounts for giantesses, witches, or trolls. Here again Tolkien follows suit. Frodo's dream of Gandalf standing on a pinnacle of stone while wolves howl below fits the pattern of wolves heralding evil, but Tolkien does even more with wolves used as mounts. In *The Hobbit*, goblins ride on wolves "like men do on horses" (VI, 112). In *The Silmarillion*, orcs ride upon "great wolves" (174). *The Two Towers* includes several references to wolf-riders; and scattered throughout *The History of Middle-earth* are still other examples of wolf-riders and orcs riding on wolves.[9]

It all makes sense, given Tolkien's fascination with the ancient Scandina-vian world. And yet, in context of that world, there is something slightly odd about these Old Norse wolves. Nearly all that remains of Old Norse writing—records, sagas, verse, and eddic mythology—came from Iceland; and Iceland has no wolves, neither wolves nor bears. Why, then, should wolves and bears show up with such regularity?

The answer is simple enough. Wolves and bears (or the *concept* of wolves and bears) were imported from the continent. They hitchhiked, you could say, in the minds and memories of Norwegians who began migrating to Iceland during the ninth century. Deep in the psyche of those new immigrants—and passed on to their children—was a vivid awareness of bears and wolves, an awareness that remained as a cultural idea, somewhat the way "lions and tigers and bears, oh my!" still remains with us. Journeys back to Norway helped keep the concept alive; but over time, both animals began to slip more and more into the realm of metaphor, not just as an easy tag for the ruthless and vicious but as creatures of the imagination, creatures of dreams and magic, creatures of the dark.

Like saga wolves, Tolkien's wolves are humanized—endowed with unnatural abilities and the worst of human traits, and they too work their machinations by dark. In *The Hobbit* they talk "in the dreadful language of the Wargs" (VI, 111) and collaborate with goblins; in *The Lord of the Rings*, the same pattern holds. "[W]here the warg howls, there also the orc prowls," says Aragorn, loosening his sword in their camp at the base of Caradhras (*FR* II, iv, 311), an aphorism with much the same ring as one from *Völsunga saga*, which claims "where wolf's ears are, wolf's teeth are near" (332).

To these *Lord of the Rings* Wargs—as compared with his *Hobbit* ones—Tolkien adds the were-magic, the werewolf horror, of shape-shifting with evil intent. These are not just talking wolves but humans shaped as wolves. Like certain skin-changers in the sagas who can send forth their spirit in animal form while asleep back in their beds, the substance of these wolves is not permanent; they leave no traces of blood or body once morning comes. "It is as I feared," Gandalf says. "These were no ordinary wolves hunting for food in the wilderness" (*FR* II, iv, 313).

Wolves of this sort serve almost as magical extensions of Saruman, as a way for Saruman to reach beyond his tower without leaving its protective walls.[10] In *The Silmarillion* and *The History of Middle-earth*, the same is true of Sauron, another master of wolves and werewolves, and of Morgoth, who disperses "his might" into "creatures of wickedness" and whose "hate" and "malice" are heard in the howls of Carcharoth (*S* 101, 185).[11] But body projection, if I may call it that, is not the only means of shape-shifting Tolkien took from the Norse. The use of animal skins, like those Sigmund and Sinfjotli steal, appears in Tolkien as well. In accounts of Beren and Lúthien (from *The Silmarillion*, *The Lays of Beleriand*, and *The War of the Jewels*), Beren enters Morgoth's fortress dressed in the "werewolf cloak" or "wolf-hame" of Draugluin (werewolf servant to Sauron).

Sauron too takes on the shape of a wolf and does so to battle Huan, wolfhound companion to Beren and Lúthien. In *The Silmarillion* and *The Lays of Beleriand* no mention is made of how Sauron (Lord of Wolves, Werewolf Lord, living on the Isle of Werewolves) achieves this transformation. In

The War of the Jewels, however, he is described as coming forth to battle "in wolf-hame" (67).

From a saga perspective, *hame* is a particularly telling term. You won't find it in most dictionaries, not with the meaning Tolkien has in mind. You will find it, however, in the *Oxford English Dictionary* as an outdated word for "skin, membrane" or the "slough of a serpent." In Old English the word is *hama*, a close cousin of the Old Norse *hamr*, meaning skin or slough; shape or form. A person capable of skin-changing in Old Norse belief is *ham-ramr*.

References to skin-changing, or suggestions of that skill, are common enough in Old Norse literature and strikingly so in the opening section of *Egils saga*, where Egil's family is introduced, beginning with Egil's grandfather, a man named Ulf (Wolf). If nothing else, this opening shows how matter-of-fact the ancient Icelanders were about their family trees. Ulf is a hard-working man, foreseeing, and generous with advice but only during the day. Once evening arrives, he grows irritable and evil-tempered. Because of this, he is considered a skin-changer and acquires the name Kveldulf (Evening-wolf).[12] Evening-wolf's own father is called Bjalf, and *Bjalf* means animal hide, a good indication that Evening-wolf is not only a skin-changer in his own right but the son of a skin-changer too. And there is more: Evening-wolf's mother, a woman named Hallbera, is the daughter of yet another man named Wolf, and both she and her brother Hallbjorn have names based on words for *bear*, adding a hint of bear blood to the family as well.

By themselves, names that include animals (most frequently wolves or bears) are not at all unusual. They were common in Medieval Scandinavia and are still common today. In Egil's family, however, more than chance is at work. Violent behavior continues down the generations, so that Egil (in his boyhood) is nearly killed by his father; and when Egil is "seven winters" of age, he intentionally kills another boy during a game of ball. As an adult, he has thick wolf-grey hair, and he attacks a man by biting him in the throat.

It all adds up to an impressive list of traits, but animal connections are not the only ones Evening-wolf can claim. There is a troll connection in the family too. The full name of Hallbjorn (Evening-wolf's uncle on his mother's side) is Hallbjorn the Half-troll, and trolls (as troublesome and commonplace as supernatural wolves) are where we are going next.

2. Trolls

If you have been reading carefully, you should already have noticed several facts about trolls: One: they are associated with magic (the "troll's lore" Siggeir's mother uses in order to change her shape). Two: that which a person wishes to curse or be rid of can be sent to the trolls (the skins Sigmund wishes "to the trolls"). Three: trolls, like witches and giantesses, are known to ride on wolves. And four: trolls can breed with humankind.

In the sagas, trolls are represented as ill-favored, oversized, solitary beings, living on the edge of humankind and sometimes interacting (generally in unpleasant ways) with the human world. In *Grettis saga*, when the hero, Grettir, swims a wintry bay by night and crashes into an isolated house,[13] he is taken for a troll—a fairly understandable mistake: Grettir is "wondrous great" of size (117) and covered with ice, and he bursts into the dwelling in true monster fashion, the way Grendel does in *Beowulf* or the way a "troll-wife" does later in *Grettis saga* in a scene highly reminiscent of Beowulf's fight with Grendel.[14]

> [W]hen it drew towards midnight, [Grettir] heard great din without, and thereafter into the hall came a huge troll-wife, with a trough in one hand and a chopper wondrous great in the other; she peered about when she came in, and saw where [Grettir] lay, and ran at him; but he sprang up to meet her, and they fell a-wrestling terribly, and struggled together for long in the hall. She was the stronger, but he gave back with craft, and all that was before them was broken ....
> She was fain to drag him from the house, but might not until they had broken away all the fittings of the outer door, and borne them out on their shoulders: then she laboured away with him down towards the river, and right down to the deep gulfs....
> All night did they contend in such wise; never, he deemed, had he fought with such a horror ....
> But now when they came to the gulf of the river, he gives the hag a swing round, and therewith got his right hand free, and swiftly seized the short-sword that he was girt withal, and smote the troll therewith on the shoulder, and struck off her arm; and therewithal was he free ....
> Now Grettir's story is that the troll-wife cast herself into the gulf when she got her wound; but the men of Bard-dale say that day dawned on her, while they wrestled, and that she burst, when he cut the arm from her; and that there she stands yet on the cliff, a rock in the likeness of a woman [194–6].

The fate of the troll-wife (as the men of Bard-dale would have it) is not unique to *Grettis saga*. It is an old motif that Tolkien would have known from other sources as well—from Scandinavian folklore[15] and from Norse mythology, where the giantess Hrimgerd is turned to stone by the sun and the dwarf Alvis is destroyed by the light of day.[16]

As a philologist, Tolkien would also have known other peculiarities associated with trolls and with words related to *troll*. He would have known that the primary meaning of *trylla* in the Old Norse language is to work magic or enchant. This meaning is still around in modern Scandinavian languages, so much so that in the Norwegian translation of *The Lord of the Rings*, Gandalf the Wizard becomes *trollmannen Gandalv* (or Gandalf the Trollman).

With his philological background and his familiarity with Old Norse literature (mythology, sagas and folklore), Tolkien would also have recognized the substantial overlap that exists between giants and trolls. This awareness shows in *The Fellowship of the Ring*, in Aragorn's description of the Ettenmoors as "the troll-fells" (I, xii, 212), a perfectly appropriate description since *etten* derives from the Old English *eoten*, meaning both giant and troll. In *Beowulf*, for example, Grendel is referred to as both eoten and troll, and this same usage appears in Tolkien's translation of *Sir Gawain and the Green Knight*, where he renders "half etayn" (*etayn* being the Middle English for *eoten*) into "half a troll" though he might just as well have written "half a giant" (28).

Like the saga writers who reduced the giants of their mythology to earth-based trolls, Tolkien too began shifting away from giants—a wise choice on Tolkien's part since the introduction of trolls gave him fresher possibilities than giants would have allowed (with their too-established, fairytale familiarity). After the stone-giants of the Misty Mountains put on their rock-hurling display in *The Hobbit*, no more giants make an appearance in Tolkien's Middle-earth. In *The Lord of the Rings*, there are rumors of giants, and Ents are referred to as giants (appropriately enough since *ent* is another Old English word commonly translated as *giant*). "[W]hat about these Tree-men, these giants, as you might call them?" Sam asks (*FR* I, ii, 53). But that is as close as we get. Tolkienian giants that started up in draft accounts (like the malevolent Giant Treebeard) are either weeded out or evolve into something new.[17]

What remains are trolls and orcs. And yet, given the literature and language they evolved from, what are orcs but another variation on the troll and giant theme? All three are hefty and brutal; all three are steeped in rough nature; all three have reason to fear the sun. There is an Old English connection between orcs and giants as well, as the word *orcþyrs* (orc-giant) indicates.[18]

Here is what Tolkien himself has to say about giant orcs and trolls in Appendix F at the end of *The Return of the King*:

> In their beginning ... [trolls] were creatures of dull and lumpish nature and had no more language than beasts. But Sauron had made use of them, teaching them what little they could learn, and increasing their wits with wickedness....
>
> But at the end of the Third Age a troll-race not before seen appeared ....That Sauron bred them none doubted, though from what stock was not known. Some held they were not Trolls but giant Orcs ....Trolls they were, but filled with the evil will of their master: a fell race, strong, agile, fierce and cunning, but harder than stone. Unlike the older race of the Twilight they could endure the Sun [410].

These newly bred trolls, "no longer dull-witted, but cunning and armed with dreadful weapons" (*FR* I, ii, 53), are not the half-trolls of saga lore. Once Tolkien decided their creation depended on Sauron's manipulation, he removed the concept of half-ness from their character—so that the black "half-trolls" found in an early version of "The Battle of the Pelennor Fields"[19] now become the "black men like half-trolls" or the "troll-men" who are driven into the East by the knights of Dol Amroth in *The Return of the King* (V, vi, 121, 123).

But "half-orcs," also called "goblin-men," still remain (*TT* III, vii, 142). Such monsters, such partially human monsters, may even walk among us and drink at our favorite inn the way Bill Ferny's squint-eyed companion does, a man who looks "more than half like a goblin" (*FR* I, xi, 193). Not a pleasant thought.

3. The Dead

And now we come to the Dead, to those who ought to be dead but refuse to accept the fact. Death and endings run throughout *The Lord of the Rings*. An age is dying; Elves are departing; the Entwives are lost; battles are taking their toll, and virtual deaths occur all around—from the hobbits' entrapment in a burial mound, to Gandalf's "death" in Moria, to Frodo's journey to Mordor, the land of shadow and death.[20] In more than one letter Tolkien acknowledged this emphasis on death, mostly calling it the theme of "Death and Immortality."[21] But when it comes to specifics, Tolkien's depiction of death is not a simple one. There is no clear answer to what death means or what death brings. What Tolkien gives us instead are possibilities: for Dwarves, an afterlife in Mandos's halls, or so the Dwarves believe (the Elves say Dwarves return to earth and stone)[22]; for Men, an "unrevealed destiny," giving "Hope without guarantees" (*Letters* 286, 237); and for Elves, a virtual immortality while the created world endures.

The Norse too had multiple ways of explaining what happens after death. In their mythology, those who die heroically in battle spend their nights drinking and feasting in Valhalla and their days in glorious battle, killing or being killed before rising up again. Those who die less gloriously are sent to the vague and somewhat inconsistent realm of Niflheim or Hel, a dreary world of darkness, chill, and starvation.

Sagas and poetry offer other possibilities. Reincarnation is one, sometimes clearly stated, sometimes only alluded to, and sometimes sought or hoped for by naming one's newborn child after a relative who has died.[23] There is also the possibility of "dying into the hills," a term used for certain favored dead who are welcomed into a mountainside. There, an afterlife much like that of Valhalla is said to continue on.[24] But, one way or another, the Norse tended to imagine some form of continuing consciousness on the part of their dead, and sometimes more than consciousness was thought to occur. Sometimes the dead got up and moved around. Those that did were said to "walk," becoming *afterwalkers*.[25]

There is a considerable difference, however, between the after-death behavior of unsavory individuals and that of decent folks. Those who were honorable and kindly in life recognize death is part of the deal. At most, they sing in their barrow mounds or allow themselves a farewell visit, or (as in the case of Thorgunna) cook up a final meal for their casket bearers.[26] Such hauntings are essentially innocuous and even welcome at times. But the violent and greedy, the ruthlessly ambitious and the overly proud are another matter. Folks of this sort not only become walkers of the worst kind; they also receive a noticeable boost from death. Their nastiness, their size, their strength are all enlarged. Their flesh remains uncorrupted, though their burial site may reek. And as often as not they turn black in color or blue.

Grettis saga is full of fine examples. In his first encounter with one of the living dead, Grettir enters the burial mound of Old Kerr, a notorious and destructive afterwalker who has been plaguing the neighborhood. It is night when Grettir finishes breaking into the mound, and he enters by descending on a rope. "[R]ight dark it was," we are told, and the smell "none of the sweetest."

> Now he groped about to see how things were below; first he found horse bones, and then he stumbled against the arm of a high-chair, and in that chair found a man sitting; great treasures of gold and silver were heaped together there, and a small chest was set under the feet of him full of silver; all these riches Grettir carried together to the rope; but as he went out through the barrow he was griped at right strongly; thereon he let go the treasure and rushed against the barrow-dweller, and now they set on one another unsparingly enough.
> Everything in their way was kicked out of place, the barrow-wight[27] setting on with hideous eagerness; Grettir gave back before him for a long time, till at last it came to this; that he saw it would not do to hoard his strength any more; now neither spared the other, and they were brought to where the horse-bones were, and thereabout they wrestled long. And now one, now the other, fell on his knee; but the end of the strife was, that the barrow-dweller fell over on his back with huge din [47–48].

At this point Grettir draws his sword and cuts off the barrow-wight's head, laying it next to the wight's thigh, an *almost* a sure-fire way of preventing further walking. From the spoils of this encounter, Grettir acquires a short but even better sword.

It is not hard to see how all of this worked its way into Tolkien's world. Burial mounds, or barrows, are fairly common throughout Middle-earth. Like Norse mounds (or Celtic ones, for that matter), these burial sites are not always quiet. And the most Norse and most troubling of all in Tolkien's literature is the one the hobbits enter on the Barrow Downs. The setting, the mood, the sheer creepiness; the darkness, the treasure, and the viciousness waiting within are straight from the sagas. Added to this are the long daggers taken from the barrow, daggers that later serve the hobbits well. Even the "rumbling sound, as of stones rolling and falling," during Tom Bombadil's rescue is quite in line with the sagas, where barrow-wights seem to move in and out of their barrows without benefit of a door but others need to break their way forcefully in (*FR* I, viii, 153).

Tolkien, however, shifts matters a bit in his own Barrow Downs account, giving us a haunting and a skirmish without maligning the one for whom the barrow was intended, a prince buried some two hundred years before the wight itself appeared.[28] This means that Tolkien's wight is not a reanimated corpse belonging to the barrow but an opportunist who has moved—the way a hermit crab does—into someone else's abode.

There are further oddities here. What Frodo (having gathered his courage) confronts is an arm walking on finger tips. If this is the barrow haunt, then who captured the hobbits, who dressed them in white rags and trinkets, who laid them in the barrow and placed a sword across three of the hobbits' throats? A lone arm, reduced to finger walking—like a yellow pages telephone ad—would have difficulty managing all of this, though the arm is described as heading toward the hilt of the sword.[29] Or was it the "tall dark figure like a shadow" that bends over Frodo before gripping him outside the barrow (*FR* I, viii, 151)? This dark, looming specter is a far more likely candidate, though it looks and speaks more like a Black Rider than a burly Norse barrow-wight committed to defending a treasure and keeping others out. But if this specter is the wight, then who is the arm? And who makes the "snarling noise" when the arm is destroyed?

It is something of a puzzle but not one that readers are likely to worry about. The scene works perfectly. Tolkien has created a thrilling barrow horror, using hobbits, a phantom, a finger-walking arm, and a minor skirmish. There is no out-and-out battle raging in the dark as there was with Grettir and Old Kerr. But these are hobbits, not warriors on a human scale; and a disembodied arm, a leftover piece of a malevolent barrow being, is adversary enough.

To some extent, the Barrow Downs encounter is a side incident, off and away from the main storyline. Nonetheless the barrow itself and events surrounding the barrow fit right in—as one in a series of burial sites where treasure is found and violence or battle occur. Where this most often happens (in *The Hobbit* and *The Lord of the Rings*) is inside Tolkien's mountains. And here again Tolkien is following Norse tradition, that belief in hills or mountains that receive and house the dead.

Tolkien does not follow the Norse pattern precisely, but—in one way or another—his mountains tend to encase the dead and include settings where treasure is found and battles occur. The Lonely Mountain (with its dragon hoard and its Battle of Five Armies) is where Thorin is laid to rest, the Arkenstone on his breast. Moria (the source of mithril, or "true-silver," and site of more than one battle) is where Balin has his tomb. Within the passages beneath Dwimorberg (The Haunted Mountain), the oathbreaking "Sleepless Dead," are waiting and the "bones of a mighty man"[30] lie before a door, a man whose belt shows "gold and garnets" and whose hauberk is "gilded," and whose helm is "rich with gold" (*RK* V, ii, 55, 60). From here the oathbreakers, warriors long dead, will rise again.[31] Mount Doom offers only a slight variation. Here is where Gollum falls to his death, carrying with him his Precious, the One Ring.

But Gollum's ending in the furnaces of Mount Doom is more a completion of death than a sudden, violent demise. Though he began in a children's story and needed some alteration to find his place within *The Lord of the Rings*, from the first Gollum is marked by traits that fit the afterwalking dead of Old Norse belief.

He is, if nothing else, a thieving, kin-murdering, treasure-hoarding, sun-hating, underground dweller who ought to be dead. And once he crawls away from the living world (driven away from family and kin) and burrows into a mountain, he continues a darkened, extended, and hungry existence, hungry in an unnatural, unfillable way. "We are lost, lost," says Gollum. "No name, no business, no Precious, nothing. Only empty. Only hungry; yes, we are hungry" (*TT* IV, vi, 298).

Compare this to the freshly dead Aran from *Egils saga einhenda ok Ásmundar berserkjabana* (*The Saga of Egil One-hand and Asmund Berserker-Slayer*). On the first night Aran eats the hawk and hound buried with him; on the second night he kills and eats his horse, and on the third night he attacks his former foster brother (who escapes with only the loss of his ears). Though Gollum's hunger is certainly less extreme, Gollum and Aran are both examples of abnormal appetite that cannot be satisfied.[32]

Like the Old Norse walking dead, Gollum is supernaturally strong and must be wrestled with hand to hand, as both Sam and Frodo do with him on the slopes of Mount Doom and within Mount Doom itself. And again like an afterwalker, Gollum is described as black. In a passage written to his illustrator, Pauline Baynes, Tolkien attempted to mitigate this image, saying Gollum may appear "dark or black" and is admittedly described this way, but this is because he "evidently had black garments." Gollum's skin, however, is white, "almost bone-white."[33] But Gollum as a contrast in black and white (*bone*-white) fits still other images of the Old Norse dead. As Helen Buckhurst, Tolkien's colleague, explained in her paper, "Icelandic Folklore," the dead who have been animated by magic are black but show one gleaming touch of white.[34]

There is this as well: Gollum is destroyed by fire, and in Norse belief, destruction by fire is an ultimate solution for stopping the restless dead. In *Eyrbyggja saga*, Thorolf Halt-foot (nasty in life and even nastier in death) wreaks havoc and destruction long after his burial. When Thorolf first grows restless after death, he is dug up and moved. This temporarily stops his walking; but after his son dies (a decent man who had previously maintained control of his troublesome father), Thorolf begins walking and killing again. This time heavier measures are required. Thorolf is dug up a second time; and with great difficulty his body ("blue as hell," uncorrupted, and supernaturally huge) is set on fire and burned to ashes that fly off into the wind (172).

In *The Lord of the Rings*, Gollum is not alone in his being destroyed by fire. Others who have lived beyond their time or have chosen to side with death also end in smoke and flame. The Nazgûl (no longer part of the living world but moving through it still) end by "shooting like flaming bolts" in "fiery ruin," crackling, withering, and going out (*RK* VI, iii, 224). Denethor, who has turned his back on life, who lives in a dying city where few children are born, who would take the life of his only remaining son, dies engulfed by flames with a treasured palantír clutched to his breast.

Even Sauron comes to such an end. As a Maia, he should not be subject to death; but in choosing to serve Morgoth, he moves himself in that direction, not only becoming "a shadow of Morgoth and a ghost of [Morgoth's] malice" (*S* 32), but assuming the title of *Necromancer*, a term used for wizards or magicians who commune with the dead.[35] Caught up as he is in death and the dead yet virtually indestructible, Sauron's undoing by fire is fully appropriate.

When Frodo puts on the Ring, claiming it as his own, Sauron is "suddenly aware." His wrath blazes in "consuming flame," even while his fear rises like "black smoke to choke him" (*RK* VI, iii, 223). Moments later the Ring is destroyed, and Sauron's fiery, smoke-filled response merges with his destruction. The world he has created begins crashing and melting amidst darkness and flickering flames; Sauron becomes a shadow filling the sky; and then, like smoke or like the ashes of Thorolf Halt-foot, this shadow is blown away.

Saruman—ever the imitator of Sauron—ends with only a slightly less dramatic version of the same. He too has challenged the natural order and entombed himself in a tower. He too should be immortal; he too has sided with death. When his time comes, he turns to "grey mist" that rises "like smoke from a fire" before a wind blows it into nothing (*RK* VI, viii, 300).

It is quite a pattern Tolkien creates for those who would take more than their due and who have aligned themselves with death. Like the afterwalkers of Old Norse sagas, they come to a final and well-deserved destruction though fires and flames that burn them fully away.

And there you have them: the werewolves, trolls, and afterwalkers of Old

Norse belief—the beasts, the brutes, and the malevolent dead—all who have been given their own form of afterlife in Tolkien's literature.

NOTES

1. Originally given as the keynote speech for the Fifth Annual Tolkien Conference at the University of Vermont. April 12, 2008.

2. "On Fairy-stories" was written as an Andrew Lang Lecture and delivered at the University of St. Andrews in 1939. An expanded version was published in 1947.

3. Sigurd's story (and variations on his story) appear in other early works as well, most notably the *Poetic Edda*, the *Prose Edda*, and the German *Nibelungenlied*.

4. This poetic rewriting was edited by Christopher Tolkien and published in 2009 (along with a second poem on the story of Gudrún) under the title *The Legend of Sigurd and Gudrún*. The original title for Tolkien's Sigurd poem was *Völsungakviða en nýja* (*The New Lay of the Völsungs*). Both poems were most likely composed in the early 1930s.

5. In 1911, while still at King Edward's School, Birmingham, Tolkien read a paper on the Norse sagas to the school's Literary Society, claiming *Völsunga saga* one of the best. By 1914 he had used part of the five pounds from his Skeat Prize for English to buy several William Morris books, including Morris's translation of *Völsunga saga*.

6. All saga quotations in this essay are from William Morris and Eiríkr Magnússon translations.

7. This similarity was first cited by T.A. Shippey as "werewolves devouring bound men in the dark" (*Road* 259).

8. See *Author* 30–1.

9. Primarily *Lost Tales* II, *Lays*, and *War*.

10. This shaman's trick is one that Odin used as well, as his two news-bearing ravens (Thought and Memory) suggest.

11. The influence of wolves from Norse mythology is also evident here. Like Odin (called Battle-wolf, as one of his many bynames), both Thû (Sauron) and Morgoth keep and feed wolves next to their thrones. (See *Lays* 252, 288.) This fraternizing with wolves does not save Odin from being swallowed by the giant wolf Fenrir during Ragnarok, the end of the world, when the sun too is swallowed by a wolf.

12. William Morris translates the name less exactly as *Nightwolf*.

13. Like Bilbo's party, Grettir and his companions have been unable to light a fire; and when one is seen in the distance, Grettir is sent to fetch some back.

14. In fairness to the race, not all of those with troll blood are as hostile and destructive as Grendel in *Beowulf* or the troll-wife in *Grettis saga*. There is also Thorir, a half-troll, who rules over a secret, thermally-warmed valley. This is where Grettir spends a pleasant winter, enjoying Thorir's accommodating daughters and ample mutton from Thorir's well-fattened sheep (the source, perhaps, of Tolkien's mutton-eating trolls).

15. Tolkien was certainly aware of the paper, "Icelandic Folklore," Helen Buckhurst, a friend and colleague, presented in 1926; the paper was later published in the proceedings of the Viking Society for Northern Research. See Anderson, 80–82.

16. See John Rateliff's *Mr. Baggins*, 102–104, for further explanation.

17. See *Shadow*, especially 253–254, for early references to giants and *Treason* (*passim*) for outlines and drafts by Tolkien showing Treebeard as malevolent.

18. See *Road* (65) and *Author* (88) for comments on this word, as well as Tolkien's own comments (Nom 761–762).

19. Cited by Christopher Tolkien in *War* 369. See as well *Peoples* 35–6, 83.

20. See Hilda Roderick Ellis, *The Road to Hel*, for how the ancient Norse saw "the journey to the land of the dead" and "the entrance into the burial mound" as closely related (193).

21. See *Letters* 246, 262, 267, 284.
22. See *S* 44.
23. See Ellis, *The Road to Hel,* 138–147.
24. The desire to provide continuity and amenities for the dead is also found in burial mounds, into which household items were placed, as well as food, animals, weapons, armor, and treasure (when these could be spared).
25. The Old Norse is *aptrgangr,* though *draugr* (*draugar* in the plural) was also used for the restless dead.
26. Thorgunna, a strong-willed, fifty-some woman dies a good distance from her intended burial site, requiring her casket bearers to make a long and difficult journey. When an ungenerous farmer along the way offers them shelter for the night but no food, Thorgunna rises out of her casket—stark nude—enters the farmer's kitchen and prepares her casket bearers a meal (*Eyrbyggja saga*).
27. Though Tolkien, in "Nomenclature," claimed *barrow-wight* was "an invented name," others were ahead of him (*Companion* 753). The *Oxford English Dictionary* attributes *barrow-wight* to Andrew Lang, citing an 1891 usage, but the word appears earlier than that, in the above passage from William Morris and Eiríkr Magnússon's translation of *Grettis saga.* See *The Ring of Words* by Peter Gilliver, Jeremy Marshall, and Edmund Weiner for a full explanation (214–16).
28. See *Companion* 144–145.
29. There are readers who assume the arm belongs to the spectral figure (not yet fully in view). Others—myself included—see the arm as one of several disembodied hands and arms that appear in Tolkien's illustrations. (See Hammond and Scull, *J.R.R Tolkien, Artist & Illustrator* 83–4) To add to the argument for an arm on its own, it seems unlikely that one still attached to a body would bother with finger walking.
30. Baldor, son of Brego. See *RK* V, iii, 70.
31. See *Companion* 530–1, for more on oathbreakers.
32. There are ways in which Grendel in *Beowulf* fits this pattern too—emerging from a treasure-filled cave and eating whole men at a go.
33. From the Bodleian Library, Department of Western Manuscripts, Tolkien Papers, A61 fols I-31, quoted by John Rateliff in *Mr. Baggins,* 186–7.
34. This mix of black and white (sometimes depicted as half flesh-color and half blue-black), is also ascribed to Hel, the ruler of Niflheim.
35. *Necromancer* comes from *nekros,* the Greek word for corpse. See *Companion* 237 for a full explanation of Tolkien's use of *necromancer* for Sauron.

WORKS CITED

Buckhurst, Helen. "Icelandic Folklore." *Saga-Book of the Viking Society for Northern Research.* Vol. 10 of Proceedings, 1919–1927. Coventry: Curtish and Beamish, 1928–1929. 216–263.

Ellis, Hilda Roderick. *The Road to Hel: A Study of the Conception of the Dead in Old Norse Literature.* Cambridge: Cambridge University Press, 1943. Rpt. Westport, Connecticut: Greenwood Press, 1968, 1977.

Gilliver, Peter, Jeremy Marshall and Edmund Weiner. *The Ring of Words: Tolkien and the Oxford English Dictionary.* Oxford: Oxford University Press, 2006.

Grettis Saga. Tr. Magnússon, Eiríkr, and William Morris. [Published as *The Story of Grettir the Strong.*] London: F.S. Ellis, 1869.

Hammond, Wayne G., and Christina Scull. *J.R.R. Tolkien: Artist & Illustrator.* Boston and New York: Houghton Mifflin, 1995.

_____. *Völsunga saga: The Story of the Volsungs and Niblungs.* The Collected Works of William Morris, Vol. 7. New York: Russell and Russell, 1966.

Morris, William, tr. *Egils saga*. [A fragment of the saga in 40 chapters, published as *The Story of Egil the Son of Scaldgrim*.] May Morris. *William Morris: Artist, Writer, Socialist*. New York: Russell and Russell, 1966. 565–636.

Morris, William, and Eiríkr Magnússon, tr. *Eyrbyggja saga*. [Published as *The Story of the Ere-Dwellers*.] London: Bernard Quaritch, 1892.

Pálsson, Hermann, and Paul Edwards, tr. *Egils saga einhenda ok Ásmundar berserkjabana*. [Published as *Egil and Asmund*.] *Seven Viking Romances*. London: Penguin, 1985.

Rateliff, John D. *The History of The Hobbit. Part One: Mr. Baggins*. London: HarperCollins, 2007.

The Red Fairy Book. Ed. Andrew Lang. London: Longmans, Green, 1890.

Tolkien, J.R.R. tr. *Sir Gawain and the Green Knight, Pearl, and Sir Orfeo*. Boston: Houghton Mifflin, 1978. 25–88.

_____. *The War of the Jewels*. Ed. Christopher Tolkien. The History of Middle-earth XI. Boston: Houghton Mifflin, 1994.

Väinämöinen in Middle-earth: The Pervasive Presence of the *Kalevala* in the Bombadil Chapters of *The Lord of the Rings*

David L. Dettman

1. Introduction[1]

From his first encounter at age 19, J.R.R. Tolkien was fascinated with the *Kalevala* and with the mythical world of the Finnish people. The *Kalevala* is a mid-nineteenth century compilation of oral formulaic poetry centered on the deeds of the ancient heroes of the mythical Kaleva District of Finland. This work was assembled by Elias Lönnrot from short chanted or sung poems collected by Lönnrot and a small group of folklorists in the early nineteenth century in what is now Finland and Russia. The first full English translation was by W.F. Kirby, published in 1907 in an Everyman Edition, which made it widely available. In an early essay introducing the *Kalevala* to a literary club at Oxford, Tolkien spoke of spending time "with this strange people and these new gods, with this race of unhypocritical low-brow scandalous heroes, and sadly unsentimental lovers ... the more I read of it, the more I felt at home and enjoyed myself" ("'The Story of Kullervo' and Essays on *Kalevala*" 263–4).[2] For Tolkien, who by the age of 19 was well versed in Old English and Old Norse literature, and who had grown up enjoying the western European legends and fairy tales of the juvenile collections of his day, this was a new mythical landscape and a new literature of legendary heroes that was extremely attractive ("Story of Kullervo" 246, 262).

The heroes of the *Kalevala* are different—they possess great magical powers over the natural world, yet they are at times easily defeated and humiliated. They live and travel in a strange, forested, small-scale world and spend much of their time building boats, singing songs, courting (and kidnapping) maidens, or fishing for pike.[3] The exotic and rather alien stories that were told, the attitudes and motivations expressed, and the mythological background were all very attractive to Tolkien as something new. In Tolkien's 1951 letter to Milton Waldman, in which he summarizes his created mythology, the impact of Finnish is singled out and emphasized when he talks about his disappointment with the poverty of English (as opposed to British) heroic legend. "There was Greek, and Celtic, and Romance, Germanic, Scandinavian, and Finnish (which greatly affected me); but nothing English, save impoverished chap-book stuff" (*Letters* 144). In 1955 he wrote to W.H Auden, "I mentioned Finnish, because that set the rocket off in story. I was immensely attracted by something in the air of the Kalevala, even in Kirby's poor translation.... But the beginning of the legendarium, of which the Trilogy is part (the conclusion), was in an attempt to reorganize some of the Kalevala, especially the tale of Kullervo the hapless, into a form of my own" (*Letters* 214).

Tolkien's first attempt at writing a mythic story in prose, this retelling of the story of Kullervo, has recently been published ("Story of Kullervo"). In 1914 he wrote to Edith, then his fiancée, "I am trying to turn one of the stories—which is really a great story and most tragic—into a short story somewhat on the lines of Morris' romances with chunks of poetry in between" (*Letters* 7). In this unfinished short story Tolkien retells the story of Kullervo, his tragic childhood, revenge on his uncle, unknowing incest with his sister, and suicide, following the plot line in the *Kalevala* closely. He begins the story using the names in the *Kalevala*, but quickly starts to change them into ones of his own creation ("Story of Kullervo" 212–4). The new names seem to show that Tolkien is starting to modify the world of the *Kalevala* "into a form of my own." This is an early example of the creative techniques that Tolkien used throughout his life, based in the creation of languages and imaginatively exploring the meaning, history, and implications of invented names.

Tolkien was intrigued by the examples of Finnish in Kirby's translation, and his interest in these stories inspired a strong desire to read them in the original language, although it was not until he entered Exeter College in Oxford (at age 20) that he was able to obtain a Finnish grammar. Of this experience he later wrote, "It was like discovering a complete wine-cellar filled with bottles of an amazing wine of a kind and flavour never tasted before. It quite intoxicated me" (*Letters* 214). At this time Tolkien began working on another of his invented languages, this one based heavily on Finnish. This was eventually to become Quenya, the High-elven language (Garth 60–63).

These two features of the *Kalevala*—the story of Kullervo, which became the Túrin story, and the language itself, which has close ties to the High-elven language—are the most discussed connections between the Finnish legends of the *Kalevala* and the world of Middle-earth (see R. Helms, Shippey, and West, among many others). Tolkien himself points out these connections in his letters, and Carpenter's biography makes them very clear. A few other papers have added to the list of influences in *The Silmarillion* and Tolkien's mythology of the First Age of Middle-earth (Himes, Dubois and Mellor, Garth, Flieger, Petty), but very few have argued for Finnish influences in Tolkien's most popular work, *The Lord of the Rings*. A recent paper on the *Kalevala* and *The Lord of the Rings* argues that the influences are "limited" and focuses its discussion on the powers that Tom Bombadil and Treebeard possess (Gay 302). I, however, have argued elsewhere that the *Kalevala* was a pervasive influence in Tolkien's best known work ("Beyond Kullervo"). A close reading of the *Kalevala*, especially in the translation available to Tolkien, reveals an extensive web of parallels and influences in the mythology of Middle-earth as presented in his early writings, and many of these influences are inherited by the narrative of *The Lord of the Rings*. This essay, however, will look at the much more overt influence of the *Kalevala* on one section of *The Lord of the Rings*, in which features of the *Kalevala* seem to have been consciously inserted into the passage in which the hobbits encounter Tom Bombadil.

2. The *Kalevala*, Tolkien, and C.S. Lewis

For a person with Tolkien's interests, the *Kalevala* represented a triumph of philology. The work was assembled from a large body of heroic and lyric songs or poems collected primarily by Elias Lönnrot and David E.D. Europaeus (*Kalevala*, tr. Magoun 353). Lönnrot was interested in the idea, first suggested by both Kaarle Akseli Gottlund and Reinhold von Becker (*Kalevala*, tr. Magoun 350), that many of the poems, with their recurring characters and stories, were short passages of much longer narratives. Lönnrot spliced the poems of this oral tradition together, wrote a few bridging passages and published the first edition of the *Kalevala* in 1835.[4] This work was nearly doubled in size and extensively reworked for publication in 1849. Lönnrot responded to commentary on and criticism of the 1835 version with a much greater emphasis on the features that appealed to the nationalist romantic sensibilities of the first half of the nineteenth century, and this contributed to the considerable enthusiasm shown for the 1849 version by romantics throughout Europe (DuBois 32–33, 113–115, 262–265; Gay 296). The 1849 version of the *Kalevala* was the basis for the Kirby translation, the English version read by Tolkien and C.S. Lewis. This work was embraced by the Finnish elite (particularly those advocating national independence) as a native literature with a mythology that demonstrated the uniqueness of Finnish culture, and it became a cultural icon pointing to the need for independence from the increasingly oppressive rule of Russia.[5] It contained a mythology and a body of legendary tales that had been hidden in the oral traditions of the dispersed people of back-country Finland and western Russia. In it was the creation of the world, the arrival of people, animals, and trees. It contained the adventures of powerful magicians, magical charms, marriages, great battles, the accomplishment of heroic tasks, and much more. There was no hint of this mythology in old writings or literature of the region ("Story of Kullervo" 249, 267; Branch 9; *Kalevala* tr. Bosley, xvi–xxi). The *Kalevala* was the work of one person, a folklorist and philologist[6] who collected much of the material and compiled and published these myths, rescuing them from the (supposed) slow attrition of traditional oral culture. This had particular resonance for Tolkien as he began the writing of his *legendarium*.

In his 1914 essay on the *Kalevala*, written while he was working on "The Story of Kullervo," Tolkien spoke of the importance of the *Kalevala* mythology. "We have here then a collection of mythological ballads full of that very primitive undergrowth that the literature of Europe has on the whole been cutting away and reducing for centuries with different and earlier completeness in different peoples" ("Story of Kullervo" 248).[7] He describes how these orally transmitted poems have come down from pre–Christian times in an unmodified form, and praises their "minor emotional key" and most poignant pathos (250, 252). The conclusion of his paper conveys his great affection for the *Kalevala*.

> But the delight of Earth, the wonder of it; the essential feeling as of the necessity for magic; that juggling with the golden moon and silver sun (such are they) that is man's universal pastime: these are the things to seek in the Kalevala. All the world to wheel about in, the Great Bear to play with and Orion and the Seven Stars all dangling magically in the branches of a silver birch enchanted by Väinämöinen; the splendid sorcerous scandalous villains of old to tell of when you have walked into "Sauna" after binding the kine at close of day .... [256–257].

The *Kalevala* ends with an invitation (written by Lönnrot) for others to follow in his footsteps. I suspect that this invitation remained in Tolkien's mind in his twenties, during which he began his writings and was spurred on in his creation by the events of the First World War. The last 108 lines of the *Kalevala* speak of these back-country poems and how they were disregarded and belittled before the publication of the *Kalevala*, how the people who created these poems were thought uneducated, but had a body of native lore that was truly valuable. Lönnrot concludes:

> But let this be as it may be,
> I have shown the way to singers,
> Showed the way, and broke the tree-tops,
> Cut the branches, shown the pathways.
> This way therefore leads the pathway
> Here the path lies newly opened,
> Widely open for the singers,
> And for greater ballad singers,
> For the young, who now are growing,
> For the rising generation [50: 611–620].[8]

Tolkien accepted this invitation, and with "The Story of Kullervo" began his lifelong work of sub-creation, giving us the myths and legendary heroes of Middle-earth.

Tolkien's close friendship with C.S. Lewis must have led to further discussion of these Finnish tales during the 1920s, '30s, and '40s, for both men had independently developed a strong interest in the *Kalevala* prior to their meeting in 1926, and they continued to be keenly interested in myth and heroic legend (King 71; Lewis, *Stand Together* 137, 266). In the mid–1930s both men published poems based on characters from the *Kalevala*, possibly influenced by the 1935 centennial of the publication of the *Kalevala*.[9] Tolkien's poem is "The Adventures of Tom Bombadil," which I will discuss below. In 1937 Lewis published a short poem reworking one of the most important passages of the Kullervo story, Kullervo's suicide (Lewis, "After Kirby's Kalevala"). This poem describes the remorse Kullervo (called Coolruff by Lewis) feels over his unknowing seduction of his sister; the conversation he holds with his sword, asking if it is willing to take his life; and finally his suicide. This is, of course, the same passage that forms the climax of Tolkien's first mythical writing, "The Story of Kullervo," and of the tale of Túrin Turambar. By 1937 Lewis had almost certainly read the Túrin story in one version or another, and the parallel would have been clear (Carpenter, *Inklings* 29–32). Although Tolkien had worked on his re-telling of the Kullervo story for more than 20 years, Lewis was the first of the two to publish a work based on that story.

The *Kalevala* seems to have remained a text that Tolkien referred to through much of his life. Writing to his son Christopher in July of 1944, when he was working on the last chapters of Book 4 of *The Lord of the Rings*, he quotes a passage on the first brewing of beer:

> Drunk was Ahti, drunk was Kauko,
> Drunken was the ruddy rascal,
> With the ale of Osmo's daughter [20: 395–397].

and a later passage:

> Thus was ale at first created
> ....
> Best of drinks for prudent people;
> Women soon it brings to laughter,
> Men it warms into good humour,
> ....
> But it brings the fools to raving [20: 415–424].

More than 30 years after he first encountered these Finnish tales, he still refers to these heroes and recommends that Christopher make time to read the *Kalevala* someday (*Letters* 87). The *Kalevala* even appears in the concluding remarks of Tolkien's valedictory address to the University of Oxford, delivered June 5, 1959, just before his retirement, in which Tolkien lists some of the most "salient" points in his academic career. Among the six scholars and events mentioned is "[s]eeing Henry Cecil Wyld wreck a table in the Cadena Café with the vigour of his representation of Finnish minstrels chanting the *Kalevala*" (*MC* 238).[10]

3. The Adventures of Tom Bombadil

In 1934, while he was finishing the manuscript of *The Hobbit*, Tolkien published a poem, "The Adventures of Tom Bombadil," in *The Oxford Magazine*. The poem sets up a number of interesting parallels between its main characters and the legendary heroes of the *Kalevala*. It is possible that the then-upcoming centennial of the *Kalevala*'s publication (1935) inspired the poem, although nowhere in Tolkien's published writings or letters does he refer to the centennial. The echoing of features from the *Kalevala* is relatively minor in the poem, and the echoes are not overt, reading more like a private joke to those in the know, who can recognize the borrowings. These parallels were to be expanded significantly in the Tom Bombadil chapters of *The Lord of the Rings*. The poem was reprinted in 1962 with only minor changes, in the collection of poetry titled *The Adventures of Tom Bombadil*. In it Tom has a series of adventures involving harassment or capture of Tom by the River's daughter, Old Man Willow, the Badgers, and the Barrow-wight.

In the *Kalevala*, Väinämöinen is the eldest and greatest of all the singers. The first to walk on solid earth after the creation of the world, he is often given the epithets "eldest" and "aged." Tom is also old; he is constantly referred to as "Old Tom Bombadil." Seven of the poem's twenty-six stanzas begin with this phrase. Väinämöinen's singing is very powerful magic, and songs are used in battle with song matched to song. Väinämöinen defeats his enemies through skillful singing, transforming their weapons into saplings or reeds and singing one enemy into a swamp, putting him in danger of drowning. In addition, he can build boats, heal wounds, and transform himself into various animals with his songs. In one case, Väinämöinen sings his opponents to sleep and thereby defeats them. Although in this poem Tom does not enchant through singing, he sings some of his familiar nonsense verses. Old Man Willow, on the other hand, uses powerful songs to capture Tom by singing him to sleep and traps him inside a crack in the tree trunk against which he was leaning. Tom's speech is notably and curiously powerful; his simple demand to be set free is immediately granted by Old Man Willow. This sequence of events is repeated when Tom is also captured by the Badgers and the Barrow-wight, both of whom immediately release him on demand, with no hint of opposition. In the poem, of course, his "speaking" is in verse and has the feel of song. In Kirby's translation powerful magic can be spoken as well as sung (e.g. 12: 371), and the verbs "speak" and "sing" are often paired in a virtually interchangeable fashion:

> Who will clasp their hands together,
> Hook their hands in one another,
> And begin to speak unto us,
> Swaying back and forth in singing... [21: 319–322].

Väinämöinen also woos a maiden, Aino, who rejects him and in despair drowns herself in a lake and becomes a daughter of the waters ("Vellamo's young water-maiden, / Me, the darling child of Ahto" (5: 132–133)—Kirby glosses Vellamo and Ahto as goddess and god "of the Sea and of the Waters" in his name index). Väinämöinen later catches a fish in the lake who reveals herself to him as his lost betrothed. The fish escapes, and Väinämöinen loses her forever, lamenting that the

> Youngest daughter of the surges,
> Who should be my friend for ever,
> And my wife throughout my lifetime,
> Came and seized the bait I offered,
> In my boat sprang unresisting;
> But I knew not how to hold her
> To my home I could not take her [5: 183–189].

This contrasts with Bombadil, who is successful where Väinämöinen failed; he captures and marries Goldberry, "the River-Daughter." While Väinämöinen "knew not how to hold her" and was unable to take her home, Tom "caught her, held her fast!" and

> Said Tom Bombadil: "Here's my pretty maiden!
> You shall come home with me! The table is all laden:

yellow cream, honeycomb, white bread and butter;
roses at the window-pane peeping through the shutter.
You shall come under Hill—never mind your mother
In her deep weedy pool: there you'll find no lover! [465].

The foods awaiting the "Riverwoman's daughter" on Tom's table are the same foods that, in the *Kalevala,* the good bridegroom should supply his bride (chapter 24), as well as wedding celebration fare, including cream-cakes, wheaten bread, lumps of butter, and honey from the taps (25: 384–402).

Tom's courtship of Goldberry is unorthodox, although apparently not unwelcome. He kidnaps her and carries her off to his house, where there is a feast waiting. Väinämöinen and the other heroes of the *Kalevala* also gain brides by kidnapping or attempt to do so. This happens frequently enough that Kirby felt the need to comment in a footnote, "There are so many instances of maidens being carried off, or enticed into sledges, in the *Kalevala,* that it seems almost to have been a recognized legal form of marriage by capture" (8: 35; Vol. 1, 322n).

4. Bombadil's Songs in *The Lord of the Rings*

Tom Bombadil and characters from this poem appear again in *The Lord of the Rings,* when Frodo and his three companions try to pass through the Old Forest at the beginning of their travels. The Tom Bombadil chapters were first written in the summer of 1938, and the parallels with the *Kalevala* characters were expanded. This was only a year after C.S. Lewis had published his Kullervo poem, and it seems likely that Lewis and Tolkien had recently discussed the *Kalevala.*

Tom is now unambiguously a singer. As with Väinämöinen, his power is in song, and it is through his singing that he makes Old Man Willow release Pippin and Merry. Tom's song also breaks open the barrow and defeats and banishes the Barrow-wight after the hobbits are again captured. "His songs are stronger songs," Tom sings of himself (*FR* I, viii, 153). Interestingly, Old Man Willow and the Barrow-wight are the only two enemies of the quest that use song to enchant and capture. Contests in song, common in the *Kalevala,* do not occur in *The Lord of the Rings* except in the small region in which Tom Bombadil lives.[11]

After the hobbits enter the Old Forest, the sounds of the forest and the strength or feebleness of voices become very significant in Tolkien's narrative. Pippin's shout "fell as if muffled by a heavy curtain" (*FR* I, vi, 122). Frodo attempts to compose a song as an overt attack on the palpable enmity of the forest, "For east or west all woods must fail," but his song lacks the power to prevail. "... his voice faded into silence. The air seemed heavy and the making of words wearisome" (*FR* I, vi, 123). The oppressive nature of the forest is too powerful. In the valley of the Withywindle, Old Man Willow's whispering and singing fill the sunny and hot valley and overwhelm the hobbits with sleepiness. Singing an enemy to sleep is a strategy used in the *Kalevala* by Väinämöinen when stealing the Sampo, a magical source of wealth, and by Lemminkäinen's mother when she recovers his body from the realm of the dead. Lemminkäinen's mother calls on the sun to "[s]hine an hour with heat excessive" and to "[l]ull to sleep" the warriors of the Land of the Dead (15: 214–231). In the hot sun of the Withywindle valley the hobbits come to the thin shade of Old Man Willow and there they feel an overwhelming urge to sleep. "There now seemed hardly a sound in the air. The flies had stopped buzzing. Only a gentle noise on the edge of hearing, a soft fluttering as of a song half whispered, seemed to stir in the boughs above" (*FR* I, vi, 127). Sam hears more clearly, muttering to himself, "I don't like this great big tree. I don't trust it. Hark at it singing about sleep now! This won't do at all!" (128). Later, after fire has failed to free the trapped Merry and Pippin, Frodo, not knowing how to save his friends from the willow, runs along the path crying "*help! help! help!* It seemed to him that he could hardly hear the sound of his own shrill voice: it was blown away from him by the willow-wind and drowned in a clamour of leaves, as soon as the words left his mouth" (130). Frodo then hears Tom's song off in the distance, and as he listens, it suddenly "rose up loud and clear," after which "The wind puffed out. The leaves hung silently again on stiff branches" (130). Old Man Willow is clearly overmastered by Tom's power; after Tom frees Merry and Pippin with his singing, "complete silence fell" (131).

Tom's voice continues to be powerful throughout these three chapters, both when contending with adversaries and when interacting with friends. Frodo and Sam, running along the path, stop short "as if they had been struck stiff" when Tom says "Whoa! Whoa! steady there!" (*FR* I, vi, 131). Tom easily gets Frodo to tell him much more about his journey and the Ring than Frodo intended to reveal and, notably, Frodo simply hands him the Ring when Tom asks for it. Although it is not clear if Tom or Goldberry is singing, during the second night in Tom's house, "Frodo heard a sweet singing running in his mind" and (because of the song?) the hobbits all sleep soundly, unlike the previous night (*FR* I, viii, 146). Tom's stories can call up visions; when Tom tells the hobbits tales of the barrows, they experience an intense vision of the men of Westernesse (157). In a curious fashion, Tom's songs can travel to distant places in his land. When Tom goes on ahead down the path toward his house, his voice fades into the distance, and one presumes that he continues his singing as loudly and clearly as always. "[T]he noise of his singing got fainter and further away. Suddenly his voice came floating back to them in a loud Halloo!" and he tells them in song how to reach his house (*FR* I, vi, 132). This happens a second time in the barrow when Tom's song is heard immediately after Frodo sings his appeal for help. This may also be implied in the sudden change in volume and rapid arrival of Tom during their first encounter at Old Man Willow. This phenomenon perhaps echoes chapter 44 of the *Kalevala*, in which Väinämöinen's singing can be heard across six villages and all creatures gather to listen to him sing.

It is not only that Tom's voice is powerful, but also that "[h]is songs are stronger songs" (*FR* I, viii, 153). He teaches one to the hobbits to be used to summon him if they encounter trouble on the Barrow-downs. The song he teaches them is simple, invoking a number of natural phenomena:

> Ho! Tom Bombadil, Tom Bombadillo!
> By water, wood and hill, by reed and willow,
> By fire, sun and moon, harken now and hear us!
> Come, Tom Bombadil, for our need is near us! [*FR* I, vii, 145].

Although I cannot find any clear parallel song in the *Kalevala*, the appeal to this list of living things and aspects of the natural world could have had its inspiration in chapter 17. There Antero Vipunen, in great distress from the tortures inflicted by Väinämöinen, calls out to many of the items in Tom's song, asking them to come to his aid. The similarity is lessened because many lines of verse are used in the appeal to each item. Vipunen requests aid from the earth and fields, the pine-forests and junipers, the waves and waters, the goddess of creation, and Ukko, the god of the heavens (17: 261–308). In the barrow, lying next to the cold bodies of the other three hobbits, Frodo listens to the cold and miserable song of the Barrow-wight and is almost defeated by it, feeling as if he were turned to stone by the song. But his courage does not fail, and he attacks the wight's long arm with a sword. Then in the dark tomb, while the wight snarls, he begins to sing Tom's summoning song. "In a small desperate voice he began: *Ho! Tom Bombadil!* and with that name his voice seemed to grow strong: it had a full and lively sound, and the dark chamber echoed" (*FR* I, viii, 153). Frodo's singing is now powerful, the wight is immediately silenced, and Tom hears the summons, answering in song. After only four lines of Tom's reply, "[t]here was a loud rumbling sound, as of stones rolling and falling, and suddenly light streamed in" (153). This sentence evokes a description of Väinämöinen's singing during his battle with Joukahainen:

> Sang the aged Väinämöinen;
> Lakes swelled up, and earth was shaken,
> And the coppery mountains trembled,
> And the mighty rocks resounded.

And the mountains clove asunder;
On the shore the stones were shivered [3: 295–300].

Both Tom and Väinämöinen are singers. When Tom is by himself, either busy outside his house in the mornings or dancing down the Withywindle path, he is constantly singing. One gets the impression that he only stops singing when the need to speak to someone intrudes. Although Väinämöinen does many other things, he is foremost a singer. After the creation of the world (chapter 1) and the planting of the dry land with trees and crops (chapter 2), the third chapter of the *Kalevala* begins:

Väinämöinen, old and steadfast
Passed the days of his existence
Where lie Väinölä's sweet meadows,
Kalevala's extended heathlands:
There he sang his songs of sweetness
Sang his songs and proved his wisdom
Day by day he sang unwearied,
Night by night discoursed unceasing,
Sang the songs of by-gone ages,
Hidden words of ancient wisdom,
Songs which all the children sing not,
All beyond men's comprehension,
In these ages of misfortune,
When the race is near its ending [3: 1–14].

There are many other examples of Väinämöinen filling days with singing. During the protracted feud with the mistress of Pohjola over the theft of the Sampo, Väinämöinen must deal with diseases and a great bear sent to ravage his land. After healing the people or driving out the bear, he returns to his singing (chapters 45 and 46). There are multiple times when all living creatures gather to hear his singing, and they listen throughout the day (or days) without stopping: "And they wondered at their pleasure" (44: 296). This is very reminiscent of what happens during the long rainy day spent in Tom's house. In the morning Tom says it is a good day for "long tales, for questions and for answers" (*FR* I, vii, 140) but he does not ask any questions or really converse with the hobbits at all. He spends all the daylight hours telling tales and singing songs to them. They have missed the noon meal and happily listened to many tales of nature and the history of the lands nearby. When Tom finishes, it is night and there is silence, and Frodo "did not feel either hungry or tired, only filled with wonder.... He spoke at last out of his wonder and a sudden fear of that silence" (142). It is only after the evening meal that Tom and the hobbits talk about the journey, the Ring, and plans for the next day. Tom takes the day to sing songs and tell tales because that is simply what he does: he is a singer like Väinämöinen.

Like the echo of the word "wonder" between the passages described above, another pair of passages also seems to echo each other in both words and imagery. Having escaped Old Man Willow with Tom's help, at the end of the long day in the Old Forest, the hobbits finally come to the edge of the forest, weary and nervous about the night. Up ahead they see the lights of Tom's house. "Suddenly a wide yellow beam flowed out brightly from a door that was opened" (*FR* I, vi, 133). As they hurry forward, they hear Tom sing a short verse and then Goldberry sings. The final sentence of the chapter is, "And with that song the hobbits stood upon the threshold, and a golden light was all about them" (133). The language used here conveys warmth and comfort, and the relief of arrival in a safe haven after a dangerous ordeal. It is strongly reminiscent of the final couplet of chapter 25 (and the final couplet of volume 1 of the Everyman edition), in which Väinämöinen finally returns to his home after a long journey to Pohjola and to the realm of the dead. His horse brings him at last:

> To his own door, widely open,
> To the threshold brought him safely [25: 737–738].

5. Bombadil's Meter

In his earliest piece of mythical writing, "The Story of Kullervo," Tolkien composes verse in the meter of the Kirby translation of the *Kalevala*. Although he calls the meter "monotonous and thin," he refers to it with some affection, calling it "capable of the most poignant pathos (if not of more majestic things)" ("Story of Kullervo" 252), and he invested time enough to write over 300 lines of poetry in this meter. The Kirby translation's meter, an unvarying trochaic tetrameter (four pairs of stressed / unstressed syllables), however, does not fare well in English. In his essays on the *Kalevala*, Tolkien points out that the meter of the Finnish *Kalevala* has considerable variation; and others have complained that the meter of the Kirby translation in English (and the earliest German translation of Schiefner, read by Longfellow) was over-regularized.[12] Using Eliot's 1890 Finnish grammar and the passages of the *Kalevala* included in it, Tolkien would have been well aware that the original meter, although it maintains a very regular eight syllable line, contains notable variation in stress and vowel length that creates a much more varied and interesting meter.

Even though Tom is a character closely related to the *Kalevala*, Tolkien rejected Kirby's meter when writing Tom Bombadil's songs. Tom's verse in both "The Adventures of Tom Bombadil" and *The Lord of the Rings* is clearly very closely related to the meter of the *Kalevala*, but Tolkien has modified it, breaking the monotonous trochaic beat and adding welcome variation.

Longfellow's famous, but parody-prone, *Hiawatha*, makes some of the problems of this over-regularized meter familiar to most readers.[13] Because the Kirby translation of the *Kalevala* is a verse translation, both narrative and speech are in this meter, and the text develops an unchanging and monotonous feel, even during passages of great conflict or high drama. Bombadil's language, both prose and song, is infused with meter and alliteration, but Tolkien gave him a much more fluid meter by frequently replacing trochees with single stressed syllables. He also lengthened the line to seven feet (made up of a four-foot half-line and a three-foot half-line), with the final three feet almost always trochees. Thus Tolkien's meter has a longer arc and many possible variants, both of which relieve the monotony. Where the *Kalevala* has:

> Now the tidings were repeated,
> And the news was widely rumoured,
> How the youthful maid had perished,
> And the fair one had departed [5: 1–4].

Tolkien's meter is much more enjoyable, yet one can still hear the underlying trochaic meter:

> Hop along, my little friends, up the Withywindle!
> Tom's going on ahead candles for to kindle.
> Down west sinks the Sun: soon you will be groping.
> When the night-shadows fall, then the door will open,
> Out of the window-panes light will twinkle yellow.
> Fear no alder black! Heed no hoary willow! [*FR* I, vi, 132].

The lingering influence of the Finnish oral formulaic verse can also be seen in the occasional repetitive pair of lines. In the *Kalevala* verse quoted immediately above, one idea is stated in a different way in the following line. This is not as common in Tom Bombadil's poetry as in the *Kalevala*, but it does happen regularly. An example is the last line of Bombadil's poem above, "Fear no alder black! Heed no hoary willow!" The idea is stated and repeated with variation. Perhaps as another attempt to recreate the atmosphere of the *Kalevala*, in which all action and conversation is in verse, Tom Bombadil cannot get away from this meter. It is there almost constantly in his prose statements as well as his verse. "Whoa! Whoa! steady there! ... where be you a-going to, puffing like a bellows? ... I'm Tom Bombadil. Tell me what's your trouble! Tom's in a hurry now. Don't you crush my lilies!" (*FR* I, vi, 131). It is not just for Tom that the distinction between speech and song becomes blurred; during that first evening in Tom's house "the guests became suddenly aware that they were singing merrily, as if it was easier and more natural than talking" (*FR* I, vii, 136).

6. In Tom Bombadil's House

As in "The Adventures of Tom Bombadil," Goldberry remains the daughter of the River in *The Lord of the Rings*. Tom addresses her in his songs as the River-daughter. She is tied to the river in most of the descriptive statements in these chapters. Among other examples, her voice is described as "like the song of a glad water flowing down," or "rippling." Her clothes rustle "like the wind in the flowering borders of a river," and "[t]he sound of her footsteps was like a stream falling gently away downhill" (*FR* I, vi, 133; I, viii, 146; I, vii, 134, 136). Goldberry is associated with a number of riverside plants in Tom's poems and in the narrative: water lilies, reeds, willows, and rushes. These plants all occur repeatedly in the relatively limited flora of the *Kalevala*. Tolkien also seems to take particular notice of Goldberry's clothing and jewelry. Although Goldberry makes only three relatively brief appearances in the narrative, her silver-green (or silver) clothing and golden jewelry are described in some detail three times and briefly mentioned another three times. These may be echoes of the passages describing Aino's rich blue dresses and the golden jewelry that she retrieves from her mother's storehouse after rejecting Väinämöinen's attempt to entice her into his sleigh to become his bride (chapter 4). Aino's mother encourages her strongly to dress in her finery and accept Väinämöinen. But weeping, Aino dresses in her finest clothes and wanders off into the forest. She eventually comes to a lake, where she lays her clothing out on the bushes, throws her jewelry on the sand, and drowns herself. This is the lake in which Väinämöinen later caught her in the form of a fish, but found himself unable to hold her or bring her back to his home.

Another feature with strong echoes of the *Kalevala* that is carried over from "The Adventures of Tom Bombadil" into *The Lord of the Rings* is the food served in Tom's house. The meals are strongly correlated with the foods served in good and prosperous households of the *Kalevala*, where a new bride is not abused. The hobbits feast on cream, honeycomb, white bread, butter, milk, cheese, green herbs, and berries—a vegetarian version of the foods presented at *Kalevala* feasts.[14] White bread and cakes of honey are particularly associated with Väinämöinen's unsuccessful courting of Aino: she refuses his advances, saying she is not interested in the "[w]heaten bread" or beautiful clothes he offers (4: 26), and he later laments the loss of a bride who would have baked "loaves of bread" and "[c]akes of honey" (5: 119–120).

7. Eldest

Like Väinämöinen, who was born during the creation of the world, Bombadil was in Middle-earth before the arrival of the elves or men, and he seems to lie outside the creation story presented in *The Silmarillion.* When asked who he is, he replies that he is the Eldest. "Tom was here before the river and the trees; Tom remembers the first raindrop and the first acorn" (*FR* I, vii, 142). Väinämöinen also is the eldest. A very frequent epithet is the "aged Väinämöinen," and the *Kalevala* begins with his conception.[15] He is the first to walk on dry land after his mother, Ilmatar, separates land from sea and creates the earth. The first raindrop and first acorn are most likely a reference to the second chapter of the *Kalevala,* in which Väinämöinen summons Sampsa, the first sower, to scatter the seeds of trees and crops to grow in this new barren land. Many plants grow well, but the acorn will not germinate and Väinämöinen tries a number of times to get it to grow. Eventually the acorn sprouts and sends down roots and grows into the Great Oak that hides the sun and moon. Later in this chapter Väinämöinen discovers six barley seeds, although they too at first fail to grow. Väinämöinen must clear a field and then call on Ukko, the sky god, to bring soft rains to nurture the new crop.

8. An Anomaly

Bombadil is an anomaly in Middle-earth. In a 1954 letter Tolkien discusses the anomalous nature of Tom Bombadil: "And even in a mythical Age there must be some enigmas, as there always are. Tom Bombadil is one (intentionally)" and "Tom Bombadil is not an important person—to the narrative. I suppose he has some importance as a 'comment.'... he represents something that I feel important, though I would not be prepared to analyze the feeling precisely" (*Letters* 174, 178). During the hobbits' stay in Tom's house, the question of "Who is Tom Bombadil?" is asked twice, but no clear answer is given. Tom says of himself that he is oldest, and that he is what he is seen to be. This repeated questioning emphasizes the question in the reader's mind and points out the fact that Tom does not fall neatly into one of the peoples of Middle-earth. Both Tom and Goldberry are creatures unique in Middle-earth. Frodo's initial impression of her compares her to the elves, but also sees her as something different. "He stood as he had at times stood enchanted by fair elven-voices; but the spell that was now laid upon him was different: less keen and lofty was the delight, but deeper and nearer to mortal heart; marvellous and yet not strange" (*FR* I, vii, 134).

Very surprising in the context of *The Lord of the Rings* is the fact that the Ring has no power over Tom and that he can see Frodo wearing the Ring. He is outside the competing powers of Middle-earth. As Tolkien wrote in another letter of 1954, "He is *master* in a peculiar way: he has no fear, and no desire of possession or domination at all. He merely knows and understands about such things as concern him in his natural little realm. He hardly even judges, and as far as can be seen makes no effort to reform or remove even the Willow" (*Letters* 192, emphasis in original). Tom Bombadil exists in a "little realm," a realm that is set apart from the rest of Middle-earth, although how this is so remains unexplained, just as Tolkien left Bombadil's true nature unexplained. The mythic world of the *Kalevala* is also set apart—its small-scale, forested environment is ahistorical and is removed from both modern and nineteenth-century Finnish culture. There is no tie to historical events, except for rather vague references to the arrival of Christianity in the final chapter. Nor is there any connection to village or urban culture. Time, place, and people are all set in the timeless and placeless context of the mythic Kaleva District.

9. A Small Land

Tom Bombadil's realm is a limited one; he has set very clear borders around a small area in Middle-earth beyond which he will not willingly go. He has great power, even over the Ring. Within the borders of his land, where battles are fought in song, Tom is easily the master. The fact that Elrond had forgotten about Tom although he does not live very far away (*FR* II, ii, 278) shows that the boundaries of Bombadil's lands are strong and have been in place for a long time. This setting has a strong echo in the landscape and people of the *Kalevala*. The world of the *Kalevala* is surprisingly small; its narrative can be seen as the various interactions and conflicts of the inhabitants of four or five farmsteads. The characters live and travel exclusively in the back-country forest. Interactions between characters are almost always one-on-one, with very little group conflict. The major characters live alone or as couples on isolated farms or in small settlements in the forest. The largest groups of people number perhaps a few dozen, gathered in a single settlement, but these larger groups, with the exception of one or two people, remain anonymous and shadowy. There are no towns. This closed, forested setting is echoed in the wilderness existence of Aragorn and of a number of characters in *The Silmarillion*, such as Túrin, and Beren and Lúthien. In *The Lord of the Rings*, not only Tom's lonely house, but also Rivendell, the emptiness of Fangorn Forest, and the secret realm of the Elves of Lórien are all reminiscent of the small land of the *Kalevala*.

It may seem that Väinämöinen is unlike Bombadil because he travels away from Kaleva, his home, to Pohjola or to the land of the Dead. Väinämöinen does not close himself up in one small region. However, the *Kalevala* makes clear that he would prefer to stay in his home region if circumstances did not draw him away. The beginning of chapter 3, quoted above, tells how he passes his days in the sweet meadows of Kaleva. After being lost at sea and arriving in Pohjola for the first time, Väinämöinen is greatly distressed because he does not know how to return to his own country, and he weeps for days, expecting never to return home (7: 117–132). He grasps any chance he is offered to return to his home.

There has been considerable debate over what or who Bombadil really is within the context of Middle-earth and where his powers come from.[16] I do not think this can be answered based on the texts we have. However, Bombadil's unique character, powers, and setting seem to be based on reimagining a hero of the *Kalevala*, Väinämöinen, as a character in Middle-earth. Tolkien's affinity for the world of the *Kalevala* led to his inclusion of many elements of Finnish mythology into the limited world of Tom Bombadil. The fact that Tolkien singles out Finnish on a number of occasions as an important influence, one that "set the rocket off in story," should be a signal to us, the readers, to take a closer look at the *Kalevala*. Many important parallels remain to be explored.[17]

NOTES

1. Thirty-five years ago I wrote an essay for the fan journal *Minas Tirith Evening-Star* on the close parallels between Tom Bombadil and Väinämöinen, the central character of the Finnish epic poem the *Kalevala* ("Vainamoinen and Bombadil"). Although that paper was designated "Part One," I never found the time or energy to assemble Part Two, which was intended to broaden the discussion of parallels beyond Bombadil. There was clearly much more of the *Kalevala* built into *The Lord of the Rings* than anyone had suspected. I would like to thank Phil Helms and the American Tolkien Society's call for papers to celebrate Prof. Tolkien's eleventy-first birthday, which finally gave me a push to assemble Part Two, entitled "Beyond Kullervo and Túrin: The Kirby translation of the *Kalevala* as a pervasive and unrecognized influence on Tolkien's writings" (later published in *Minas Tirith Evening-Star*: "Beyond Kullervo"). This paper is a greatly reworked version of the Bombadil section of my presentation for that celebration, September 22, 2003. Since then, a group of essays on Tolkien and Finnish myth has been published; one essay in particular pointed out a number of the parallels that I discuss here (Gay). While the *Kalevala* can no longer be said to be an unrecognized influence on *The Lord of the Rings*, I disagree with Gay's assessment that Finnish folklore's influence is minor. I would like to thank Bill Fliss of the Marquette University Library and Don W. King for assistance in gaining access to texts. I also thank John Rateliff and John Houghton for very helpful editing and suggestions.
2. This is from a revised version of the original talk, given to Oxford University essay clubs in November 1914 and February 1915. The date of the revision is unclear, but seems to be from the period from 1918 to the early 1920s ("Story of Kullervo" 213).
3. The literature in English on the *Kalevala* is growing; for a good introduction to the *Kalevala* see the Introduction of the Bosley translation of the *Kalevala* and references therein. For Finnish mythology, much derived from the *Kalevala*, see Pentikäinen.
4. This edition is now referred to as the *Old Kalevala*.
5. See Wilson (4–66) and Hautala's monograph for more information on how the romantic nationalist movement in Finland made use of philology and traditional oral legends in the eighteenth and nineteenth centuries.

6. Lönnrot also compiled a massive dictionary of the Finnish language.

7. Tolkien later added a more personal note in the revised version of the essay, "I would that we had more of it left—something of the same sort that belonged to the English" ("Story of Kullervo" 265).

8. All *Kalevala* quotations are from Kirby's translation. They will be cited by chapter (also called Runo) and line number.

9. At least two short notices on the centennial celebrations were published in *The Times* (28 February and 1 March 1935).

10. H.C. Wyld was Merton Professor of English Language and Literature at Oxford from 1920 to 1945.

11. There are two other major associations of song and (magical) power in Tolkien's writings. In the "Ainulindalë," the universe and the Earth are created through the physical manifestation of the song of Ilúvatar and the Valar (*S* 15–19). This emphasizes the power of song in Tolkien's mythology; song determined the flow and structure of the creation. Battles in song also occur in the various versions of the Tale of Beren and Lúthien. See B.S.W. Barootes, "'He chanted a song of wizardry,'" elsewhere in this volume.

12. See the introduction to the Bosley translation of the *Kalevala* xlvi–lii for a good discussion of translators and meter.

13. H.W. Longfellow also developed an interest in the *Kalevala*, based on Schiefner's German translation. Interestingly, he was also inspired to write an epic based on legendary tales of another culture and history, that of the Iroquois, in *The Song of Hiawatha* (1855).

14. With the exception of cheese, which is not mentioned in the *Kalevala*.

15. Curiously Väinämöinen is described as "old" while still in his mother's womb (1:289).

16. Much of this debate is summarized in Noad.

17. I have recently discussed two areas of parallelism between the *Kalevala* and Tolkien's First Age writings: "Trees and the light of celestial objects in Tolkien's writings and the Kalevala" and "Lúthien, Beren, and the Kalevala," both in *Minas Tirith Evening-Star*.

WORKS CITED

Branch, Michael. "Finnish Oral Poetry, *Kalevala,* and *Kanteletar.*" *A History of Finland's Literature.* Ed. George C. Schoolfield. Lincoln: University of Nebraska Press, 1998. 3–33.

Carpenter, Humphrey. *The Inklings: C.S. Lewis, J.R.R. Tolkien, Charles Williams, and Their Friends.* Boston: Houghton Mifflin, 1979.

Dettman, David L. "Beyond Kullervo and Túrin: The Kirby translation of the Kalevala as a pervasive and unrecognized influence on Tolkien's writings." *Minas Tirith Evening-Star* 32.4 (Winter 2003): 3–19.

_____. "Lúthien, Beren, and the Kalevala." *Minas Tirith Evening-Star* 40.1 (Spring-Summer 2011): 3–19.

_____. "Trees and the light of celestial objects in Tolkien's writings and the Kalevala." *Minas Tirith Evening-Star* 39.3 (Year-End 2010): 3–21.

_____. "Vainamoinen and Bombadil: Finnish Folklore in *The Lord of the Rings,* Part One." *Minas Tirith Evening-Star* 8.4 (July 1979): 5–12.

DuBois, Thomas A. *Finnish Folk Poetry and the Kalevala.* New York: Garland, 1995.

DuBois, Thomas, and Scott Mellor. "The Nordic roots of Tolkien's Middle-earth." *Scandinavian Review* 90 (2002): 35–40.

Eliot, C.N.E. *A Finnish Grammar.* Oxford: Clarendon, 1890.

Flieger, Verlyn. "A Mythology for Finland: Tolkien and Lönnrot as Mythmakers." *Invention* 277–283.

Garth, John. *Tolkien and the Great War: The Threshold of Middle-earth.* Boston: Houghton Mifflin, 2003.

Gay, David Elton. "J.R.R. Tolkien and the *Kalevala*: Some thoughts on the Finnish Origins of Tom Bombadil and Treebeard." *Invention* 295–304.

Hautala, Jouko. *Finnish Folklore Research 1828–1918*. History of Learning and Science in Finland 1828–1918, Vol. 12. Helsinki: Finnish Society of Sciences, 1968.

Helms, Randel. *Tolkien and the Silmarils*. Boston: Houghton Mifflin, 1981.

Himes, Jonathan B. "What J.R.R. Tolkien Really Did with the Sampo?" *Mythlore* 22.4 (#86) (Spring 2000): 69–85.

The Kalevala. Comp. Elias Lönnrot. Tr. Keith Bosley. Oxford: Oxford University Press, 1989.

Kalevala: Land of Heroes. Comp. Elias Lönnrot. Tr. W.F. Kirby. Everyman's Library. 2 volumes. London: J.M. Dent, 1907.

The Kalevala or Poems of the Kaleva District. Comp. Elias Lönnrot. Tr. Francis Peabody Magoun. Cambridge, MA: Harvard University Press, 1963.

King, Don W. "After Kirby's Kalevala." *C.S. Lewis Reader's Encyclopedia*. Ed. J.D. Schulz and J.G. West, Jr. Grand Rapids, MI: Zondervan, 1998. 71.

Lewis, C.S. "After Kirby's Kalevala." *The Oxford Magazine* 55 (13 May 1937): 595.

_____. *They Stand Together: The Letters of C.S. Lewis to Arthur Greeves (1914–1963)*. Ed. Walter Hooper. New York: Macmillan, 1979.

Noad, Charles E. "The Natures of Tom Bombadil: A Summary." *Leaves from the Tree: J.R.R. Tolkien's Shorter Fiction*. London: Tolkien Society, 1991. 79–83.

Pentikäinen, Juha Y. *Kalevala Mythology*. Tr. Ritva Poom. Bloomington: Indiana University Press, 1989.

Petty, Anne C. "Identifying England's Lönnrot." *Tolkien Studies* 1 (2004): 69–84.

Tolkien, J.R.R. "The Adventures of Tom Bombadil." *The Oxford Magazine* 52.13 (15 Feb. 1934): 464–465.

_____. "'The Story of Kullervo' and Essays on *Kalevala*." Ed. Verlyn Flieger. *Tolkien Studies* 7 (2010): 211–278.

West, Richard C. "Setting the Rocket off in Story: The *Kalevala* as the Germ of Tolkien's Legendarium." *Invention* 285–294.

Wilson, William A. *Folklore and Nationalism in Modern Finland*. Bloomington: Indiana University Press, 1976.

"Lack of Counsel Not of Courage": J.R.R. Tolkien's Critique of the Heroic Ethos in *The Children of Húrin*

RICHARD C. WEST

In an earlier essay on "Túrin's Ofermod"[1] I argued that the story of Túrin in all of its various recensions contains Tolkien's fictional musings on the virtues and flaws of the heroic ethos that informs so much myth and literature from ancient times to modern. Túrin son of Húrin is a great hero in the classic mode, a mighty warrior in the defense of his people, but he also wreaks havoc wherever he goes and brings tragedy to the very people he is trying to defend. While martial courage is admirable, it takes wisdom to distinguish it from foolhardiness, and Túrin, though he is an Elf-friend and far from stupid, has a tendency to be hot–tempered and overly bold. He shows "ofermod" in Tolkien's interpretation of this Old English word.

In this essay I wish to argue further that Tolkien constructed the story to examine this theme through many of the secondary characters as well, both by their similarity to the protagonist and by contrast.

The story of Gwindor son of Guilin is especially instructive in this regard. Gwindor starts out very much in the same mode as Túrin and other classical heroes. He goes with the army of the Elf kingdom of Nargothrond to assault Morgoth's stronghold of Angband, partly out of a subject's duty to his King Fingon, it is true, but also partly out of fraternal duty to his brother Gelmir, missing in action after an earlier battle. Thus he combines many of the traditional heroic motives, the political one of fighting for his people against a powerful threat with the more personal ones of rescue or revenge, a mixture we also see in Túrin. When the captive Gelmir is slaughtered in front of him, Gwindor leads his forces in a furious attack, as Túrin might well have done in such circumstances. They succeed in breaking into Angband so that even the powerful "Morgoth trembled upon his deep throne, hearing them beat upon his doors" (*Narn* 56). This is as heroic a feat as any in Tolkien's *legendarium*, but it is unwise, throwing into disarray the battle tactics of the Elves and leading to their defeat. The result of Gwindor's daring is that he is cut off from the rest of the army and captured, and suffers hard, debilitating labor in the mines for years. He eventually fights his way out but (in the *Narn* version of the story) loses a hand in the process, joining many another Tolkien character whose physical maiming images a deeper psychological hurt (Frodo of the Nine Fingers being the most obvious example: and these two share what we now call post-traumatic stress disorder). When Beleg finds him hiding in the forest he is "but a bent and timid shadow of his former shape and mood" (152), to the extent that he is barely recognized when he returns home. He nonetheless helps Beleg to rescue Túrin, and gets him to safety after Beleg's death.

His counsels thereafter are very much on the side of caution. Tolkien provides a set-piece (160–163) of a debate carried out with both sides having strong arguments. Túrin is for boldness and martial glory even in the face of defeat: "... though mortal Men have little life beside the span of the Elves, they would rather spend it in battle than fly or submit" (161). Gwindor is for saving as much as possible, "for not all can fight and fall, and those we must keep from war and ruin, while we can" (162). When Túrin's rashness wins out, Gwindor does "fight and fall," mortally wounded while battling courageously to protect his people. His last words to Túrin are an exhortation to rescue Finduilas (the Elf maiden whom they both love and who loves them both, in their fashion) and flee with her to some place of safety.

It takes but a little reflection to see that Túrin would have been far better off had he heeded Gwindor's wise counsel. Finduilas is killed because he does nothing to help her, as he eventually discovers to his shame and grief. Had he been able to rescue her, a good possibility had he pursued her captors promptly instead of letting the false counsel of the dragon Glaurung send him astray, they might have married, which would have forestalled his marrying his sister later. Even if they had not wed, he would certainly have taken her to some refuge, and the most likely place was Doriath. Earlier Túrin's stubborn pride has kept him from accepting King Thingol's pardon and returning there, but even he might have been able to go back with his head held high if he went as the escort of as many Elves as he could rescue from the sack of Nargothrond. And in Doriath at this time he would have been re-united with his mother and the sister he had never seen, and thereby prevented the tragedy that was to come to all three of them. As Gwindor presciently warns Túrin, Finduilas "alone stands between you and your doom. If you fail her, it shall not fail to find you" (177).

Andróg has a story arc that is almost the opposite of Gwindor's, starting out as an outlaw who preys on any convenient victim, whose hastily loosed arrow kills one of the sons of Mîm, and who takes the lead in tormenting the captured Beleg. He seems more a villain of the piece than a potential hero. He changes when Túrin re-shapes the outlaw band into a guerrilla army, and especially after Beleg earns his gratitude (in spite of their mutual distrust) by healing him of what should have been a mortal wound. When the Orcs overwhelm Túrin's stronghold on Amon Rûdh it is, surprisingly, Andróg who is described as the "[m]ost valiant" (150) of the defenders, and even though he knows he is near death he spends the last of his strength to rescue Beleg. It is only by this heroic act that Beleg is saved to pursue the Orcs who have carried off Túrin. Perhaps Andróg never gains very much wisdom, but at least his violent nature is channeled in more productive ways, and he dies well, saving the life of another.

Beleg himself is a warrior who is both courageous and wise, but he frequently acts against his better judgment for love of Túrin. His most unwise act is, when he needs "a sword of worth" (96) and is given his choice among the armory of his King, to select a mighty sword indeed, but one forged by a dark heart who set malice in the blade (97). It is emblematic of the proverb that one who lives by the sword shall also perish by the sword, and, since it is the weapon with which Túrin kills Beleg by a tragic accident, it also embodies how a hero's rashness can harm those dear to him.

Dorlas is a man after Túrin's own heart, declaring "I would ever go forward rather than wait for a foe" (227) as he is the first to volunteer to accompany Túrin in a seemingly hopeless fight against the dragon Glaurung. While courageous in battle, he cannot bring himself to cross the raging river Teiglin in the dark. As his compatriot Hunthor wisely observes, "a man may love war, and yet dread many things" (235). Dorlas deserts Túrin and Hunthor and hides in the forest in shame, unable to live up to his own idea of what constitutes heroism or to settle for something else that might be within his capabilities. As Brandir later tells him, it would still have been an act of courage just to watch the dragon from a distance, and if he had then speedily brought back news of Túrin's fight with Glaurung he might have forestalled much trouble.

It is Hunthor, the man of peace, who braves the river crossing and, as they scale a cliff afterward, saves Túrin from falling to his death. But he himself is killed in the perilous climb, simply by being in the way of a falling rock. For all the destruction that follows in Túrin's wake, Hunthor's death is the clearest demonstration that heroes are dangerous to be around. As Túrin puts it, "by my wrath and rash deeds I cast a shadow wherever I dwell ..." (192) and "It is ill to walk in my shadow!" (237).

Hunthor is one of the few to heed his kinsman Brandir, the irenic leader of the People of Haleth who tries to keep them safely hidden in the Forest of Brethil rather than going openly into battle, a tactic similar to that of the Elves of Nargothrond under King Orodreth prior to the coming of Túrin. Lamed by a leg broken in childhood, Brandir can never be a warrior but he is a healer, whose ministrations help many including Túrin and his sister Nienor. Hunthor says of him that his weakened "limbs by ill hazard cannot do as his heart would" (227), but he nevertheless limps into dangerous places trying to help others. He hears the dying Glaurung tell Nienor that her brother is "a stabber in the dark, treacherous to foes, faithless to friends, and a curse unto his kin" (243), a malicious twisting of the truth that Túrin unconsciously echoes in accusing Brandir of similar treachery. "Then Brandir, seeing his death in Túrin's face, stood still and did not quail, though he had no weapon but his crutch ... 'you slander me, son of Húrin. Did Glaurung slander you? If you slay me, then all shall see that he did not. Yet I do not fear to die....'" (252). Indeed when the wrathful Túrin kills Brandir the people whom he has just saved from the dragon flee from him in terror.

A healing role somewhat similar to that of Brandir is played by Túrin's kinswoman Aerin. When the Easterlings took over Túrin's homeland of Dor-lómin, their chief Brodda forcibly wed Aerin, a tactic common among conquerors in early human history wishing to cement their hold on their new territories by such a match with a leading family of the natives. Brodda is anything but a good husband, but Aerin is able to use her position to ameliorate the sufferings of her people. Túrin calls her faint of heart, but he is corrected by a man who knows better: "Many a man of arms misreads patience and quiet. She did much good among us at much cost. Her heart was not faint ...." (190).

Túrin's sister Nienor has as strong a heart as their aunt Aerin. When their mother Morwen insists on going in person to fallen Nargothrond to seek news of what became of her son instead of waiting for the report of experienced scouts (it will be seen that Túrin comes by his stubborn pride honestly), Nienor disguises herself and accompanies the reconnaissance. She knows she will eventually be found out, and when that happens she is resolute that she will accompany her mother either back to Doriath or on to Nargothrond as Morwen decides, for "nothing that you fear not do I fear" (202). She hopes that her mother will take the excuse to return to safety at Thingol's court, which she realizes would be the wiser course, and the tactic almost works. Morwen has no qualms about putting herself in unnecessary danger, but is less ready to do the same for her daughter. So she does waver. But we are told that "she could not overcome her pride, and would not (save the fair words) seem thus to be led back by her daughter, as one old and doting" (203) and so they both press on, the wife and daughter of Húrin the Steadfast, ultimately to their tragic deaths. Mablung, the leader of the Elvish scouting party, says in exasperation: "Truly, it is by lack of counsel not of courage that Húrin's kin bring woe to others!" (203), neatly summing up this major theme of the Túrin story.

Now these people are frequently wise enough to see the doubtful nature of many of their undertakings, but they are also caught up in circumstances they realize are often beyond their control. This is mythically represented by the curse Morgoth speaks to his prisoner Húrin: "...upon all whom you love my thought shall weigh as a cloud of Doom, and it shall bring them down into darkness and despair. Wherever they go, evil shall arise. Whenever they speak, their words shall bring ill counsel. Whatsoever they do shall turn against them. They shall die without hope, cursing both life and death" (64). Thus they are, as Christopher Tolkien notes in his Introduction, "condemned to live trapped in a malediction of huge and mysterious power..." (14). It is a grim thought about a grim story. Yet this is the human condition writ small and expressed in myth. We are each and every one of us just a small part of a much larger world, even the most powerful among us, and whatever freedom of will and action we may possess, we are always constrained by forces outside ourselves. The tension between fate and free will is a regular theme in much of Tolkien's fiction, but he is careful never to resolve it too definitively one way or the other. Morgoth's curse appears at the beginning of the story and remains solidly in the background, with an occasional reminder that it is there, but what we mostly see are well-developed characters making decisions very much in keeping with their individual characters.

World War I demonstrated to Tolkien and many of his "lost generation" that martial glory could be foolish and the human cost of war tremendous. The tragedy of the Great War was fresh in his mind when he was composing the early recensions of the Túrin story in the mid-teens to mid-twenties of the last century, and not forgotten when he was making additions and embellishments in the re-writings of the thirties and the fifties that led to *The Children of Húrin* as we now have it. This is a work of fiction and not an essay, but in it he expresses a great deal. He wrote to his son Christopher late in life about "...my nature, which expresses itself about things deepest felt in tales and myths..." (*Letters* 420–421). In the tale and myth of Túrin and his kindred Tolkien produced a tragic and a great work of literature.

NOTE

1. "Túrin's *Ofermod*: An Old English Theme in the Development of the Story of Túrin," *Tolkien's* Legendarium: *Essays on The History of Middle-earth*, ed. Verlyn Flieger and Carl F. Hostetter, Contributions to the Study of Science Fiction and Fantasy, no. 86 (Westport, CT and London: Greenwood Press, 2000), 233–245.

"Alone Between the Dark and Light": "The Lay of Aotrou and Itroun" and Lessons from the Later *Legendarium*

KRISTINE LARSEN

Numerous scholars (as well as Tolkien himself) have acknowledged the importance of Tolkien's Christianity in general, and Catholicism in particular, in understanding fundamental aspects of the *legendarium* (Coloumbe 53–66, Dickerson, Moseley, Wood). Tolkien himself acknowledged in a 1953 letter that "*The Lord of the Rings* is of course a fundamentally religious and Catholic work; unconsciously so at first, but consciously in the revision" (*Letters* 172). Tolkien's writing is informed, not only by basic tenets of his faith, but also by its prohibitions and taboos. An interesting example is the Catholic Church's long-time stance against occult practices and superstitions. For example, the 1997 *Catechism of the Catholic Church* articulates clear and definitive prohibitions against "all forms of divination" including astrology, palmistry, and "conjuring up the dead," as well as against "all practices of magic and sorcery, by which one attempts to tame occult powers" even if the intent is to heal the sick (3.2.1.1.III, 2117). As noted by several authors (e.g., Moore, Quainton), numerous Biblical passages are the root source of these prohibitions. For example, Isaiah 47:12–14 warns

> Persist in your spells and your monstrous sorceries,
> Maybe you can get help from them, maybe you will yet
>   inspire awe.
> But no! In spite of your many wiles you are powerless.

Let your astrologers, your stargazers
Who foretell the future month by month, persist, and save
    you! [New English Bible].

Despite the Catholic Church's early condemnation of occult practices (dating back to the edicts of Constantine and the writings of St. Augustine), certain arcane practices—most notably astrology—crept back into popular practice in the late Medieval times, lasting well into the Renaissance. Astronomy and astrology were at times virtually interchangeable, and the practitioners of the former (such as Johannes Kepler) found a lucrative business in making observations of the heavens in the service of the latter. Kepler said of his horoscope casting, "Nature, which has conferred upon every animal the means of sustenance, has designed astrology as an ally of astronomy" (Baker 315). Kings, emperors, and even popes succumbed to the lure of this fashionable superstition, complete with the creation of the desirable and powerful position of court astrologer (Jacobi). While court astrologers are now mercifully rare (with the all-too-recent exception of the Reagan White House), one can argue that astrology and related occult practices have remained in vogue in certain quarters even to this day. For example, polls have shown that between 1979 to 2010 a third or more of the American public consistently answered that astrology has some scientific basis (National Science Board A 7–19).

Astrology and other arcane superstitions were certainly in vogue during the time of Tolkien's writing of the early *legendarium* through *The Lord of the Rings*. For example, in 1943 the California State Assembly briefly considered a bill which would have established a special State Board of Astrological Examiners for the purpose of licensing astrologers (Connor 226). Presumably the state would have made a considerable amount of money if it had gone through with the plan, as there were an estimated 30,000 astrologers in the United States at that time (228). In response, a number of scientists declared rather public war on these beliefs (Bok and Mayall, Chant, Leavitt). It can be argued that Tolkien would have agreed with these scientists, although perhaps from the angle of faith rather than the scientific method. Tolkien's Catholic intolerance for such beliefs could easily explain why he was not able to follow the lead of his friend C.S. Lewis and include astrology as a plot device in his writings, despite the fact that numerous scholars have argued that Lewis only did it to maintain the consistency of a medieval—yet clearly Christian—universe (Duriez, Ford, Zambreno). In *Planet Narnia*, Michael Ward has argued that Lewis's entire Narnia series (and to a lesser extent, the Space Trilogy) is directly based on an interpretation of the seven classic astrological "planets." Tolkien might even have been sympathetic to biologist J.B.S. Haldane's criticism of the Space Trilogy, when Haldane claimed that Lewis's work "defended beliefs in astrology [and] black magic" (251).

In Lewis's defense, he openly defended the intrinsic beauty and power of the medieval geocentric cosmology despite its scientific inaccuracies, and argued quite eloquently in his famous work *The Discarded Image* (1964) that it is still relevant in a modern society. In that work he noted that the "[c]elestial bodies affect terrestrial bodies, including those of men. And by affecting our bodies they can, but need not, affect our reason and our will" (103–4). It is certainly possible that Lewis might have been speaking of the supposed behavioral problems associated with the full moon—so-called "lunacy"—for which repeated statistical studies have shown no evidence, despite stubbornly persistent folklore to the contrary (Kelly et al.). But even if he were to be admitting the possibility (or even probability) of such pseudoscientific beliefs, it is important to note that Lewis is arguing that even if these influences exist, they need not rule human behavior—they "can, but need not." He instead argues that "the wise man will over-rule the stars," but admits that "more often it will not be resisted, for most men are not wise; hence like actuarial predictions, astrological predictions about the behavior of large masses of men will often be verified" (104). Lewis's rather tongue-in-cheek answer here exposes his real thoughts on astrology. If this is not obvious enough, one need look no further than Lewis's "A Reply to Professor Haldane," in which he states,

> There is thus a great deal of scientific falsehood in my stories: some of it known to be false even by me when I wrote the books. The canals in Mars are not there because I believe in them but because they are part of the popular tradition; the astrological character of the planets for the same reason [*Of Other Worlds* 76].

Lewis therefore has no difficulty separating his personal beliefs from those of the larger culture; Tolkien appears to have a much more complicated relationship with such a detachment in his own writings.

In *J.R.R. Tolkien: Author of the Century* and *The Road to Middle-earth*, Tom Shippey explored this tension between personal belief and artistic license (as applied to fiction set in a pre–Christian society), using as his examples two of Tolkien's non-*legendarium* works, "The Homecoming of Beorhtnoth Beorhthelm's Son" and "The Lay of Aotrou and Itroun." Tolkien admits in Manuscript B of the essay "On Fairy-stories" that Faërie is "the occult power in nature" and therefore "fairies have thus acquired a diabolical aspect" (*TOF* 264). Shippey argues that "The Lay of Aotrou and Itroun" clearly demonstrates Tolkien's belief that "getting involved with Faërie was deeply dangerous" (*Road* 280), but as this essay will further explore, the danger may be philological and philosophical as well as ethical and moral.

"The Lay of Aotrou and Itroun" (Breton for "lord and lady") is an alliterative rhymed poem written in octosyllabic couplets which Tolkien composed at least as early as September 1930, and published in the *Welsh Review* in 1945

(Carpenter 168, 272). Shippey, Kocher, and Yates have individually explored the various Celtic and Norse literary sources for the lay (*Road* 280, Kocher 159–168, Yates 63–71). While Tolkien's version has plot points which can be clearly traced back to several predecessor stories, Shippey notes that his main original contribution to the tale is "a heavy weight of faith" (*Road* 280). In Tolkien's lay, a childless Lord invokes the occult influence of a witch—a Corrigan—in the form of a magic potion in order to conceive twins with his Lady wife. Yates notes that it might be the fact that the children were twins (twins being considered supernatural in some traditions) that suggested to Tolkien that their conception might have been an occult rather than a divinely inspired event (69). After the children are born, the Corrigan demands the Lord's affections (including his hand in marriage) as her belated payment. While in some source versions of the tale the Lord betrays his Lady by having sexual relations with the witch, Tolkien's Christian Lord remains faithful to his bride and is condemned to death in three days' time by the Corrigan. His wife dies of grief soon after, and the ultimate fate of the ill-begotten offspring is unclear. Tolkien successfully turns the cautionary tale from one about the dangers of infidelity to one's spouse to one about the dangers of infidelity to one's faith—infidelity in one's relationship with God. As Shippey argues, Aotrou "would have done better to trust in 'hope and prayer,' even if the prayer were unanswered" (280). Yates adds that if Aotrou had just been patient, "he might have been rewarded with children born naturally" (70). It is as Tolkien warns in Manuscript B of "On Fairy-stories": part of the power of the "inhabitants of Faerie ... is power to play on the desires of our bodies and of our hearts" (211).

Thus, as Shippey explains, while the death of the Lord also appears in Breton versions, in Tolkien's version the death is

> deserved, or at least prompted by Aotrou's attempt to sway Providence by supernatural forces. Tolkien's moral is clear and unequivocal. Aotrou's sin lay not in submitting to the Corrigan ...—it lay in having any dealings with her at all [*Author* 294].

Indeed, Tolkien's lay ends with the invocation

> God keep us all in hope and prayer
> from evil rede and from despair,
> by waters blest of Christendom
> to dwell until at last we come
> to joy of Heaven where is queen
> the maiden Mary pure and clear ["Aotrou" 266].

The final invocation of Mary demonstrates unequivocally that she is the only "supernatural" woman with whom Tolkien believes we should have contact. Similarly, Shippey notes that the poem is a "complete rejection of supernatural allure" which goes "several stages" beyond his other poems which discuss the intersection between humans and Faërie (*Author* 294).

This same lesson is repeated throughout Tolkien's Middle-earth *legendarium*. One of the most obvious occult practices against which Tolkien warns is the direct worship of the dark powers, in the form of Melkor and Sauron. In Tolkien's account of the downfall of humans, "The Tale of Adanel" (part of the "Athrabeth Finrod ah Andreth"), early humans in Middle-earth mistakenly believed the voice of Melkor to be that of God (and that of Ilúvatar to be an evil power which wanted to ensnare them). They prayed to their Master, bowed to him, and "received his commands," driving them to commit evil acts against each other (*Morgoth* 347). Too late did they realize the folly of their ways. Melkor easily ensnared the humans by promising them hidden knowledge that Ilúvatar had withheld from them (Ilúvatar desiring instead for the humans to discover things for themselves). Melkor successfully turned the humans against each other by playing favorites, as "to some he began to show favour; to the strongest and cruellest, and to those who went most often to the House. He gave gifts to them, and knowledge that they kept secret ...." (348). Tolkien's lesson here is obvious, and this "fall" has clear parallels with the fall in the Book of Genesis. Tolkien admitted in a 1951 letter to Milton Waldman that "There cannot be any 'story' without a fall—all stories are ultimately about the fall" (*Letters* 147). Indeed, in the *legendarium* there are multiple "falls," not only of humans, but of elves and even the Ainur themselves.

Another of the falls of humankind appears in the multiple versions of the tale of the fate of Númenor. The royal house of Númenor fell under the sway of Sauron, and the culture declined into a form of Satan worship of the Lord of Darkness (Melkor), including human sacrifice. Their ultimate sin was to declare open war on the Valar and attempt to break the Ban by sailing West to the Blessed Lands in order to somehow wrestle immortality from the hands of the Valar. All of these bad behaviors were a natural outgrowth of their obsessive and unnatural desire to attain some arcane knowledge with which they might achieve immortality (*S* 274 ff.). This central motivation for the self-destructive behavior of the Númenóreans dates all the way back to the first version of "The Fall of Númenor," written circa 1936, and remains consistent in the various retellings and retooling of the tale (*Lost Road* 21). The survivors of Númenor (we may think specifically of the residents of Gondor) were quick to forget the lessons of their forefathers. In the first version of "The Fall of Númenor" it is said

> But all alike were filled with desire of long life upon earth, and the thought of Death was heavy upon them .... And they built mightier houses for their dead than for their living, and endowed their buried kings with unavailing treasure. For their wise men hoped ever to discover the secret of prolonging life and

maybe the recalling of it.... [T]hey achieved only the art of preserving uncorrupt for many ages the dead flesh of men [*Lost Road* 16].

We also find an overview of this in *The Lord of the Rings*, when Faramir explains to Frodo that many of the exiled Númenóreans

> became enamoured of the Darkness and the black arts .... Death was ever present, because the Númenoreans still, as they had in their old kingdom, and so lost it, hungered after endless life unchanging. Kings made tombs more splendid than houses of the living .... Childless lords sat in aged halls musing on heraldry; in secret chambers withered men compounded strong elixirs, or in high cold towers asked questions of the stars [i.e., engaging in both potion-making and astrology] [*TT* IV, v, 286].

The reference to "childless lords" in the description of the fallen and exiled Númenóreans brings us once again to consider "The Lay of Aotrou and Itroun." Tolkien's lesson both there and in the case of the Númenóreans is quite clear: God's gifts—both granted (the gift of mortality) and withheld (the gift of heirs)—must be accepted with grace, and vain attempts to use the occult arts to "play God" never come to good ends.

Another supernatural activity against which Tolkien generally admonishes is speaking with disembodied spirits. In the "Laws and Customs Among the Eldar" (part of "The Later *Quenta Silmarillion*"), we read that such communication is

> a foolish and perilous thing, besides being a wrong deed forbidden justly by the appointed Rulers of Arda .... They will not speak truth or wisdom. To call on them is folly. To attempt to master them and to make them servants of one's own will is wickedness. Such practices are of Morgoth; and the necromancers are of the host of Sauron his servant [*Morgoth* 224].

Note that the root of the issue in all these examples is the desire for power over others (including over the will of Ilúvatar), to bend individuals and the laws of nature toward one's will. This, above all else, is central to Tolkien's definition of the black arts, as we shall see.

It should be noted that in these cautionary tales, Tolkien is clear to differentiate between astronomy and astrology. For example, while the court of Gondor are to be condemned for their attempts at astrological prognostication, characters of good heart are often cheered by gazing upward at the stars. Thus in the years before ascending the throne of Númenor, Tar-Meneldur's "chief delight was in the watching of the stars" and he built an observatory tower especially for this purpose (*UT* 173). Likewise, before Saruman perverted the beautiful tower of Isengard "to his shifting purposes," "wise men" used the tower to view the heavens (*TT* III, viii, 160). After leaving Hobbiton on his way to Bree, Frodo spends time with Gildor Inglorion's company of

Elves, and upon the rising of Orion (Menelvagor to the Elves), the company breaks into "speech and merriment" (*FR* I, iii, 91). This is in keeping with Biblical passages which describe the constellations as signs of God's greatness: Amos calls God "He who made the Pleiades and Orion" (5:8) and God asks Job if he (presumably like God) could "bind the cluster of the Pleiades or loose Orion's belt?" (38:3).

The examples given so far are distinctly black and white—sin is clearly defined and unequivocal. However, Tolkien dares to walk where angels fear to tread, having characters witness signs in the heavens. For example, Durin was given a sign of the legitimacy of his kingship when he looked into the Mirrormere "And saw a crown of stars appear" (*FR* II, iv, 329). Even more curious are instances where signs are purposefully placed in the heavens by the Valar, such as Varda's creation of the Valacirca (the Big Dipper) as "a challenge to Melkor ... and sign of doom" (*S* 48). Another example is Eärendil wearing his Silmaril and sailing the heavens in his ship Vingelot. The Elves termed the sailor, jewel and ship together "Gil-Estel"— "Star of High Hope"— and "took it for a sign"; and upon viewing the star "Morgoth was filled with doubt" (*S* 250). It is certainly true that heavenly signs do appear in the Bible, such as in Joel 2:30–31, where we read,

> I will show portents in the sky and on earth,
> Blood and fire and columns of smoke;
> The sun shall be turned into darkness and the moon into blood
> Before the great and terrible day of the Lord comes [NEB].

But how well-defined is the line between godly portent and ungodly horoscope? Are the Valar, as proxies of Ilúvatar, automatically granted such divine powers without question? How does one differentiate between true and false signs? For example, in the second version of "The Fall of Númenor," Tolkien writes that Sauron "beguiled the Númenóreans with signs and wonders" (*Lost Road* 27)

Tolkien himself notes in Manuscript B of "On Fairy-stories" that "Miracle and magic are not so easy to distinguish from one another. They have in fact only become distinguished by Christian theology" (252). He continues to explain that "God performs *miracles* in answer to prayer, or through the mediation of a person (human or angelic) who is in that particular operation the agent of a specifically divine purpose" (253). In his discussion of Tolkien and the power of faith, Birzer gives the example of blinding of the magician Elymas by St. Paul as a clear example of "the superiority of the miracle to magic" (102). As applied to Middle-earth, this would seem to include Ilúvatar and the Valar (including Varda, who fashioned the Valacirca). However, does this satisfactorily explain how Galadriel's mirror—a scrying mirror which shows visions to its user—is not in the same forbidden class as the black arts practiced by the Kings of Gondor? Galadriel herself notes to Sam that her mirror is "what your folk would call magic, I believe ... and they seem also to use the same word of the deceits of the Enemy," i.e. Sauron (*FR* II, vii, 377). She warns the hobbit that her mirror shows some events which "never come to be, unless those that behold the visions turn aside from their path to prevent them. The Mirror is dangerous as a guide of deeds" (378). Likewise, is the line between the phial of the Corrigan (containing the fertility potion which Aotrou secretly feeds to his wife) and the phial of Galadriel, whose light has the power to repel Shelob the monstrous spider, black and white, or an uncomfortable shade of gray? Tolkien himself saw a significant difference, and admitted that Galadriel's characters owes much "to Christian and Catholic teaching and imagination about Mary" (*Letters* 407). But is the difference always consistent and clear to the reader?

Tolkien understood well that he had encountered considerable difficulties in clearly articulating the sometimes subtle differences between Elvish and "black" magic (*Letters* 146, 199). In fact, numerous pages of Tolkien's various drafts and revisions of "On Fairy-stories" as well as a number of published letters are devoted to attempts to clarify this division, possibly in his own mind as well as those of his readers. Indeed, the period of his crafting of the initial lecture through revisions to the final version for publication (circa 1942–47) falls within the middle of the time during which Tolkien was writing *The Lord of the Rings*. This period was clearly one in which Tolkien was struggling to articulate a clear and self-consistent definition of the types of "magic" in his subcreation, definitions which would be consistent with his own personal beliefs and used consistently within his *legendarium*. In a 1954 draft for a letter, Tolkien admits that he has "been far too casual about 'magic' and especially the use of the word.... It is a v. large question, and difficult" (*Letters* 199). In another letter he explains that he has not used the term magic "consistently," and blames this in part on a lack of a clear term for Elvish magic (as opposed to the black magic of "the Enemy") (*Letters* 146). Perhaps the clearest distinction possible (despite the lack of a proper terminology) is found in Manuscript B of "On Fairy-stories" in which he explains that "Magic is evil when it is sought as a means of personal power (especially over our fellows)" (261). By this definition, the works of Melkor, Sauron, and the Corrigan of "The Lay of Aotrou and Itroun" are clearly evil. Since the childless Lord desired power as well—the power to counteract his wife's infertility, in effect to create life where naturally there would be none—his deal with the Corrigan is clearly sinful and his subsequent punishment of death deserved.

But the issue of "magic" in Tolkien's *legendarium* cannot be wrapped up quite so neatly. Tolkien spent decades trying to find consistent language (and apply that language in some consistent way). Nowhere is this clearer than in the multiple drafts of his famous lecture "On Fairy-stories." For example, Flieger and Anderson include four different versions of a particular passage concerning definitions of (and relationships between) such terms as "*Art, Enchantment, Wizardry, Magic, Science, delusory belief, elvish craft,* [and] *Fantasy*" and characterize Tolkien's ever-changing hypothesis as "confusing and ... itself confused" (140). While he does not achieve complete consistency or clarity, there are two important points made in both the drafts and the final essay: Elvish "magic" is more closely aligned with what we would normally call art and enchantment (in terms of fantasy and not harmful delusion), and the "magic" of the Enemy is more closely aligned with control, domination, and mechanism/technology. This final identification is perhaps the most consistent piece of the definition, and is clearly seen in what Tom Shippey calls "Sandyman's disease." Shippey describes the advanced form seen in Saruman when he explains it "starts as intellectual curiosity, develops as engineering skill, turns into greed and the desire to dominate, corrupts further into a hatred and contempt of the natural world which goes beyond any rational desire to use it" (*Author* 171). Tolkien continues this identification through his later letters, such as the 1951 communication with Milton Waldman. Here he explains that the Fall is caused by a possessive attachment to one's own sub-creations and a desire for immortality, either one of which will "lead to the desire for Power, for making the will more quickly effective,—and so to the Machine (or Magic)" (*Letters* 145).

Like Tolkien himself, Tolkien scholars and critics have also struggled with describing and defining just what "magic" means in the *legendarium*. For example, Birzer argues that Tolkien believed in two forms of magic which he described as "*magia* and *goeteia*"—which Birzer defines as "enchantment" and "power derived from a demonic source and intended to dominate others and deprive its victim of their free will" (102). But in a 1954 letter draft Tolkien points out the problems with this dichotomy: "*magia* could be, was, held good (per se), and *goeteia* bad. Neither is, in this tale, good or bad (per se), but only by motive or purpose or use. Both sides use both, but with different motives" (*Letters* 200). For example, Tolkien explains in the same draft that "the Enemy" (Sauron, and presumably Melkor) uses his *magia* "to bulldoze both people and things" while the Elves (and Gandalf) use their *magia* "sparingly" and "for specific beneficent purposes." The Enemy uses "*goeteia* to terrify and subjugate" while the Good Powers' goetic powers are "entirely *artistic* and not intended to deceive" (although he admits they could deceive mere humans) (*Letters* 200, emphasis in original). Tolkien's working definition appears to be the following: magic can be divided into two kinds of dichotomies: by motive into Art and Domination, and by outcome into Effect (what he calls in this draft *magia*) and Delusion/Enchantment (here called *goeteia*). Here we see the closest thing to clearly articulated definitions of the uses of magic in his subcreation. One can construct a 2 × 2 matrix of forms of magic, and a test of the consistency of this two-dimensional classification would be to try and assign specific examples within the *legendarium* into a single, unambiguous box (such as the following):

	Art	Domination
Effect	good (but used sparingly)	worst
Enchantment	best	bad

An example of an Art-Effect would be Gandalf's fireworks, while a Domination-Effect would be Saruman's explosives. The Elvish cloaks given to the members of the Fellowship would be an example of Art-Enchantment, while Domination-Enchantment would include the signs Sauron used to ensnare the Númenóreans. The Corrigan's fertility potion is clearly an example of Domination-Effect as well. In Tolkien's worldview, most machines/technologies have at least the strong potential to fall under the Domination-Effect category. This is seen in the 1954 letter draft when Tolkien explains that "The Enemy, or those who have become like him, go in for 'machinery'—with destructive and evil effects—because 'magicians,' who have become clearly concerned to use *magia* for their own power, would do so" (*Letters* 200).

The clear connection between magic and mechanism (technology) is especially interesting in light of another attempt to classify types of magic, namely that done by fellow Inkling C.S. Lewis. In his 1954 *English Literature in the Sixteenth Century* (based on the 1944 Clark Lectures) Lewis first differentiates between "mere witchcraft—traditional, perhaps Satanistic, rites practiced by the poor, the ignorant, or the perverted" (which he dismisses out of hand) and "high magic: not concealed but avowed and vindicated by eloquent scholars who draw much of their strength from the New Learning" (i.e. the Scientific Revolution) (7). Lewis also carefully notes the change in depictions of magic in literature between the Middle Ages and the Sixteenth Century. For example, references to medieval magic have "the note of 'faerie' about them. They could arouse a practical or quasi-scientific interest in no reader's mind.... [M]agic, like knight-errantry, is part of the furniture of romance" (8). In contrast, in the works of Shakespeare and his contemporaries "books are opened, terrible words pronounced, souls imperilled.... [I]t might be going on in the next street" (8). This new form of "practical" magic (one that causes palpable effects rather than enchantment, to translate this into Tolkien's classification) can only steer clear of sliding into Black Magic through the careful selection of its source of power. Lewis explains that the basis for this "High Magic" is the existence of "theologically neutral" spirits or "aethereals" that are clearly distinct from the standard angels and demons of Christian theology (9). In Tolkien's mind, this could hardly be "High" magic; all power ultimately derives from God, either through miracles, or the use of personal talents and/or knowledge given to one from God (even if those gifts are later perverted, as in the case of Melkor). Therefore Varda's power to create the stars is already inherent in her nature, as is Melian's ability to create the Girdle that (temporarily) protects her kingdom. But these are actually both subcreations, as they derive from a greater (and thus the only true) creation, that of Ilúvatar. Whatever "powers" the early humans receive from cavorting with Melkor are only perversions of their own nature or the limited "magic" Melkor can muster by destroying and distorting the natural world. Hence they are doomed to disappointment (and disaster). Therefore even if the existence of these "aethereals" could be accepted by Tolkien, they would either have to be aligned with God or not—neutrality is not an option when it comes to "power." Finally, as we have already noted, Tolkien wrote a definitive prohibition against consulting with disembodied spirits in "Laws and Customs Among the Eldar."

We see another clear difference between Tolkien's and Lewis's concepts of "magic" in their relationship to science and technology. Lewis explains that this new type of Sixteenth Century magic

> falls into its place among the other dreams of power which then haunted the European mind. Most obviously it falls into place beside the thought of Bacon. His endeavor is no doubt contrasted in our minds with that of magicians; but contrasted only in the light of the event, only because we know that science succeeded and magic failed [13].

This "magic" could also include alchemy and astrology, and other pseudo-sciences for which, as we have seen, Tolkien had no patience in his *legendarium*. The reference to Francis Bacon is interesting, if one considers his views on the relationship between science and the natural world. In the words of feminist science historian and philosopher Evelyn Fox Keller, Bacon's "central metaphor—science as power, a force virile enough to penetrate and subdue nature—has provided an image that permeates the rhetoric of modern science" (48). According to Bacon, scientists seek to find the "nature of things" through experiments that express "the spirit of action, of a 'doing' devoted to 'finding out.' Science controls by following the dictates of nature, but these dictates include the requirement, even demand, for domination" (37). The use of the words "power" and "domination" in describing both this "magic" and the "science" that developed in parallel to it would negate the possibility that Tolkien would include it as anything other than Domination-Effect, and points to another clear distinction Tolkien makes in his *legendarium*, namely that of pure science versus technology. For example, in a draft to a 1954 letter to Peter Hastings, Tolkien explains that Tom Bombadil is then an 'allegory,' or an exemplar, a particular embodying of pure (real) natural science: the spirit that desires knowledge of other things, their history and nature.... a spirit coeval with the rational mind, and entirely unconcerned with 'doing' anything with the knowledge: Zoology and Botany not Cattle-breeding or Agriculture. Even the Elves hardly show this: they are primarily artists [*Letters* 192].

Tolkien is not "anti-science"; he is, however, a vehement critic of the misuse and overuse of technology, and warns against the slippery slope that leads from scientific discovery to technological application. Perhaps the best known example is found in a 1956 draft to a letter to Joanna de Bortadano:

Of course my story is not an allegory of Atomic power, but of *Power* (exerted for Domination). Nuclear physics can be used for that purpose. But they need not be. They need not be used at all. If there is any contemporary reference in my story at all it is to what seems to me the most widespread assumption of our time: that if a thing can be done, it must be done. This seems to me wholly false [*Letters* 246].

Just because the Corrigan *can* induce fertility in Itroun, it need not be done. Tolkien clearly demonstrates that it *should not* be done. It would be interesting to consider what Tolkien might have thought about the wide array of reproductive technologies available today, from *in vitro* fertilization to surrogate mothers. Personally, this author assumes he would have considered this technology in a similar vein as the Corrigan's phial.

It has been shown above that it is possible to unambiguously classify some specific examples from Tolkien's works using the system laid out in his 1954 letter draft. However, what of the more interesting examples found in the *legendarium*? As one might suspect, as with all classification systems which rely on dichotomies rather than continua there are exceptions which cannot be so clearly pigeonholed. Melian and her daughter Lúthien both use enchantment to thwart the Enemy and his hordes, for example in the case of the Girdle that surrounds Doriath and the disguises that Lúthien devises for herself, Beren, and Huan in order to fool Sauron and Morgoth. Melian seeks to preserve the lives and safety of the residents in her and Thingol's realm. While the couple's isolationist politics are dubious in intent (and ultimately unsuccessful), the initial purpose of Melian's Girdle to protect the residents of Doriath from attacks of orcs and other foul creatures is a justified one. But what of Lúthien? She first sought to rescue Beren from Sauron's dungeon, but the ultimate goal of their quest was to steal a Silmaril from Morgoth's iron crown as a dowry prize for her father. As a part of her plan to acquire the cursed jewel from Morgoth, Lúthien sang a song "of such surpassing loveliness, and of such blinding power, that he listened perforce; and a blindness came upon him, as his eyes roamed to and fro, seeking her. All his court were cast down in slumber, and all the fires faded and were quenched" (*S* 180–81). While her actions at first sound like her mother's enchantment, they move into power and effect. While one may or may not argue whether the ends justify the means, the point is that this is an example open to interpretation, and serves as a sign that Tolkien's classification is not completely unambiguous or consistent.

Another important example is the Rings of Power. As Tolkien notes in a 1951 letter, the object of Elvish magic is "Art not Power, sub-creation not domination and tyrannous re-forming of Creation" (*Letters* 146). But Tolkien himself agrees that the Elves "came their nearest to falling to 'magic' and machinery" when with "the aid of Sauron's lore they made *Rings of Power* ('power' is an ominous and sinister word in all these tales, except as applied to the gods)" (*Letters* 152, emphasis in original). Tolkien further explains that the "chief power" (note the use of that "ominous" word again) of the rings was

> the prevention or slowing of *decay* ... the preservation of what is desired or loved, or its semblance—this is more or less an Elvish motive. But also they enhanced the natural powers of a possessor—thus approaching 'magic,' a motive easily corruptible into evil, a lust for domination [*Letters* 152].

Is Tolkien's definition truly consistent here or is he splitting hairs? Just how convincing is his argument that the Elvish rings have indeed stayed on the right side of the rather nebulous line between good and evil magic? Has he backed himself into a corner from which he cannot escape in a self-consistent manner, regardless of his literary gymnastics? This particular case, and the case of Galadriel's mirror, this author will leave for each reader to draw his or her own conclusions from.

Hence we see that the "The Lay of Aotrou and Itroun" is a reflection of the greater evolution of Tolkien's thoughts on magic as described in the *legendarium* at large, an evolution from tackling clear examples of "right and wrong" to a more interesting gray area at the multiple intersections of morality, intention, action, and result. Tolkien's views on "magic" approached, but apparently never ultimately reached, a self-consistent completion (rather like the *legendarium* itself). Therefore perhaps it is Tolkien himself, rather than Aotrou, who ultimately stands "alone between the dark and light" ("Aotrou" 255) as he attempts to reach a definitive and consistent differentiation between miracle, magic, enchantment, mechanism, science and art in his pre–Christian (yet admittedly Catholic) sub-creation.

WORKS CITED

Baker, Alfred. "Astrology." *Journal of the Royal Astronomical Society of Canada* 15.9 (1921): 309–21.

Birzer, Bradley. *J.R.R. Tolkien's Sanctifying Myth: Understanding Middle-earth*. Wilmington: ISI Books, 2002.

Bok, Bart J., and Margaret W. Mayall. "Scientists Look at Astrology." *The Scientific Monthly* 52.3 (1941): 233–44.

Catechism of the Catholic Church. Vatican City: Vatican Library, 1993. Part III, Section 2, Chapter 1, Article 1, III, 2117. May 5, 2011. http://www.vatican.va/archive/ENG0015/__P7E.HTM.

Chant, C. E. "Astrology Again." *Journal of the Royal Astronomical Society of Canada* 36 (1942): 55–60.

Coloumbe, Charles A. "*The Lord of the Rings*—A Catholic View." *Tolkien: A Celebration*. Ed. Joseph Pearce. San Francisco: Ignatius Press, 2001. 53–66.

Connor, Elizabeth. "Astrology Is Not Extinct." *Publications of the Astronomical Society of the Pacific* 55 (1943): 226–32.

Dickerson, Matthew T. *Following Gandalf: Epic Battles and Moral Victory in* The Lord of the Rings. Grand Rapids: Brazos Press, 2003.

Duriez, Colin. *A Field Guide to Narnia*. Downer's Grove: InterVarsity Press, 2004.

Flieger, Verlyn, and Douglas A. Anderson. "The History of 'On Fairy-stories.'" *TOF* 122–158.

Ford, Paul F. *Companion to Narnia*, rev. ed. New York: HarperOne, 2005.

Haldane, J.B.S. *Everything Has a History*. London: George Allen and Unwin, 1951.

Jacobi, Maximilian. "Astrology." *The Catholic Encyclopedia*, v. 2. New York: Robert Appleton Company, 1907. May 5, 2011. http://www.newadvent.org/cathen/02018e.htm.

Keller, Evelyn Fox. *Reflections on Gender and Science*. New Haven: Yale, 1985.

Kelly, I.W., James Rotton, and Roger Culver. "The Moon was Full and Nothing Happened: A Review of Studies on the Moon and Human Behavior and Human Belief." *The Outer Edge*. Ed. Joe Nickell, Barry Karr, and Tom Genoni. Amherst, NY: CSICOP, 1996. 16–34.

Kocher, Paul H. *Master of Middle-earth: The Fiction of J.R.R. Tolkien*. New York: Ballantine, 1977.

Leavitt, Eugene E. "Superstitions: Twenty-Five Years Ago and Today." *American Journal of Psychology* 65.3 (1952): 443–49.

Lewis, C.S. *The Discarded Image*. Cambridge: Cambridge University Press, 1964.

_____. *English Literature in the Sixteenth Century, excluding Drama. The Completion of the Clark Lectures, Trinity College, Cambridge, 1944*. Oxford: Clarendon, 1954.

_____. "A Reply to Professor Haldane." *Of Other Worlds: Essays and Stories*. San Diego: Harvest, 1994. 74–85.

Moore, Joan Andre. *Astronomy in the Bible*. Nashville: Abingdon, 1981.

Moseley, Charles. *J.R.R. Tolkien*. Plymouth: Northcote House Publishers, 1997.

National Science Board. *Science and Engineering Indicators 2012*. Arlington: National Science Foundation, 2012. A 7–19.

Quainton, Cecil S. "The Astronomy of the Bible." *Journal of the Royal Astronomical Society of Canada* 29 (1926): 193–7.

Tolkien, J.R.R. "Manuscript B." *TOF* 206–296.

_____. "On Fairy-stories." *TOF* 27–84.

Ward, Michael. *Planet Narnia*. Oxford: Oxford University Press, 2008.

Wood, Ralph C. *The Gospel According to Tolkien*. Louisville: Westminster John Knox Press, 2003.

Yates, Jessica. "The Source of 'The Lay of Aotrou and Itroun.'" *Leaves from the Tree*. Ed. Trevor Reynolds. London: The Tolkien Society, 1991. 63–71.

Zambreno, Mary F. "A Reconstructed Image: Medieval Time and Space in *The Chronicles of Narnia*." *Revisiting Narnia*. Ed. Shanna Caughey. Dallas: Benbella Books, 2005. 253–66.

Appendix: Recent Work—Shippey on Tolkien Since 2004

For a bibliography of Tom Shippey's earlier writing on J.R.R. Tolkien, see Douglas A. Anderson, "Tom Shippey on J.R.R. Tolkien: A Checklist," *Tolkien Studies* 1 (2004), 17–20.[1] Professor Shippey also maintains a current list (on which this one is based) on his Saint Louis University web-page, http://www.slu.edu/x23819.xml.

"'A Fund of Wise Sayings': Proverbiality in Tolkien." *The Ring Goes Ever On: Proceedings of the Tolkien 2005 Conference: 50 Years of* The Lord of the Rings. Ed. Sarah Wells. 2 vols. Coventry: Tolkien Society, 2008. I: 279–286.

"History in Words: Tolkien's Ruling Passion." *Scholarship* 25–39.

"Imagined Cathedrals: Retelling Myth in the Twentieth Century." *Myth in North-west Europe*. Ed. Stephen Glosecki. Tempe, AZ: MRTS, 2007. 307–32.

"Introduction." J.R.R. Tolkien, *Tales from the Perilous Realm*. London: HarperCollins, 2008. ix–xxviii.

"Introduction: Why Source Criticism?" *Tolkien and the Study of his Sources*. Ed. Jason Fisher. Jefferson, NC: McFarland, 2011. 7–16.

"Light-elves, Dark-elves, and Others: Tolkien's Elvish Problem." *Tolkien Studies* 1 (2004). 1–15.

"New Learning and New Ignorance: Magia, Goeteia and the Inklings." *Myth and Magic: Art According to the Inklings*. Ed. Eduardo Segura and Thomas Honegger. [Zollikofen]: Walking Tree, 2007. 21–46.

Roots and Branches: Selected Papers on Tolkien. Cormarë Series 11. [Zollikofen]: Walking Tree, 2007. ["Tolkien and the *Beowulf*-Poet" (1–18); "Tolkien and the Appeal of the Pagan: *Edda* and *Kalevala*" (19–38); "Tolkien and the West Midlands: The Roots of Romance" (39–59); "Tolkien and the *Gawain*-Poet" (61–77); "Grimm, Grundtvig, Tolkien: Nationalism and the Invention of Mythologies" (79–96); "The Problem of the Rings: Tolkien and Wagner" (97–114); "Goths and Huns: The Rediscovery of Northern Cultures in the Nineteenth Century" (115–136); "Fighting the Long Defeat: Philology in Tolkien's Life and Fiction" (139–156); "History in Words: Tolkien's Ruling Passion" (157–173); "A Look at *Exodus* and *Finn and Hengest*" (175–186); "Tolkien and Iceland: The Philology of Envy" (187–202); "Tolkien's Academic Reputation Now" (203–212); "Light-Elves, Dark-Elves and Others: Tolkien's Elvish Problem" (215–233); "Indexing and Poetry in *The Lord of the Rings*" (235–241); "Orcs, Wraiths, Wights: Tolkien's Images of Evil" (243–265); "Heroes and Heroism: Tolkien's Problems, Tolkien's Solutions" (267–283); "Noblesse Oblige: Images of Class in Tolkien" (285–301); "'A Fund of Wise Sayings': Proverbiality in Tolkien" (303–319); "Tolkien and 'The Homecoming of Beorhtnoth'" (323–339); "The Versions of 'The Hoard'" (341–349); "Allegory versus Bounce: (Half of) an Exchange on *Smith of Wootton Major*" (351–362); "Blunt Belligerence: Tolkien's *Mr. Bliss*" (363–364); "Another Road to Middle-earth: Jackson's Movie Trilogy" (365–386)].

"Tolkien and the Appeal of the Pagan: *Edda and Kalevala*." *Invention* 145–61.

"Tolkien e la tessitura degli eventi: La filosofia della provvidenza ne 'Il signore degli annelli.'" *L' Osservatore Romano.* 27 May 2010: 5.

The Tolkien Encyclopedia. Ed. Michael D.C. Drout. London and New York: Routledge, 2007. [Entries on: Alliterative verse by Tolkien; John Buchan; Cruces in medieval literature; Ylfe, Alfar, Elves; Germanic mythology; Haigh's *Glossary of the Huddersfield Dialect*; Tolkien's influence on 20th century literature; C.S. Lewis; *The Owl and the Nightingale*; Uncollected Poems; Poems by Tolkien in other languages [asterisk-poems]; Old Norse language; Scholars of medieval literature; *The Adventures of Tom Bombadil*].

"Tolkien, Medievalism, and the Philological Tradition." *Bells Chiming from the Past: Cultural and Linguistic Studies on Early English*. Ed. Isabel Moskowich-Spiegel and Begona Crespo-Garcia. Costerus NS 174. Amsterdam and New York: Rodopi, 2007. 265–79.

"Tolkien's Two Views of Beowulf: One Hailed, One Ignored. But Did We Get This Right?" *The Lord of the Rings* Fanatics Plaza: Scholars Forum. Lord of the Rings Fanatics Network, July 25, 2010. July 24, 2012. http://www.lotrplaza.com/forum/forum_posts. asp?TID=238598&PN=1.

"Writing into the Gap." Rev. of J.R.R. Tolkien, *Legend of Sigurd and Gudrún. Tolkien Studies* 7 (2010): 291–324.

NOTE

1. Also on-line at: http://muse.jhu.edu/journals/tolkien_studies/v001/1.1anderson02. html.

About the Contributors

B.S.W. **Barootes** is a PhD candidate in the Department of English at McGill University in Montreal. His dissertation addresses how 14th- and 15th-century English poets used the dream vision genre to engage contemporary debates about language. His interests include Middle English literature, heroic literature, book history and print culture, 19th-century medievalisms, and, of course, Tolkien.

David **Bratman** wrote his first Tom Shippey review in 1983, in *Mythprint*, the bulletin of the Mythopoeic Society, of which he served as editor. Since then he has reviewed Shippey's other works, including in *Tolkien Studies: An Annual Scholarly Review*, of which he is co-editor. Other publications include articles on Tolkien in *Mythlore* and *Mallorn*, in Diana Pavlac Glyer's *The Company They Keep*, and an edition of *The Masques of Amen House* by Charles Williams. He holds an MLS from the University of Washington and has worked as a librarian at Stanford University.

Marjorie **Burns** taught 19th- and 20th-century British literature at Portland State University for more than thirty years. Her doctoral dissertation on 19th-century British fantasists led her to a study of J.R.R. Tolkien. Her study of Celtic and Norse mythology and research as a Fulbright professor in Norway inform her book *Perilous Realms: Celtic and Norse in Tolkien's Middle-earth*. She has lectured on Tolkien throughout the world and published extensively on Tolkien.

Janet Brennan **Croft** is head of access services and associate professor of bibliography at the University of Oklahoma libraries. She is the author of *War in the Works of J.R.R. Tolkien* and several essays on the Peter Jackson films; has published articles on authors including J.R.R. Tolkien, J.K. Rowling and Terry Pratchett; and is editor of three collections of literary essays. She has also written widely on library and copyright issues. She edits *Mythlore* and serves on the board of the Mythopoeic Press.

David L. **Dettman** is a research scientist in the Geosciences Department of the University of Arizona. In addition to a PhD in geology, he holds a BA in Medieval and Renaissance studies and an MA in history from the University of Michigan. He is one of the Board of Founders (the Boffins) of the American Tolkien Society and has published numerous articles in the Society's journal, the *Minas Tirith Evening-Star* (americantolkiensociety.org).

Jason **Fisher** is an independent scholar specializing in J.R.R. Tolkien, the Inklings, and Medieval Germanic philology. He edited *Tolkien and the Study of His Sources* and *Mythprint*, the publication of the Mythopoeic Society. He has published essays and reviews in *Tolkien Studies, Mythlore, Beyond Bree, The Journal of Inklings Studies, Sehnsucht*, and other publications. He blogs at *Lingwë—Musings of a Fish* (http://lingwe.blogspot.com).

Verlyn **Flieger** is professor emerita in the Department of English at the University of Maryland, where she taught courses in Tolkien, medieval literature, and comparative mythology. She is the author of four critical books on the work of J.R.R. Tolkien and the editor of three more, as well as being co-editor of *Tolkien Studies*. She has also published two fantasy novels, *Pig Tale* and *The Inn at Corbies' Caww*, and an Arthurian novella, *Avilion*.

John R. **Holmes** teaches English (including Tolkien and Old English) at Franciscan University of Steubenville (Ohio). He also has contributed essays to several books on Tolkien and the *J.R.R. Tolkien Encyclopedia*. He has published numerous articles on Tolkien, particularly Tolkien's verse. He is working on a monograph on Tolkien's poetry.

John Wm. **Houghton** has contributed to *Beyond Bree, Mythlore, Mythprint, Tolkien the Medievalist, Tolkien Studies* and the *J.R.R. Tolkien Encylopedia* and has been active in Tolkien fandom since the 1970s. An Episcopal priest, he is the Firestone Endowment Chaplain and chair of the Department of Religious Studies and Philosophy at the Hill School, Pottstown, Pennsylvania. He received a PhD at the Medieval Institute of the University of Notre Dame. He is the author of a fantasy novel, *Rough Magicke*, and of *Falconry and Other Poems*.

Todd **Jensen** lives in St. Louis. He first discovered Tolkien's works through a copy of *The Hobbit* which he read during a visit to England when he was around eight years old, and has enjoyed him ever since. He has also enjoyed Tom Shippey's works on Tolkien, both *The Road to Middle-earth* and *J.R.R. Tolkien: Author of the Century*. He is working on an Arthurian fantasy novel for children, and is a frequent contributor to *Beyond Bree*.

Yvette **Kisor** is an associate professor of literature at Ramapo College of New Jersey. Her essays on Tolkien have appeared in *Tolkien Studies* and *Mythlore*, as well as *Picturing Tolkien: Essays on the Peter Jackson* Lord of the Rings *Trilogy*, and *The J.R.R. Tolkien Encyclopedia*. Her essays on medieval literature have been published in *Anglo-Saxon England, The Chaucer Review*, and *ANQ*, as well as the collections *On the Aesthetics of Beowulf and Other Old English Poetry, Translating the Past: Essays on Medieval Literature in Honor of Marijane Osborn*, and *Medieval Sexual Culture*.

Kristine **Larsen** is a professor of astronomy at Central Connecticut State University. Her research and teaching focus on issues of science and society, including the preparation of science educators, science outreach, and science and literature. Her publications include *Stephen Hawking: A Biography* and *Cosmology 101*, and two co-edited volumes, *The Mythological Dimensions of Doctor Who* and *The Mythological Dimensions of Neil Gaiman*.

John B. **Marino** studied medieval literature under Tom Shippey at Saint Louis University. An associate professor of English at Maryville University, he is working on a project about how history is presented in fantasy literature, particularly Tolkien. He is also planning a collection tentatively titled "All I Really Needed to Know I Learned from Reading *The Lord of the Rings*." He is the author of *The Grail Legend in Modern Literature* and regularly presents papers about the work of Thomas Malory.

Nancy **Martsch** discovered the works of Tolkien in 1966 and has been an avid fan ever since. In 1980 she became the coordinator of the Tolkien Special Interest Group of American Mensa and since 1981 has edited its magazine *Beyond Bree*. She has given talks on Tolkien at various conferences, contributed to the *Proceedings of the J.R.R. Tolkien Centenary Conference* and *The Ring Goes Ever On: Proceedings of the 2005 Tolkien Conference*, and authored *Basic Quenya*, a primer of Elvish.

John D. **Rateliff** spent many years researching Tolkien's manuscripts at Marquette University. Out of this work grew *The History of The Hobbit*. He holds a PhD from Marquette and has a special interest in the history of fantasy and in the Inklings. He has contributed to two essay collections on Tolkien: *Picturing Tolkien: Essays on Peter Jackson's* The Lord of the Rings *Film Trilogy* and *Tolkien and the Study of His Sources*.

Robin Anne **Reid** earned a doctorate in English from the University of Washington and teaches at Texas A&M University-Commerce. Her areas of scholarship include fan studies, speculative fiction, corpus stylistics, and adaptation studies in film. Works in progress include collaborative efforts to create networks focused on developing an online Tolkien Corpus. She is working on a website for the Tolkien Scholarship Project (http://earendel.net/) with the goal of summarizing and documenting Tolkien scholarship.

E.L. **Risden** is a professor of English at St. Norbert College in Wisconsin, where he teaches medieval and Renaissance literature, classical myth, and linguistics. His fifteen books include *Beowulf: A Translation for Students* and *Alfgar's Stories from Beowulf*, and also *Shakespeare and the Problem Play: Complex Forms, Crossed Genres, and Moral Quandaries*.

Leslie **Stratyner** is a professor of English at Mississippi University for Women. She teaches courses in Anglo-Saxon literature, medieval literature, history of the English language, Greek and Roman myth, and popular culture. She has been teaching, presenting and publishing on Tolkien for more than twenty years. She has co-edited, with James Keller, four volumes of essays on everything from fantasy film to Shakespeare to *South Park*.

Robert T. **Tally**, Jr., is an associate professor of English at Texas State University. He is the author of *Fredric Jameson: The Project of Dialectical Criticism*; *Poe and the Subversion of American Literature: Satire, Fantasy, Critique*; *Spatiality*; *Utopia in the Age of Globalization: Space, Representation, and the World System*; as well as books on Kurt Vonnegut and Herman Melville. He is also the editor of *Geocritical Explorations: Space, Place, and Mapping in Literary and Cultural Studies* and *Kurt Vonnegut: Critical Insights*.

Richard C. **West** has graduate degrees in English and in library science. He is on the board of advisors of the Mythopoeic Society and the editorial board of *Tolkien Studies*. He has published articles on Peter S. Beagle, C.S. Lewis, Mervyn Peake, T.H. White, and J.R.R. Tolkien, as well as the book *Tolkien Criticism: An Annotated Checklist*. Now retired, he was most recently senior academic librarian and head of serials at the Kurt F. Wendt Commons Library, University of Wisconsin–Madison.

Jessica **Yates** studied English at Lady Margaret Hall, Oxford. She was a school librarian and worked successively in three school libraries in London. She is a long-standing member of the Tolkien Society and has served as its secretary and editor of its bulletin *Amon Hen*. She is also a member of the William Morris Society and the British SF Association and is a keen Discworldian. She has published many reviews and articles on Tolkien, on fantasy, and on children's and teenage literature.

Extended Acknowledgments

The editors wish to thank:

Houghton Mifflin Harcourt and HarperCollins for extensive permissions to reprint copyrighted material.

Excerpts from AMERICAN HERITAGE DICTIONARY OF INDO-EUROPEAN ROOTS 2/E by Calvert Watkins. Copyright © 2000 by Houghton Mifflin Harcourt Publishing Company. Used by permission. All rights reserved.

Excerpts from THE ANNOTATED HOBBIT by J.R.R. Tolkien, annotated by Douglas A. Anderson. Reprinted by permission of HarperCollins Publishers Ltd. Copyright © 1937 by George Allen & Unwin Ltd. Copyright © 1966 by J.R.R. Tolkien. Copyright © renewed 1994 by Christopher R. Tolkien, John F.R. Tolkien and Priscilla M.A.R. Tolkien. Copyright © restored 1996 by the Estate of J.R.R. Tolkien, assigned 1997 to the J.R.R. Tolkien Copyright Trust. Introduction and annotations copyright © 2002 by Douglas A. Anderson. Reprinted by permission of Houghton Mifflin Harcourt Publishing Company. All rights reserved.

Excerpts from THE BOOK OF LOST TALES, PART I (The History of Middle-earth I) by J.R.R. Tolkien. Reprinted by permission of HarperCollins Publishers Ltd. Copyright © 1983 by Frank Richard Williamson and Christopher Reuel Tolkien as Executors of the Estate of J.R.R. Tolkien. Reprinted by permission of Houghton Mifflin Harcourt Publishing Company. All rights reserved.

Excerpts from THE BOOK OF LOST TALES, PART II (The History of Middle-earth II) by J.R.R. Tolkien. Reprinted by permission of HarperCollins Publishers Ltd. Copyright © 1984 by Frank Richard Williamson and Christopher Reuel Tolkien as Executors of the Estate of J.R.R. Tolkien. Reprinted by permission of Houghton Mifflin Harcourt Publishing Company. All rights reserved.

Excerpts from THE CHILDREN OF HURIN by J.R.R. Tolkien, edited by Christopher Tolkien. Reprinted by permission of HarperCollins Publishers Ltd. Copyright © 2007 by the J.R.R. Tolkien Copyright Trust and Christopher

EARTH by J.R.R. Tolkien. Reprinted by permission of HarperCollins Publishers Ltd. Copyright © 1980 by J.R.R. Tolkien Copyright Trust. Reprinted by permission of Houghton Mifflin Harcourt Publishing Company. All rights reserved.

Excerpt from THE WAR OF THE RING: THE HISTORY OF THE LORD OF THE RINGS, PART THREE (The History of Middle-earth VIII) by J.R.R. Tolkien. Reprinted by permission of HarperCollins Publishers Ltd. Copyright © 1990 by J.R.R. Tolkien Copyright Trust. Reprinted by permission of Houghton Mifflin Harcourt Publishing Company. All rights reserved.

Dover Publications, Inc., for permission to reprint Lancelot Speed, "The Princess and the Spiders," from *The Red Fairy Book*, ed. Andrew Lang (Rpt. Mineola, NY: Dover, 1966), 232.

Nancy Martsch, editor of *Beyond Bree*, the newsletter of the J.R.R. Tolkien Special Interest Group of American Mensa, for permission to reprint David Bratman, "Shippey: The Philologist and the Critics," and Todd Jensen, "A Talk by Tom Shippey," from the September, 2009, issue.

Catherine Shippey, the photographer, for permission to reproduce the cover and frontispiece photographs of Professor Shippey, copyright © 2012.

Roger Hill, Patrick Wynne, and Janet Brennan Croft, editor of *Mythlore*, for permission to reproduce Mr. Wynne's cover drawing of J.R.R. Tolkien, copyright © 1987, which originally appeared on the back cover of *Mythlore* 14.2, #52 (Winter 1987), and was based on Mr. Hill's original photograph.

Index

Numbers in **_bold italics_** indicate pages with photographs.